A History of the
Last Church of God and His Christ

Copyright 2018 Wezi Makuni Gondwe

All rights reserved. No part of this publication may be reproduced, stored in a retrieval system, or transmitted in any form or by any means, electronic, mechanical, photocopying, recording or otherwise, without prior permission from the publishers.

Published by
Mzuni Press
P/Bag 201
Luwinga, Mzuzu 2
Malawi

ISBN 978-99960-60-18-2

eISBN 978-99960-60-19-9

Mzuni Press is represented outside Malawi by:

African Books Collective Oxford (also for e-books)
(orders@africanbookscollective.com)

www.mzunipress.blogspot.com

www.africanbookscollective.com

Index and editorial assistance: Daniel Neumann

Printed in Malawi by Baptist Publications, P.O. Box 444, Lilongwe

A History of the Last Church of God and His Christ in Malawi from 1916 to 2015

Wezi Makuni Gondwe

MZUNI PRESS

A Mzuni Monograph
Mzuzu
2018

Abbreviations

AAC	African Abraham Church
AIC	African Independent (Instituted, Indigenous) Church
CCAP	Church of Central Africa Presbyterian
CAP	Church of Africa Presbyterian
EAM	Evangelical Association of Malawi
MCC	Malawi Council of Churches
MCP	Malawi Congress Party
MP	Member of Parliament
NRM	New Religious Movement(s)
PIM	Providence Industrial Mission

Contents

Introduction		7
Chapter 1:	The Last Church of God and His Christ as an "African Independent Church"	9
Chapter 2:	The Last Church of God and His Christ between 1916 and 1936	27
Chapter 3:	The Growth of the Last Church of God from 1935 to 1962	47
Chapter 4:	The Last Church of God and His Christ ("Reformed Last")	76
Chapter 5:	The Last Church of God and His Christ International (African Last)	94
Chapter 6:	Marriage and Polygamy in the Last Church of God and His Christ	128
Chapter 7:	Charismatic and Pentecostal Tendencies	148
Chapter 8:	The Sunday Worship and Preaching Service in the Last Church of God and His Christ International	171
Chapter 9:	Becoming Mainline Again	197
Bibliography		205

Illustrations

Figure 1	The General Principal Rev O. Masinda	77
Figure 2	Kazando Reformed Last Church of God	78
Figure 3	The pastors of the Reformed Last Church of God	79
Figure 4	Part of the gathering during the 2010 women's conference at Phiri	81
Figure 5	Three women preachers from Nkhotakota at Phiri (2010)	81
Figure 6	*Amayi Achikondi* members at Phiri (2010)	82
Figure 7	*Amayi Achikondi* from Kasitu Last Church	82
Figure 8	A youth choir from Nkhafu	83
Figure 9	A choir from different churches in Nkhatabay	84
Figure 10	Munkhokwe Last Church of God	99
Figure 11	Katoto Last Church of God (Chintheche, 2010	105
Figure 12	African Last Church Msondozi headquarters	106
Figure 13	*Amayi Achikondi* Choir at Munkhokwe (African Last)	114

Introduction

The Last Church of God and His Christ International, Malawi, owes its origin in this country to Jordan Msumba. He was from Usisya, village headman Mabuli in Nkhatabay district. Jordan Msumba came in touch with this church while in South Africa.[1] In 1916 he started the church in Malawi, but it was officially registered only on 29th April 1925. Jordan Msumba originally intended to establish the church at Usisya, in his home village, but the church was not welcome there. He therefore came to Nkhatabay and established the church at Msondozi, which eventually became the headquarters of the church.[2]

Jordan Msumba left Msondozi for Tanzania in 1928 and planted the church at Mwanza. In 1936, he died in Tanzania. Meanwhile the church in Malawi was left in the hands of Rev Isaac Mkhuta Banda, who became the second Archbishop of the church after Msumba. From Msondozi the church spread to other areas in Malawi as well as to neighbouring countries.[3]

Since its establishment, a lot has happened in the church. What developments and changes have taken place over the years? What has been the relationship of the church to African culture? How has the church grown or expanded? Has the church been able to maintain its unity? And what has been the relationship of the church with other churches? These are some of the questions I intend to answer in this book.

While some attention has been paid to the origins and distinct features of the Last Church of God in Malawi, there seems to be a gap in terms of a consolidated and comprehensive history of the church over the years. The church has spread to many areas and has undergone many changes. As the church is counted among the African Independent Churches, what did this mean and what does it mean now, but also what changes have taken place over the years?

---

[1] Int. Rev Chiuli Manda, retired Area Bishop, Munkhokwe, 17.9.2011.
[2] Ibid. 17.9.2011.
[3] Ibid. 17.9.2011.

The aim of the book, therefore, is to examine the history of the Last Church of God and His Christ International in Malawi from its beginning (1916) through the years and to portray a picture of its current existence in its various branches.

Chapter 1: The Last Church of God and His Christ as an "African Independent Church"

Some scholars classify the Last Church of God and His Christ under the ecclesiastical-cultural bloc known as African Indigenous Churches (AICs).[1] David Barret has divided the world's Christians into seven major ecclesiastical blocs. Three of these are: Roman Catholicism, Orthodoxy, and Protestantism.[2] These three are major Christian blocs which have arisen during the course of Christian history.

However, there are many large churches and denominations which do not define themselves under any of these three terms, and often reject all three.[3] Therefore David Barret's survey recognizes the existence of three further distinct worldwide blocs of Christianity:[4] Anglicanism, marginal Protestantism[5] and Catholicism (non-Roman).

However, as far back as 1549 (Japan) and 1741 (USA), new types of Christianity have emerged that do not fit readily into any of these preceding six major blocs.[6] These consist of denominations, churches and movements that have been initiated, founded and spread by black, Non-White or non-European peoples without European assistance, mainly in the Global South, but also among Black and Non-White minorities in the Western World. The African Indigenous Churches fall under this category.[7]

---

[1] David Barret (ed.), *World Christian Encyclopaedia: A Comparative Survey of Churches and Religions in the Modern World AD 1900-2000*, New York: Oxford University Press, 1982, p. 60.

[2] Ibid. p. 62.

[3] Ibid. p. 56.

[4] Ibid. p. 56.

[5] These are Para-Christian, quasi Christian deviations from mainline Protestantism claiming a second or supplementary or ongoing source of divine revelation in addition to the Bible. Ibid. p. 56.

[6] Ibid. p. 56.

[7] Ibid. p. 60.

In tracing the origins of the religious phenomenon in question and the challenges encountered in trying to categorize this religious phenomenon under one umbrella or category, it is argued is that this religious phenomenon should not be categorized under one block of AICs simply because it consists of movements and churches that are very different from one another; but rather each movement or church should be studied in its' own right. The Last Church of God should therefore be studied simply as any other church, not as an Independent Church.

The Beginning of African Independent Churches (AICs)

The beginning of African Church independence is traced back to the early 19th century (at least in West Africa).[8] Some argue that in the first wave of independency was a reaction against the evil of "humiliation and shame" caused by missionaries' disrespect or contempt.[9] Thus some Africans broke away from missionary churches motivated by the desire to have the leadership of the church in African hands, and not so much due to questions of doctrine or worship practice. Still others broke away or started their own churches for a variety of other reasons.[10] These Africans established churches of their own, referred to collectively as African Independent Churches.[11]

The first signs of independency made their appearance particularly in the form of what was called Ethiopianism (the separation of churches from the missionary churches).[12] Ethiopianism was promoted by the Ethiopian

---

[8] Charles Okechekwu Ifemeje, *African Independent Churches: A Pastoral Challenge to the Church in Igboland-Nigeria*, Aachen: Shaker, 2002, p. 110.

[9] Steven Paas, *The Faith Moves South: A History of the Church in Africa*, Zomba: Kachere, 2006, p. 142.

[10] Ibid. p. 142.

[11] Charles Okechekwu Ifemeje, *African Independent Churches: A Pastoral Challenge to the Church in Igboland-Nigeria*, Aachen: Shaker, 2002, p. 110.

[12] Martin Pauw, "African Independent Churches in Malawi: Background and Historical Development" in M.C. Kitschoff (ed.), *African Independent Churches Today. Kaleidoscope of Afro-Christianity,* Lewiston: Edwin Mellen, 1996, p. 19.

victory over Italian invaders in 1896 and it looked forward to an all-African theocracy of racial justice and hope.[13] This Ethiopianism was,

however, fed by biblical references to Africa in the Old and New Testament with texts such as Psalm 68:31, "Ethiopia shall soon stretch out her hands unto God."

In Malawi, the first "independent" church was born 25 years after Christianity was introduced into the country. This church was the Providence Industrial Mission (PIM), which was started by John Chilembwe in 1900.[14] Klaus Fiedler, however, argues that Providence Industrial Mission was not an AIC but that it was a (Black) American Mission Church. Patrick Makondesa, the current President of PIM, shares the same view as did his predecessor Rev Chipuliko.[15] This was followed later on in 1908 by Elliot Kamwana who started his church in Nkhatabay.[16] These were followed by several other "independent" churches.

The Problem of Definition

There are a variety of terminologies that have been coined to try to describe the religious phenomenon in question. These terms include; African Independent Churches, African Indigenous Churches and African Instituted Churches. All these are simply referred to as AICs. Other scholars still prefer the term New Religious Movements. However, there

---

[13] Steven Paas, *The Faith Moves South: A History of the Church in Africa*, Zomba: Kachere, 2006, p. 142.

[14] Martin Pauw, "African Independent Churches in Malawi: Background and Historical Development" in M.C. Kitschoff (ed.), *African Independent Churches Today Kaleidoscope of Afro-Christianity,* Lewiston: Edwin Mellen, 1996, p. 25.

[15] Patrick Makondesa, *The Church History of Providence Industrial Mission*, Zomba: Kachere, 2006.

[16] Martin Pauw, "African Independent Churches in Malawi: Background and Historical Development" in M.C. Kitschoff (ed.), *African Independent Churches Today Kaleidoscope of Afro-Christianity,* Lewiston: Edwin Mellen, 1996, p. 25.

is yet no general consensus as to which is the most appropriate term for such a religious phenomenon.[17]

African Independent Churches

The term "African Independent Churches" was the first neutral term used for these movements after more biased terms like "sects" and "nativistic," "messianic," "separatist" and "syncretist" movements.[18] Sundkler opted for the term "Bantu Independent Churches" against such terms as mentioned above. The labels, Native, Separatist and his own use of "Bantu" were regarded offensive and thus received severe criticism in the very political atmosphere that characterized apartheid South Africa.[19] Thus the term "African" came and appeared as a suitable replacement of Bantu. In spite of the criticism it received, "African Independent Churches" received a fair nod of acceptance as a working definition.[20]

Turner defined an "African Independent Church" as a church which has been founded in Africa, by Africans and primarily for Africans. The term "independent" was chosen because it signified the fact that these churches claimed to be independent of foreign origin and domination. Turner's definition may appear to hold water, especially when located within the specific period within which Turner first wrote. However, contemporary expansion of these churches now renders his definition short sighted.[21]

The term "independent" became increasingly inadequate in the post-colonial reconstruction of African church history. Among other things, in

---

[17] H.L. Pretorius, *Historiography and Historical Sources Regarding African Indigenous Churches in South Africa: Writing Indigenous Church History*, Lewiston: Edwin Mellen, 1995, p. 5.

[18] Harri Englund, "Christian Independency and Global Membership: Pentecostal Extraversions in Malawi" in *Journal of Religion in Africa*, vol. 33, 2003, pp. 83-111.

[19] Ogbu U. Kalu (ed), *African Christianity: An African Story*, Trenton: African World Press, 2007, p. 272.

[20] Ibid.

[21] Ibid.

the beginning these churches were largely viewed as political protest groups which were expected to automatically die in the aftermath of independence across Africa. However, the continuity and spread and the various forms which these churches took in post independent Africa necessitated new alternative terminologies other than "independent" churches.[22]

Apart from that, all African churches, including the mainline churches, became independent in the second half of the 20th century.[23] Again, even from the beginning of classical missions (these are missionary organizations related to mainline churches from Europe and North America) in Africa, there was the powerful factor of African initiative.[24] Therefore, it is impossible to separate the history of African Instituted Churches after 1890, from early features of independency inside the main mission founded churches.[25] These limitations led to the introduction of another term, namely African Indigenous Churches.[26]

African Indigenous Churches

Barret defines indigenous churches as "those originating within a country or race of people, or produced naturally by nationals of that country or members of that race or people as opposed to churches of foreign or alien origin imported from abroad or introduced from outside the group, such as immigrant churches or mission related churches."[27] In this case it

---

[22] Ogbu U. Kalu (ed), *African Christianity: An African Story*, Trenton: African World Press, 2007, p. 272.

[23] Steven Paas, *The Faith Moves South: A History of the Church in Africa*, Zomba: Kachere, 2006, p. 140.

[24] Ibid.

[25] Ibid.

[26] Harri Englund, "Christian Independency and Global Membership: Pentecostal Extraversions in Malawi" in *Journal of Religion in Africa,* vol. 33, 2003, pp. 83-111.

[27] David Barret (ed.), *World Christian Encyclopaedia: A Comparative Survey of Churches and Religions in the Modern World AD 1900-2000*, New York: Oxford University Press, 1982, p. 62.

refers to those churches originated within Africa and by Africans as opposed to mission-founded churches.

However, as used and defined here, this term says nothing about whether or not the people involved are indigenous to, or the original inhabitants of the country they happen to be in, the term refers only to the production of Christian movements within their midst.[28] This term "indigenous" also became inadequate with the movement and the efforts of many mission-founded churches towards inculturation and their attempt to be seen as "indigenous."[29]

Again, the idea that AICs are indigenous to Africa has had to be surrendered, as AICs can now be found in Europe (e.g. Germany, Britain and the United States).[30] In such cases, the term "African" suggests the continent of origin, rather than of location.[31]

Those researchers who wish to point out that AICs exhibit African cultural forms, describe them as "indigenous." It should be mentioned here that the differences in names correspond to the aspect that a researcher wishes to emphasize. In favour of "indigenous" it can also be argued that it carries the connotation of authenticity, of belonging naturally to or being native to a certain place or environment, in this case Africa.[32]

African Instituted Churches

African Instituted Churches is a term which avoids the difficulties mentioned above by simply indicating that these many different kinds of

---

[28] David Barret (ed.), *World Christian Encyclopaedia: A Comparative Survey of Churches and Religions in the Modern World AD 1900-2000*, New York: Oxford University Press, 1982, p. 62.

[29] Harri Englund, "Christian Independency and Global Membership: Pentecostal Extraversions in Malawi," *Journal of Religion in Africa*, vol. 33, 2003, p. 83-111.

[30] Wikipedia, "African_Initiated_Churches," 13.7.2013.

[31] Ibid. 13.7.2013.

[32] H.L. Pretorius, *Historiography and Historical Sources Regarding African Indigenous Churches in South African: Writing Indigenous Church History*, Lewiston: Edwin Mellen, 1995, p. 5.

churches were initiated by Africans, and not by Europeans.[33] But the problem here is that the term disregards all theological considerations so that churches with very different theologies are lumped together under it. In this case, the emphasis is on the absence of Whites or of a clear mission connection.[34] The problem with this as observed by some scholars is that this will mean that most Charismatic churches are to be considered as African Instituted Churches. Yet, these churches are very different from the classical AICs.[35] It is clear that these terms have been imposed upon such groups, and may not be the way they would describe themselves.[36]

New Religious Movements

For some scholars, the term New Religious Movements is a neutral way of referring to these "groups."[37] These movements are neither traditional nor Christian but have a mixture of both. These scholars argue that these "groups" are new because they came to have their present form after the Second World War, and also because they present themselves as alternatives to the official institutional religions (mostly Christianity and Islam) and the prevailing culture.[38]

They are religious because they profess to offer a vision of religious or spiritual illumination and self-realization, or they offer their members answers to fundamental questions. Again, they are called movements (instead of churches), because some of them do not consider themselves Christian or see themselves as churches, as they do not want to be associated or confused with the mission oriented churches.[39] One rare

---

[33] Harri Englund, "Christian Independency and Global Membership: Pentecostal Extraversions in Malawi," *Journal of Religion in Africa*, vol. 33, 2003, p. 83-111.

[34] Klaus Fiedler, "The Charismatic and Pentecostal Movements in Malawi in Cultural Perspective" in *Religion in Malawi,* 1999, pp. 28-38.

[35] Ibid.

[36] Wikipedia, "African_Initiated_Churches," 13.7.2013.

[37] Charles O. Ifemeje, *African Independent Churches: A Pastoral Challenge to the Church in Igboland-Nigeria,* Aachen: Shaker, 2002, p. 155.

[38] Ibid. p. 156.

[39] Ibid. p. 156.

example of such a movement is the Brotherhood of the Cross and Star in Nigeria.

However, against the use of the term New Religious Movements is the fact that many groups do not and would not want to be regarded as movements, but rather as Christian churches, and again the term puts very different groups under the same label.

AICs, NRMs: A Working Definition?

Having looked at the above terminologies, it is observed that terms like African Instituted Churches and African Indigenous Churches, although positive, are sociological terms, they disregard theological considerations of this religious phenomenon. They are sociological terms in the sense that their emphasis is on the absence of Whites as far as the starting of those churches is concerned and not on their theology.

Likewise, the term African Independent Churches, apart from being a sociological definition, is also a negative term in that it regards the growth of AICs mainly as a reaction to western mission founded churches. This definition fails to emphasize the positive and dynamic religious thrust which is intrinsic to many of these movements.[40] The AICs kept on growing and changing the face of African Christianity without any reference to Western Missions whatsoever.[41]

All the definitions above define these churches (AICs) with regard to the absence of the Whites and not their theological implications which is important. Inasmuch as sociological considerations are important in trying to discuss a religious phenomenon, these should come only after theological tools have been considered in order to have a meaningful theological discussion.[42]

---

[40] J.C. Chakanza, *Voices of Preachers in Protest. The Ministry of Two Malawian Prophets: Elliot Kamwana and Wilfred Gudu*, Blantyre: CLAIM-Kachere, 1998, p. 9.

[41] Harri Englund, "Christian Independency and Global Membership: Pentecostal Extraversions in Malawi," *Journal of Religion in Africa*, vol. 33, 2003, p. 83-111.

[42] Klaus Fiedler, "The Charismatic and Pentecostal Movements in Malawi in Cultural Perspective," *in Religion of Malawi*, 1999, pp. 28-38.

Apart from that, these definitions of AICs and NRMs often include both Christian and non-Christian groups in the same category. Due to such limitations of the definitions, some scholars like Klaus Fiedler reject the idea of AICs, instead they argue that every church or movement be studied in its own right. There is as yet no scholarly consensus as to which of these phrases is most appropriate and concise to delineate the phenomenon.[43] As such the search for a more embracing term continues among scholars.

Several scholars have treated the Last Church of God as an "African Independent Church" emphasizing the fact that the founder wanted to be independent from mission domination as far as certain practices were concerned. The Last Church of God can be regarded as an Independent Church in so far as it broke away from mission churches and also in that it adopted some typical Independent Churches' features. But now the Last Church of God wants to be like any other church, they have cast out almost all "independent" paraphernalia, leaving them with nothing special anymore.

Typologies of AICs

Several scholars have tried to classify these African Indigenous Churches into several categories. Although there is a possibility of classifying churches according to some kind of typology, this must be done with care, as there is "certainly a danger of generalizing and of forcing groups to fit into a certain pattern to such an extent that the result may even be somewhat caricaturistic."[44] Some of the scholars that have attempted a typology of theses AICs include Sundkler and Turner.

---

[43] Ogbu U. Kalu (ed.), *African Christianity: An African Story*, Trenton: African World Press, 2007, p. 272.

[44] M.C. Kitschoff (ed.), *African Independent Churches Today. Kaleidoscope of Afro-Christianity*, Lewiston: Edwin Mellen, 1996, p. 19.

Sundkler's Typology

One of the earliest scholars to attempt such a typology of African indigenous churches is Bengt Sundkler.[45] He conducted his research in rural Zululand during the mid-forties. He talks about two main types of Independent Bantu churches, "Ethiopian" and "Zionist."[46] Initially he argued that African Independent Churches were bridges back to a pre-industrial culture. However, he later recognized instead that African Independent Churches helped their affiliates to adapt to a modernizing world that was hostile to their cultural beliefs so that for him they became bridges to modern culture.[47]

Ethiopian Type

The Ethiopian type comprises churches not necessarily named Ethiopian, but rather those churches which originated in secession from White churches, mostly on racial grounds. These churches were formed as a reaction against the White conquest of the African peoples, and yet their church organization and Bible interpretation are largely copied from the patterns of the Protestant mission churches from which they have seceded.[48]

Ethiopianism in West Africa started in about 1860, but in South Africa the earliest example of this type began in 1884, when Nehemiah Tile left the White controlled Wesleyan Methodist Church in Thembuland and founded the Thembu National Church; however, he did not call his church "Ethiopian". The first so-called "Ethiopian" church was founded on the Witwatersrand in 1892, when one of the Wesleyan ministers, Mangena M. Mokone, opposed what he regarded as racial segregation

---

[45] Allan Anderson, *Bazalwane: African Pentecostals in South Africa*, Pretoria: UNISA, 1992, p. 57.
[46] Ibid. p. 57.
[47] Wikipedia "African_Initiated_Churches."
[48] Allan Anderson, *Bazalwane: African Pentecostals in South Africa,* Pretoria: UNISA, 1992, p. 56.

within the church. He therefore resigned from the Wesleyan Church in 1892 and formed a new church.[49]

The name of the new church was of great significance: the "Ethiopian Church."[50] Mokone had heard missionaries who referred in their sermons to Psalm 68:31, ["Ethiopia shall soon stretch out her hands unto God."] and who gave other references such as Acts 8:27 ["Now an Ethiopian eunuch, who was an important official in Ethiopia, was on his way home. He had been to Jerusalem to worship God and was going back home in his carriage"]. The missionaries interpreted this as a promise of the evangelization of Africa. Mokone, however, took this to mean the self-government of the African church under African leaders.[51]

In Malawi Chilembwe's Providence Industrial Mission, Elliot Kamwana's Watchman Healing Mission and the Blackman's Church founded by Yesaya Zerenji Mwase are some examples of churches that may fall under this category. However, these may not fit exactly the Ethiopian type as suggested by Sundkler, because they did not start as a reaction against the White conquest of the Malawian people. Again, some of the churches mentioned above, like Elliot Kamwana's Watchman Healing Mission, also display some Zionist characteristics.[52] It was after 1900 that the Ethiopian movement became Africa wide.

The Zionist Type

Sundkler's second type of African Indigenous Churches is the Zionist type. This comprises those churches which refer to themselves as *amaZiyoni*.[53] The beginning of these churches goes back to an apocalyptic church in the USA, the Christian Catholic Apostolic Church in Zion, founded in 1896

---

[49] Allan Anderson, *Bazalwane: African Pentecostals in South Africa,* Pretoria: UNISA, 1992, p. 39.

[50] Ibid. p. 39.

[51] Ibid. p. 39.

[52] J.C. Chakanza, *Voices of Preachers in Protest. The Ministry of Two Malawian Prophets: Elliot Kamwana and Wilfred Gudu*, Blantyre: CLAIM-Kachere, 1998.

[53] Bengt Sundkler, *Bantu Prophets in South Africa*, Cambridge: James Clarke, 1948, p. 54.

by John Alexander Dowie, "First Apostle and General Overseer."[54] Ulf Strohbehn points out three hall marks to identifying a church as Zionist: first, all churches which have historical links in their genesis to other Zionists may fall under this category.[55] The second marker is the doctrinal tenets and practices by Zionists, such as faith healing, dietary laws, purification ceremonies, uniforms and their unique way of preaching. Third is the self-designation of the church, most Zionists have "Zion" in their name.[56]

As time passed some Zionist groups began to mix aspects of traditional African beliefs, such as ancestor veneration, with Christian doctrine.[57] Such churches were named by some scholars as nativistic.[58] Some observe that in Malawi such labeling will not hold true. While a wide range of Zionist Churches in the country does include some groups, which are closer to traditional tenets, it would, however, be difficult to put any denomination into one single box.[59] The explanation being that these churches do display strong Christian beliefs, Pentecostal liberties, Baptist practices and traditional elements all at the same time.[60]

The churches which Sundkler refers to as Zionists in the South African context are often referred to as Prophet Healing, Pentecostal, Spirit type or Aladura churches.[61] These are generally more Africanized than the Ethiopian church movement.[62] Examples of Zionist Churches in Malawi

---

[54] Bengt Sundkler, *Bantu Prophets in South Africa*, Cambridge: James Clarke, 1948, p. 54.
[55] Ulf Strohbehn, *The Zionist Churches in Malawi: History-Theology-Anthropology*, Mzuzu: Mzuni Press 2016, pp. 5-6.
[56] Ibid. pp. 5-6.
[57] Wikipedia, "African_Initiated_Churches, 13.7.2013.
[58] Ulf Strohbehn, *The Zionist Churches in Malawi: History-Theology-Anthropology*, Mzuni, 2016, p. 7.
[59] Ibid. p. 7.
[60] Ibid. p. 7.
[61] Charles O. Ifemeje, *African Independent Churches: A Pastoral Challenge to the Church in Igboland-Nigeria*, Aachen: Shaker, 2002, pp. 110-111.
[62] Ibid. pp. 110-111.

include, Ifa-ifa Zion Christian Church by Adiyele Katsichi, Zion ya Bata in Salima and Jordan Zion ya Bata Church.[63]

It should be mentioned that even in 1948 Sundkler acknowledged that the distinctions between these two types of churches were not always clear, and that some "Ethiopian Churches" displayed "Zionist" tendencies and vice versa.[64]

Messianic Type

In his 1961 edition Sundkler added a third type of African Initiated Churches, called Messianic. The churches that have been called Messianic focus on power and attach special importance to their leaders. Often the leaders are thought by their followers to possess Christ like characteristics. In most cases a myth about what they did while in the womb, at birth, in the course of their ministry or at the point of death is circulated to show that they were extraordinary prophets.[65]

Many scholars are prone to identify the Messianic Churches with either the Zionist or the Ethiopian group.[66] Eliade points out that those messianic groups tend to experience a crisis and a decline in their appeal after the founder dies or disappears. The prophetic message remains closely tied to the leader and his charismatic attraction.[67]

Denominations described as Messianic include: the Kimbanguist Church in the Democratic Republic of Congo, the Nazareth Baptist Church of Isaiah Shembe in KwaZulu-Natal, South Africa, and the Zion Christian Church of Engenas Lekganyane with headquarters in South Africa's

---

[63] Ulf Strohbehn, *The Zionist Churches in Malawi: History-Theology-Anthropology*, Mzuzu: Mzuni Press, 2016, pp. 103-108.

[64] Allan Anderson, *Bazalwane: African Pentecostals in South Africa*, Pretoria: UNISA, 1992, p. 73.

[65] Wikipedia, "African_Initiated_Churches," 13.7.2013.

[66] Charles O. Ifemeje, *African Independent Churches: A Pastoral Challenge to the Church in Igboland-Nigeria,* Aachen: Shaker, 2002, pp. 110-111.

[67] Ibid. pp. 110-111.

Limpopo Province.[68] In Malawi, Gudu's *Zion ya Yehovah (Ana a Mulungu)* falls between the Zionist type and the Messianic type.[69]

Using Sundkler's typology one observes that the Last Church of God hardly fits into any of the above typologies. Hence there is need probably for Sundkler's threefold typology to be revised so that it becomes more inclusive of churches like the Last Church of God.

Turner's Typology

Harold Turner developed his own typology of African Independent Churches using Sundkler's work as his starting point. Turner distinguishes between neo-primal, syncretist, Hebraist movements and Independent churches.[70] The latter "represent the Christian end of the spectrum, and since they intend to be Christian and retain the whole Bible and usually some kind of Christology, they may properly be called churches."[71] Turner classifies these movements into five categories and these are:

Politico Messianic Movements

These groups aim at cultural and political liberation, for instance the United Native African Church of Nigeria that was already active in 1886.[72]

Neo-Traditionalism

Turner's second category is called Neo-Traditionalists.[73] These are movements, which deliberately seek to revitalize traditional religious

---

[68] Wikipedia, "African_Initiated_Churches," 13.7.2013.

[69] J.C. Chakanza, *Voices of Preachers in Protests. The Ministry of Two Malawian Prophets: Elliot Kamwana and Wilfred Gudu,* Blantyre: CLAIM-Kachere, 1998, pp. 55-96.

[70] H.L. Pretorius, *Historiography and Historical Sources Regarding African Indigenous Churches in South Africa: Writing Indigenous Church History*, Lewiston: Edwin Mellen, 1995, p. 5.

[71] Ibid. p. 5.

[72] Chanju Mphande, "The History of Independent Churches in Malawi: An Investigation of the Last Church of God and His Christ among the Tonga of the Lakeshore (Nkhatabay)," BA, Mzuzu University, 2009, p. 17.

practices.[74] Examples of this type are the Cargo Cults in New Guinea, the Church of the Ancestors in Malawi,[75] and the Herero Church in Namibia among others.[76]

Syncretistic Cults

Another category are the syncretistic cults. These cults include a mixture of borrowings from African traditional beliefs and practices, and from Christian beliefs and practices. I am not aware of such a cult in Malawi, but perhaps the Chisumphi Cult, though not consciously syncretistic, may be included here, as the worship is clearly traditional but the cult officials are almost all Christians.[77]

Monotheist or Hebraist Movements

The fourth category are the monotheist or Hebraist movements. These consider themselves to be the Old Testament people of God, but are not actually Christian.[78] They reject completely all traditional religions and are tuned towards monotheism as revealed in the Old Testament.[79] The difficulty with this type is that some of these movements do consider themselves Christian and so one wonders by what criteria they are

---

[73] Harri Englund, "Christian Independency and Global Membership: Pentecostal Extraversions in Malawi," *Journal of Religion in Africa*, vol. 33, 2003, p. 83-111.

[74] Ibid.

[75] J.C. Chakanza, *African Ancestors' Religion – Chipembedzo cha Makolo Achikuda*, Zomba: Kachere, 2004.

[76] Harri Englund, "Christian Independency and Global Membership: Pentecostal Extraversions in Malawi," *Journal of Religion in Africa*, vol. 33, 2003, p. 83-111.

[77] Isabel Apawo Phiri, "African Traditional Women and Ecofeminism: The Role of Women at Chisumphi Cult in Preserving the Environment," *Religion in Malawi*, 1996, pp. 14-19.

[78] Harri Englund, "Christian Independency and Global Membership: Pentecostal Extraversions in Malawi," *Journal of Religion in Africa*, vol. 33, 2003, p. 83-111.

[79] Chanju Mphande, "The History of Independent Churches in Malawi: An Investigation of the Last Church of God and His Christ among the Tonga of the Lakeshore (Nkhatabay)," BA, Mzuzu University, 2009, p. 17.

categorized.[80] This is an example of the dangers of categorizing.[81] Again, I did not find any group of this category in Malawi.

Prophetic and Healing Churches

Turner's fifth category is the prophetic and healing churches. These proclaim themselves to be Christians, believing in Jesus Christ as the saviour and placing great weight on the revelations of the Holy Spirit. For this reason, they are often known as churches of the Holy Spirit.[82] The Prophetic and Healing type corresponds to the Zionist type of Sundkler or the Spirit type of Daneel.[83]

Looking at Turner's typology one wonders how he defines the Church, especially when one looks at the three types: Neo Traditionalists, Syncretism Cults and the Monotheist or Hebraist Movements, which he includes within the African Independent Churches. These cannot be described as churches in the biblical sense and they do not regard themselves as Christian or as churches.

The Malawian Context

The various typologies of independent religious movements, which have been suggested, are not greatly helpful for the classification of such movements in Malawi.[84] The groups found in Malawi do not fall easily into categories such as "Zionist" or "prophet-leaders." No great prophet-type leaders like Shembe, Kimbangu or even Lenshina have emerged,

---

[80] Harri Englund, "Christian Independency and Global Membership: Pentecostal Extraversions in Malawi," *Journal of Religion in Africa*, vol. 33, 2003, p. 83-111.

[81] Ibid.

[82] Chanju Mphande, "The History of Independent Churches in Malawi: An Investigation of the Last Church of God and His Christ among the Tonga of the Lakeshore (Nkhatabay)," BA, Mzuzu University, 2009, p. 17.

[83] Harri Englund, "Christian Independency and Global Membership: Pentecostal Extraversions in Malawi," *Journal of Religion in Africa*, vol. 33, 2003, p. 83-111.

[84] M.C. Kitschoff (ed.), *African Independent Churches Today. Kaleidoscope of Afro-Christianity*, Lewiston: Edwin Mellen, 1996, p. 19.

except perhaps Kenani Kamwana.[85] But it is difficult to place even Kamwana and his Watchman Healing Mission in a particular category. For Kamwana, like Wilfred Gudu and his Ana a Mulungu Church, shared characteristics of both the Zionist type and the Ethiopian type and also the Messianic type.[86]

Again, not even John Chilembwe, the first independent church leader, fits into a single particular model. For Chilembwe neither acquired a kind of Messianic status nor became a Prophet-type leader as it happened in other countries.[87] Chilembwe does not fit specifically under the Ethiopian type or the Zionist type, even though he seems to lean more to the Ethiopian model. The "Ethiopian" movements in Malawi during the first decades of the century do not really fit into the type of Ethiopianism such as described by Sundkler.[88]

The Last Church of God and His Christ International thus does not specifically fit into any of the above typologies whether by Sundkler or Turner. Msumba did not secede from mission churches on racial grounds and he did not organize his church on the pattern of Protestant churches. His church's beliefs and doctrines were distant from the Zionists. Msumba never claimed to be a Prophet or Messiah, nor did his supporters attribute such titles to him. However, the church does share some aspects of the typologies above, especially the traditional aspect of the movements (which have been largely given up by now).

With regard to the problems observed in attempting to define and categorize this religious phenomenon, like mixing in one basket both Christian churches and non-Christian cults, insisting to regard some movements as churches while they themselves refuse to be regarded as

---

[85] M.C. Kitschoff (ed.), *African Independent Churches Today. Kaleidoscope of Afro-Christianity*, Lewiston: Edwin Mellen, 1996, p. 19.

[86] J.C. Chakanza, *Voices of Preachers in Protest: The Ministry of Two Malawian Prophets: Elliot Kamwana and Wilfred Gudu,* Blantyre: CLAIM-Kachere, 1998, pp. 12-57.

[87] M.C. Kitschoff (ed), *African Independent Churches Today. Kaleidoscope of Afro-Christianity*, Lewiston: Edwin Mellen, 1996, p. 19.

[88] Ibid.

such, and further still to fail to find a comprehensive typology or definition that is inclusive of all "independent churches" like the Last Church, I agree with Klaus Fiedler in negating the idea of Independent Churches,[89] but rather that each movement or church should be treated simply as a movement or as a church in its own right.

These movements are of a great variety, such that placing them into categories may not accurately reflect the true nature of each category and it does not always help to increase our understanding and sometimes actually may be misleading.[90] Thus, the Last Church of God and His Christ International is simply one of the many churches and not one of the African Independent Churches as some would regard it.

---

[89] Rhodian Munyenyembe, *Christianity and Socio-Cultural Issues: The Charismatic Movement and Contextualization in Malawi*, Mzuzu: Mzuni Press, 2011, p. 25.

[90] M.C. Kitschoff (ed.), *African Independent Churches Today. Kaleidoscope of Afro-Christianity*, Lewiston: Edwin Mellen, 1996, p. 19.

Chapter 2: The Last Church of God and His Christ between 1916 and 1936

The history of the Last Church of God in Malawi from 1916 to 1936 is attributed much to the founder, Jordan Msumba. Not much is known about Msumba's personal life. However, with regard to his education it is said that he got his education from Livingstonia Mission of the Free (Presbyterian) Church of Scotland.[1]

With regard to his religious life some of his followers assume that in his early life he might have belonged to Livingstonia Mission.[2] However, it is further said by others that Msumba did join the Watch Tower Society later in his life around 1907 or 1909.[3]

How did the Last Church of God develop between 1916 and 1936, and what prompted Msumba as the founder to start the church? What was his theological basis and what were the doctrines of the church? And since the church was started during the colonial era, what was the relationship of the church with the colonial government?

The discussion of the first twenty years of the church's history shows first that Msumba established the Last Church as a "vanguard" of African culture; and forgetting that culture is dynamic, it happened with time that what seemed highly relevant at the beginning, started losing its "saltiness," forcing later generations to repudiate the very "pillars" of the church,[4] so that, when Jordan Msumba established the church on polygamy, it seemed a positive action; but that, from the beginning,

---

[1] Godfrey A. Banda and Peter G. Forster, "The Last Church of God and His Christ" in *Journal of Religion in Africa*, vol. 29, p. 442.

[2] Int. Rev Chiuli Manda, Retired Area Bishop, Munkhokwe, 17.9.2011.

[3] Godfrey A. Banda and Peter G. Forster, "The Last Church of God and His Christ" in *Journal of Religion in Africa*, vol. 29, p. 442.

[4] Rhodian Munyenyembe, *Christianity and Socio-Cultural Issues: The Charismatic Movement and Contextualization in Malawi*, Zomba: Kachere; Mzuzu: Mzuni Press, 2011, p. 26.

painted a dark picture of the church, which later generations would seek to repudiate.

Msumba and the Beginning of the Last Church of God

Msumba, like many other Malawians during his time, went to South Africa to seek greener pastures. It is believed that, while in South Africa, he met Joseph Booth.[5] Langworthy noted that Msumba was attracted to Watch Tower while in South Africa.[6] For some months he accompanied Booth and Kamwana to Pretoria and Durban, but after they parted Msumba remained loyal to Kamwana and the Watch Tower. Msumba returned to Nyasaland by early 1910 to lead the struggle against the Seventh Day Baptists.[7] Msumba, together with Timon Chirwa, did successfully woo Tonga congregations to return to Watch Tower.[8] This account sounds more tangible against the one which states that Msumba was forcibly sent back to Malawi in 1920 on the grounds that he was "lunatic."[9] This claim, especially the dating by Shepperson and Price, cannot be sustained when one considers the fact that the Last Church of God was actually started in Malawi in 1916 and not in 1920.[10] The first account verifies that Msumba was already in Malawi by 1916; therefore, the dating by Shepperson and Price with regard to Msumba's deportation might have been misplaced.

The story of Msumba as a "lunatic" and his deportation from South Africa is not mentioned by members of the church. The colonial government might indeed have had their suspicions on Msumba, as was the case with other independent church leaders. But the question still stands, was Msumba really a "lunatic"? It seems the government was more worried

---

[5] Int. Rev Chikosera Phiri, Archbishop Msondozi, Masasa, 4.4.2012.

[6] Harry Langworthy, *"Africa for the African" The Life of Joseph Booth*, Blantyre: Kachere-CLAIM, 1996, pp. 222-247.

[7] Ibid. pp. 222-247.

[8] Ibid. pp. 222-247.

[9] Godfrey A. Banda and Peter G. Forster, "The Last Church of God and His Christ" in *Journal of Religion in Africa*, vol. 29, p. 444.

[10] Int. Bishop Chimuliwu Chirwa, Area Bishop, Msondozi, 20.10.2011.

with the African National Church and its members rather than with Msumba and the Last Church of God as evidenced by the report from the Provincial Commissioner in Karonga.

The Provincial Commissioner said about the African National Church "But the African National Church includes in its members several natives of doubtful character."[11] On the other hand, this was what was said with regard to the Last Church of God "As far as I am aware their doctrine is not subversive."[12] If certainly Msumba was "lunatic," could this not have been evidenced or reflected in his doctrines or teachings? If indeed Msumba was a "trouble maker," then one might be right to conclude that after establishing his church he quieted down.

It may, however, not do justice to just dismiss the claim by others that Msumba was a "lunatic," especially when one considers Msumba's involvement with characters like Booth and Kamwana and also his Watch Tower offensive against the Seventh Day Baptists in Nkhatabay. An explanation for the change in Msumba's character may probably be found in the Watch Tower's ideology, especially of looking forward to 1914. Kamwana preached that the millennium would see the end of taxes, bring free schools, self-rule, equality and the end of European domination.[13] However, the year 1914 proved contrary, Msumba and the others might have been disappointed and felt let down by something they had been fighting for. In my opinion that was the turning point for Msumba. If he were lunatic while in Watch Tower, he was forced to change by what had happened upon starting his own church. This probably also explains why major doctrines of the Watch Tower are *not* reflected in Msumba's Last Church of God.

While Msumba was in South Africa, it is also believed that he met a man by the name of Joseph Smith in Cape Town, who influenced his religious beliefs. It is stated that Smith belonged to the Tomorrow Morning Church

---

[11] The Provincial Commissioner Northern Province - The Chief Secretary of the State, 18.10.1927.

[12] Ibid.

[13] Harry Langworthy, *"Africa for the African" The Life of Joseph Booth*, Blantyre: CLAIM-Kachere, 1996, pp. 222-247.

that was founded in 1816.[14] However, how much Msumba was influenced by this man is difficult to ascertain. Some church members claim that Smith and his church believed in the Old Testament and also accepted polygamy (based on stories of Abraham and others), but that it was banned from South Africa.[15]

If the above account is true, then probably that might be where Msumba got the belief in Christian polygamy. On a related issue, it is claimed that Msumba was excommunicated from Watch Tower in 1923 for polygamy.[16] It could be true that Msumba was excommunicated from Watch Tower. However, the year could again be misplaced, since by 1923 Msumba had already started the church in Karonga, even though it was not yet registered according to the claims by church members.[17]

Return of Msumba from South Africa (1916)

Upon his return to Malawi Msumba went to Karonga in 1916 to look for a job.[18] It was in Karonga that he first introduced the Last Church of God. Msumba met Ben Ngemela, who embraced the faith and continued spreading the church even after Msumba had left Karonga.[19] Ngemela was a Nyakyusa, his father having emigrated to Karonga and married one of the Kyungu's daughters.[20] Ngemela dominated the church not only in Karonga but also in the Rungwe area in Tanzania, such that it was known almost everywhere as *BaNgemela*.[21]

---

[14] I was not able to find the "Tomorrow Morning Church" on the web or elsewhere.

[15] Int. Bishop Chimuliwu Chirwa, Area Bishop, Msondozi, 20.10.2011.

[16] Godfrey A. Banda and Peter G. Forster, "The Last Church of God and His Christ" in *Journal of Religion in Africa,* vol. 29, p. 444.

[17] Int. Bishop Chimuliwu Chirwa, Area Bishop, Msondozi, 20.10.2011.

[18] Int. Bishop Chiuli Manda, retired Area Bishop, Munkhokwe, 17.9.2012.

[19] Ibid. 17.9.2012.

[20] Terence O. Ranger, *The African Churches of Tanzania*, Historical Association of Tanzania, Paper No. 5, Nairobi: East African Publishing House, 1972, p. 21.

[21] Ibid. 1972, p. 21.

The first church in Karonga was at Mwangasi village. It is believed that many people were attracted to the Last Church of God because "it was founded on the parable of the ten virgins and it also upheld polygamy."[22] Probably the parable of the ten virgins was important in the sense that it taught about the imminent second coming of Jesus Christ. While polygamy indeed attracted many people to join the church, it was also polygamy that caused the outsiders to look at the church as if its main objective was to uphold polygamy and not salvation for its members. Hence from the beginning many outsiders never took the Last Church seriously. They even gave it the name: *Tchalitchi la mitala* (Church of the polygamists).[23]

Msumba met Isaac Chazuka Kaunda in Karonga, who was also working there.[24] Kaunda too had been in South Africa and, like Ngemela, joined the Last Church of God and became an active member.[25] From Karonga Msumba came to his home area in Usisya, but his people did not welcome the church. He therefore decided to go to Nkhatabay, in 1925.[26] He first came to a place called Phiri (Nkhatabay). At Phiri, he found a man called Harrison Truegodi Mhone, who joined the Last Church of God. But it is said that Mhone was slow in understanding the teachings as he had little education. So Msumba proceeded to Msondozi where several "educated" individuals joined the church. These people included: Luka Nyirenda who worked as a clerk in government, Khumbo Banda (preacher), Katongo Mphande, Mutepelera Ng'oma, and Isaac Mkhuta Banda.[27] Msumba established a church at Msondozi with the assistance of these people, and Msondozi eventually became the headquarters of the church.

---

[22] The Provincial Commissioner Northern Province - The Chief Secretary of the State, 18.10.1927.
[23] In Tonga "Chalichi la Mta."
[24] Int. Bishop Chiuli Manda, Kamsita, retired Area Bishop, 17.9.2012.
[25] Ibid. 17.9.2012.
[26] Ibid. 17.9.2012.
[27] Ibid. 17.9.2012.

Msumba finally succeeded in registering the church with the government on 29th April 1925 and the name of his church was the "African Last Church of God and His Christ." This was approved by H.D. Aplin, the Provincial Commissioner at Nkhatabay. The biblical verses that Msumba used in the establishment of the church included: Rev 3:7 ["To the angel of the church in Philadelphia write: "This is the message from the one who is holy and true. He has the key that belonged to David, and when he opens a door, no one can close it."] Acts 15:16 ["After this I will return, says the Lord, and restore the kingdom of David. I will rebuild its ruins], Isaiah 52:10 ["The Lord will use his holy power; he will save his people, and all the world will see it."], Isaiah 56:5 [Then your name will be remembered in my temple and among my people longer than if you had sons and daughters. You will never be forgotten."] and Amos 9:11 [The Lord says, "A day is coming when I will restore the kingdom of David, which is like a house fallen into ruins. I will rebuild it and make it as it was long ago."].[28] The above verses talk mainly about the destruction of Jerusalem or Israel by their enemies. God promises to save his people with His mighty arm and to rebuild Jerusalem. And no one will stop God when he decides to save Israel.

From the above verses, one may interpret that probably Msumba meant that there was hope for those who were rejected (destroyed) in some churches because of polygamy and thereby were denied salvation, but that God, through the Last Church of God, had opened the door for them to be saved and that no one was going to shut that door. Again, some of these texts specifically mention the figure of David, so in a way Msumba seems to have been pointing out that God chose, anointed and made lasting promises to David, who was a polygamist. Hence there is no need to reject polygamists in the churches.

Jordan Msumba and Isaac Kaunda between 1925 and 1936

The activities of Jordan Msumba after 1925 are not much known, but one thing that happened after 1925 was the split with Kaunda. There are two accounts concerning the split. One account holds that Isaac Kaunda bade farewell to the leaders of the church at Karonga to go to his home in Chintheche, but eventually teamed up with Msumba again. These two together later set out to Mzimba to introduce the church there, and it

---

[28] Int. Bishop Chiuli Chirwa, Kamsita, 17.9.2012.

was while in Mzimba that Kaunda dissociated himself from Msumba and started his own church, called Messenger of Covenant, that later became known as Chipangano.[29]

The second account, popular among the church members today, is that, after some time in Karonga, Kaunda decided to return to his home (Chintheche). He peacefully bid farewell to the church members there and the leadership gave him K1.00 *phoso* (money to use on his journey). Apparently Msumba had gone to Tanzania (1928). Upon his arrival in Nkhatabay Kaunda started using the name Messenger of Covenant instead of Last Church of God.[30]

Some members of the Last Church defected to Chipangano. When Msumba came back from Tanzania (probably in 1934) he was told of a new church besides the Last Church that allowed polygamy.[31] Msumba confronted Kaunda to show him where he got the name Messenger of Covenant that he was using. Kaunda showed Msumba the "letters" that he had brought with him from South Africa on which was written the name Messenger of Covenant.[32] Msumba tried to negotiate with Kaunda on the possibility of leaving the name Chipangano and return to the use of the name Last Church of God.

It is stated that the first meeting of the negotiations took place at Msondozi on 7th July 1934. Kaunda refused to change his mind on the issue at this meeting. Another meeting took place at Phiri in the same year. This time Kaunda accepted to return to the use of the name Last Church of God. This news was welcomed with joy by many members of the Last Church of God since the issue had ended peacefully.[33]

However, it seems Kaunda still had his own doubts and misgivings, especially when it came to the question of leadership. Kaunda asked Msumba that in the case the two churches became one, who was going to be the leader? In response Msumba said that he was not looking for

---

[29] Int. Rev Chiuli Manda, retired Bishop, Munkhokwe, 31.8.2012.
[30] Minutes Msondozi Synod, nd.
[31] Minutes, Msondozi Synod, nd.
[32] Ibid.
[33] Ibid.

leadership as he was most of the times moving up and down to Karonga.[34] Therefore, the leadership was given to Kaunda.

Nevertheless, Kaunda was not really convinced, for shortly there was a meeting at Mukuwazi where Kaunda and others announced their continued allegiance to Chipangano. This caused some confusion among the members. Some members defected to Chipangano again, while others remained in the Last Church of God.[35]

Kaunda then went to the District Commissioner (DC) to register his church. But the DC sent him back to call the leaders of the Last Church, since the teachings and beliefs of these two churches were similar.[36] It is said that Msumba willingly offered his consent to the DC for his friend to register the church. This happened on 8th July 1934 and 12th July 1934 respectively. [37]

The following are the biblical verses that Kaunda is said to have quoted in establishing his church: Matt. 18:16 ["But if he will not listen to you, take one or two other persons with you, so that every accusation may be upheld by the testimony of two or more witnesses, as the scripture says."], Mark 8:17 ["Jesus knew what they were saying, so he asked them, "Why are you discussing about not having any bread? Don't you know or understand yet? Are your minds dull?], Deut. 17:16 [The king is not to have a large number of horses for his army, because the Lord has said that his people are never to return there."], Deut. 19:15 ["One witness is not enough to convict a man of a crime; at least two witnesses are necessary to prove that a man is guilty."], and Num. 35:3 ["These cities will belong to the Levites, and pasture land will be for their cattle and all their other animals."].[38]

Unlike the verses that Msumba used in establishing his church, there seems to be no clear thought running across the verses Kaunda is said to have used. Thus, it is difficult to deduce the message he wanted to convey. But probably from Matt. 18:16 and Deut. 17:16 one may interpret that Kaunda wanted to convince the Provincial Commissioner

---

[34] Minutes, Msondozi Synod, nd.
[35] Ibid.
[36] Ibid.
[37] Ibid.
[38] Ibid.

that there were no ill feelings between him and Msumba. These two verses talk about the need to have two witnesses in a case, and support the fact that Msumba had agreed to act as a witness for him when Kaunda went to register the church.

From the above account, one can conclude that Kaunda separated from the Last Church of God on the grounds of leadership. Probably Kaunda thought what would happen if Msumba finally decided to come home and settle down? There seems to have been no other disagreements between Msumba and Kaunda apart from that. The peaceful separation encouraged the peaceful coexistence thereafter between these two churches, even up to now.

In 1935 Msumba decided to go back to Tanzania where it is believed that he started a church at Mwanza. By then Ngemela had already started the church in the Rungwe area from Karonga.[39] Meanwhile Msumba appointed Malangani Munthewe to oversee the church in Malawi.[40] Munthewe did not stay long in the position, he died in 1936 and Isaac Mkhuta was chosen to replace him. This event took place at Msondozi where members of the church from all parts of Malawi had gathered for a conference. It was at this time that the Last Church of God rejected the use of the title Bishop for the top leader; instead they opted for the title General Principal.[41]

Msumba left behind a simple leadership hierarchy consisting of the overseer known as the General Principal (who had a personal secretary), the General Secretary and the General Treasurer.[42] These were assisted by the Pastors of the congregations.

Msumba did not return from his second visit to Tanzania. It is said that he died and was buried in Mwanza in Tanzania in 1936.[43] A memorial

---

[39] Terrence O. Ranger, *The African Churches of Tanzania*, Historical Association of Tanzania, Paper No. 5, Nairobi: East African Publishing House, 1972, p. 21.

[40] Minutes, Msondozi Synod, nd.

[41] Ibid. nd.

[42] Int. Bishop Chiuli Manda, retired Area Bishop, Munkhokwe, 19.2.2012.

[43] Ibid. 19.2.2012.

tombstone has been erected recently in his home village Mabuli in Usisya.[44] Those that were left behind continued to run the church.

Theological Basis of the Last Church of God

Founders of churches usually have a basis on which their teachings are based. Surely Msumba should have had such a base. Msumba himself wrote concerning the establishment of his church:

> The desire of the establishment of this church is, she is pity for the people of Africa. Many Brethren from Europe and America came here to help us be a husband of one woman. We believed but many of us failed. It is not our law. It is not God's law. Therefore, this church is coming out from every sect which rejects to worship God with one husband and many wives; she believes and co-operates with the faith of Abraham, the father of us all.[45]

From the above quotation, it is clear that Msumba started his church with an intention to cater mainly for those like himself who were not accepted in the mainline churches due to polygamy and not necessarily to reach out to those who were not yet saved. In this case, the Last Church of God was started mostly as a reaction against mission churches, protesting against certain cultural prohibitions in the mainline churches.[46] Msumba did not only try to accommodate Christianity to indigenous culture but he actually based the faith on it. At that time, this seemed a positive step, since many people practiced polygamy and society encouraged it. But times have changed, polygamy no longer appeals to as many people today as it used to be the case in the past. Therefore, as much as polygamy seemed to have been a positive action at the time, it

---

[44] Int. O. Masinda, General Principal, Kazando, 15.4.2012.

[45] Terence O. Ranger, *The African Churches of Tanzania*, Historical Association of Tanzania Paper No. 5, Nairobi: East African Publishing House, 1972, p. 21.

[46] Rhodian Munyenyembe, *Christianity and Socio-Cultural Issues: The Charismatic Movement and Contextualization in Malawi*, Zomba: Kachere, Mzuzu: Mzuni Press, 2011, p. 26.

was also in itself "a seed of self- destruction" for the future as far as it being the basis of the church is concerned.[47]

Again, from the name of his church itself, Last Church, we can deduce some theological foundation. The name had two implications. Firstly, Msumba was saying that even them that were regarded as the "least" by many due to polygamy. were now given a chance to worship and find salvation. Another possible interpretation would be that Msumba thought that this church was the last before the second coming of Jesus Christ.

This would mean that Msumba believed in the imminent second coming of Jesus Christ. One should not forget that Msumba at one point in his life had belonged to the Watch Tower Movement. From the above explanations, one may conclude that Msumba established his church with the aim of reaching out to the "least" people with the good news of salvation before Christ returned. No wonder the Provincial Commissioner wrote in one of his letters that the church was "based on the parable of the ten virgins."[48] We know that in this parable Jesus was warning the Church to always be ready for the groom (Christ), otherwise they might miss salvation.

Even though Msumba considered the name "Last Church" in a positive light, for outsiders it had and somehow continues to have a negative undertone to it namely, that the church is the "least" church compared to other churches around.

Before Msumba went to Tanzania, he left guiding rules for the church, which were later moulded and added to as well as enshrined in the constitution of the church. These rules might have been compiled between the 1940s and 1950s, since they mention *Umanyano*, a name that came into existence in Livingstonia Synod in the 1940s.

---

[47] Ronald L. Johnstone, *Religion in Society: A Sociology of Religion*, Upper Saddle River, New Jersey: Roberts, 2004, p. 98.

[48] The Provincial Commissioner Northern Province, Nkata – The Chief Secretary to the State, 18.10.1927.

The Constitution of the Last Church of God and His Christ

Some of the rules in the Constitution of the Last Church of God and his Christ are as follows: [49]

> It is acceptable in our church to practice polygamy. However, the person is supposed to have the marriage blessed at the church (Numbers 12:1, Genesis 29:21).
>
> It is acceptable in our church to drink beer. However, the person should not get drunk (1 Timothy 5:1).
>
> It is agreed in our church that members should choose their own pastor because they choose from deep down their hearts (Acts 6:3, Exodus 18:21).
>
> It is agreed in our church that pastors should not be paid (John 10:12).
>
> It is agreed in our church for members to work with and collaborate with the government in areas such as schools, hospitals and maintaining peace.
>
> It is agreed in our church that any member or leader should not be allowed to preach if they put on short trousers because it is disgracing and disrespectful to the church.
>
> It is agreed in our church to give offerings because the money helps in solving some problems in the church (Exodus 25:1, 1 Corinthians 16:1).
>
> It is agreed in our church to have women's guild (*Umanyano*) and youth guild (*Ukilano*) because they are parts of the church (Joel 2:28, Judges 4:1, Acts 2: 17).
>
> It is agreed in our church to conduct Holy Communion (1 Corinthians 11:23).
>
> It is agreed in our church to conduct baptism (Mathew 3:16, John 3:1, Acts 2:37).

---

[49] Constitution of the Last Church of God and His Christ, nd.

For a long time, the above constitution governed the church, however, the recent years have seen some of the rules in the constitution changed with regard to the changing of the times and the needs of the members.

The Doctrine of the Last Church of God and His Christ

The Last Church of God does not have a well-organized or written doctrine. However, they do believe in one God and that Jesus is the Son of God and the Saviour of humankind. They also believe in the Trinity of God (God the Father, God the Son and God the Holy Spirit).[50] However, the understanding of many members about the Trinity is not that deep (as it is oftentimes true for local Christians in various churches). They generally understand God to be the father, Jesus the son and also as the intermediary sent to do the work of the father on earth. The Holy Spirit is seen as the power of God and not necessarily as a person.[51]

They believe that Jesus will come again to judge the world and that those who believe in Jesus Christ and do God's will shall be saved, whereas sinners will be condemned forever. To be saved means to believe in Jesus Christ as one's personal Lord and Saviour and to do good. That means that a person can have faith in Christ, but when she or he dies while having a particular sin unconfessed, they go to hell.[52] Here the theological issues of whether salvation can or cannot be lost are irrelevant for many members.

The Last Church of God believes that Holy Communion is just a remembrance of Jesus' suffering, death and resurrection. The Last Church also believes in the believers' need for baptism by immersion. Baptism symbolizes sharing in the death and resurrection of Jesus Christ as well as repentance of one's sins. Thus, when a person is baptized, it is proof that his or her sins have been forgiven.[53]

---

[50] Int. Rev Kaundama, Kamsita, 9.10.2012.

[51] Ndongolera Mwangupili, "Grassroots Perception of the Trinity: The Case of the Catholic Church and the Last Church of God in Champhira," MA module, Mzuzu University, 2009.

[52] Int. Rev Kaundama, Kamsita, 9.10.2012.

[53] Ibid.

The Last Church of God and the Colonial Government

Msumba started his church in a political climate when independent churches were viewed with suspicion by the colonial government, especially due to the 1915 Chilembwe uprising. For Msumba the suspicion was increased "because of his previous association with Watch Tower."[54] Even though this was the case, Banda and Forster observe that "in its formative years the Last Church came into conflict more with the already established Mission Churches than with the colonial government."[55]

It seems Msumba just wanted to concentrate on his church, and it was clearly stated in the constitution that members were to cooperate with the government. Up to now the Last Church does not involve itself in political matters.[56] Members are clearly told that the church shall not take any responsibility if they find themselves in trouble with the government. However, this does not mean that members are forbidden to participate in politics, but they should do so as individuals and not in the name of the church.[57]

In 1939, over two decades since the establishment of the church in Malawi, the Acting Chief Secretary to the Government (Malawi), confessed in his letter to the Chief Secretary (Lusaka) that "No complaints have been received as far as I am aware as to the manner in which these Missions have been conducted."[58] The Missions being referred to in the letter were the Last Church of God and the African National Church.[59]

---

[54] Godfrey A. Banda and Peter G. Forster, "The Last Church of God and His Christ" in *Journal of Religion in Africa,* vol. 29, pp. 455-456.

[55] Ibid, p. 447.

[56] Constitution of the Last Church of God and His Christ, nd.

[57] Ibid. nd.

[58] Acting Chief Secretary - the Government to the Chief Secretary Lusaka, Northern Province, 21.10.1939.

[59] Godfrey A. Banda and Peter G. Forster, "The Last Church of God and His Christ" in *Journal of Religion in Africa,* vol. 29, pp. 455-456.

Even though Msumba seems to have been pursuing a peaceful co-existence with the colonial government, his church still faced some challenges due to its expansion. The Provincial Commissioner (Northern Province - Nkata) wrote to the Chief Secretary to the State in 1939 saying,

> When I was recently at Karonga the leaders of the sect, Ben Ngemela and Sam Sichinga, asked for permission to build two more churches in villages where the Headmen and villagers have no objection to their presence. I have deferred granting their request for I feel that these people are going to be so numerous and that there will be many more applications for churches.[60]

Some government administrators tried to discourage this rapid expansion of the church. For instance, in 1929 the Acting Provincial Commissioner, Karonga, wrote to the Chief Secretary in Zomba to the effect that "Msumba was not of good character, having been detained in 1924 by the District Commissioner for Chintheche as being a danger to the peace."[61] This probably was aimed at convincing the Chief Secretary that the Last Church was a danger to the state hence some action should be taken against the church.

In 1934, there was again pressure to ban the Last Church. Chief Kyungu Peter in Karonga, who was a modernizer and also active in the Native Association, petitioned the government to ban the church. His official reason was that its practice of baptism by total immersion was potentially dangerous.[62] However, "The Governor saw no reason to ban the church as it had given no trouble, and he merely agreed that places of baptism would be inspected."[63] Thus, neither Msumba nor his church were of any danger to the colonial government, even though some people thought that they were and tried to suppress them.

---

[60] The Provincial Commissioner Northern Province, Nkata - the Chief Secretary to the State Nyasaland, 22.9.1939.

[61] Godfrey A. Banda and Peter G. Forster, "The Last Church of God and His Christ" in *Journal of Religion in Africa,* vol. 29, pp. 455-456.

[62] Ibid. p. 447.

[63] Ibid. pp. 455-456.

The Relationship with other Churches

The Last Church of God came into conflict with the already established mission churches, especially when it came to certain behavioural patterns that were condoned by the Last Church of God, but were condemned by the mission churches.[64] Some of the practices that some of the mission churches did not agree with included acceptance of polygamy, beer drinking, consulting African doctors as well as the issue of baptism by the mission churches. The fact that those who were seen as not "ready" for baptism and those who had been expelled could be welcome in the Last Church of God did not go well with the mission churches.[65]

Due to the above reasons, it is said that the Church of Central Africa Presbyterian (CCAP) for instance, would not sell Bibles to members of the Last Church of God claiming that they were sinners. Apart from that, members of the Last Church of God were forbidden to sing songs that were sung in CCAP. This made them to come up with their own songs and a hymn book. The third edition of the hymn book was done in 1987 and it contains 208 songs. The people who composed many of these songs were pastors in the church like Maxwell Mvula, C.C. Mvula, M.J. Mvula, L.L. Jere, Yakobe Mkweu, Y. Mbizi and G. Mwanza. The members of the Last Church interpreted the act of the CCAP as a campaign to have the members of the Last Church of God join CCAP.[66] In other words, the CCAP thought that by not selling the Bibles to the members of the Last Church of God they would be forced to leave the Last Church of God and join CCAP.[67] In the 1970s cases were recorded of refusal of Presbyterians and Last Church of God members to attend each other's funerals. In those cases where attendance was permitted, conflicts often erupted.[68]

---

[64] Godfrey A. Banda and Peter G. Forster, "The Last Church of God and His Christ" in *Journal of Religion in Africa,* vol. 29, pp. 455-456.

[65] Ibid. p. 447.

[66] Int. Rev Chiuli Manda, retired Rev African Last Church, Kamsita, 19.2.2012.

[67] I record this as perceived by the Last Church. There may be no documentary evidence by Livingstonia Synod.

[68] Godfrey A. Banda and Peter G. Forster, "The Last Church of God and His Christ" in *Journal of Religion in Africa,* vol. 29, pp. 455-456.

It is mentioned that in one case, members of the Last Church of God were told by a lay member to stop singing their own hymns while on the way to the funeral of a Presbyterian member.[69]

The Last Church of God further claims that the CCAP would not even accept offerings from them during the funeral of a CCAP member. This still continues in certain areas like at Kamsita (Nkhatabay). When I asked Agness Kachali (the wife of the CCAP Rev Mughogho responsible for Kamsita area), she said that she was not aware of this but would find out. But she said that if it was true that this was taking place then it was wrong. She, however, confessed that according to the Synod rules they do not exchange choirs with the Last Church of God and other similar churches because CCAP considers them as sects.[70] One however questions if it is wrong to exchange choirs even with sects. Nevertheless, every church has its own principles.

The other thing was that, whereas the Last Church of God would and still does recognize the baptism of the members from mission churches, this was and still is not the case with the mission churches. These mission churches would still require someone from the Last Church of God to be re-baptized after going through certain required instructions in order to become a member of the church.[71]

The *Amayi Achikondi* also met some challenges from some members of *Umanyano* (CCAP) as these would tell them *(Amayi Achikondi)* to stop putting on their uniform. Apparently the *Amayi Achikondi* had adopted almost the same uniform as the *Umanyano*, which is a white blouse, black skirt and black shoes. The difference was the belt, while the *Amayi Achikondi* had a black belt the *Umanyano* had a white belt.

From the above account, one would notice that conflicts were mainly between the Presbyterians and the Last Church of God. However, this does not mean that there were no conflicts between the Last Church of God and other mission churches. But it appears "that relations with

---

[69] However, the pastor later apologized about this. Ibid. p. 447.

[70] Int. Mrs Rev Mughogho, wife to CCAP Rev K.T.R. Mughogho, Bandawe Station, 19.2.2012.

[71] Int. Rev Chiuli Manda, retired Rev African Last Church, Kamsita, 19.2.2012.

Roman Catholics were sometimes more accommodating at the local level."[72] For instance, it is stated that the Roman Catholic Mission at Nkhamenya helped its Last Church of God neighbours with food when a major conference was held and there were cases of joint Easter services taking place.[73] But it is not clear as to how exactly these joint Easter services were conducted.

One should, however, be careful not to think that the mission churches dictated or authorized everything that their members did towards the Last Church of God members or vice versa. Sometimes members would do certain things towards other churches based on their own reasons and personal attitudes. However, we can again not rule out that there were some decisions that came from the leadership of the church. For instance,

> The Livingstonia Synod of the Presbyterian Church expressed the view that if one of its own ministers were asked to give a funeral sermon for any member of the Last Church (or any other Independent Church), he should take the whole service without the participation of an Independent Church member.[74]

There were also certain cases where the Last Church of God co-existed well with some of the already established missions and actually wanted to amalgamate with them. The Provincial Commissioner (Northern Province-Nkata) wrote to the Chief Secretary to the State in 1927 that,

> Mr D.R. Mackenzie of the Scottish Mission informs me that the members of the Last Church of God have often strongly urged Scottish Mission to take them under their charge, but that naturally it is impossible for him to countenance polygamy. He looks upon them as good Christians who are mistaken in their interpretation of scriptures.[75]

---

[72] Godfrey A. Banda and Peter G. Forster, "The Last Church of God and His Christ" in *Journal of Religion in Africa,* vol. 29, pp. 455-456.

[73] Ibid. pp. 455-456.

[74] Ibid. pp. 455-456.

[75] The Provincial Commissioner Northern Province, Nkata - the Chief Secretary to the State, 18.10.1927.

With time, however, the relationship between the Last Church of God and mission churches, even with the Presbyterians, improved. Rev Masinda for instance recalls how Rev Mphande of the CCAP (Kachere congregation) brought together the leaders from various churches (including Last Church) and chiefs at Kachere (Nkhatabay) in the early 1990s.[76] Mphande called for this meeting, where he discussed the need and importance of unity among people from various churches. People were able to air their concerns and challenges they were facing with regard to the issue of unity. From that time the relationships between CCAP and Last Church of God greatly improved as the CCAP would even accept offerings from the Last Church of God during the funeral of a Presbyterian member.[77] However, there is still a general tendency for the Last Church of God to feel that the Presbyterians look down upon them.[78] And it is true that to some extent the Presbyterians do look down on the Last Church, for even today they do not exchange choirs with them and demand rebaptism, among other things.

On the other hand, there seems to have existed good relationships between the Last Church of God and other Independent Churches from the beginning. For example, White Longwe (the General Principal after the split of the church) was the one who ordained the leader of the New Testament Church in Nkhatabay. Sometimes a pastor from Chipangano or African National Church or Emanuel Church could take the service during the funeral of a member of the Last Church of God and vice versa.[79] Apart from that, members from these churches are free to partake in Holy Communion in the other churches, and these churches recognize each other's baptism.

In some cases, if someone had a position in the other churches and then joins the Last Church of God, they still recognize his position, but the person may not be given a church if he was a pastor, since there is already another pastor. For instance, in Nkhatabay there is missionary

---

[76] Int. Rev Masinda, Archbishop, Kazando, 21.9.2011.

[77] Int. Rev Masinda, Archbishop, Kazando, 21.9.2011.

[78] Godfrey A. Banda and Peter G. Forster, "The Last Church of God and His Christ" in *Journal of Religion in Africa,* vol. 29, pp. 455-456.

[79] Int. Rev Kaundama, Kamsita, 16.2.2011.

Matridi who came from Chipangano Church where he was the Head Pastor. He is recognized as a missionary in the Last Church of God, but he has not been given any section, since all sections are already occupied.[80]

One can argue of course that the warm relationships that exist (or existed) between the Last Church and other Independent Churches as described above are due to the fact that these churches share or for years had shared many things in common, such as acceptance of polygamy etc. But with the mission churches the point of departure seems to have been "permanently" marked that very time when Msumba "defiantly legalized" polygamy in his church.

For many years mainline churches chose to look at the Last Church only negatively. This is the case even when the Last Church is trying to repudiate the very same things that negatively tainted the church, of course doing so for other reasons. Unfortunately, other churches, which came later, to a large extent, also share the negative attitude against "AICs," including the Last Church.

When Msumba died, he had left the headquarters of the church at Msondozi, which became the headquarters of not only the Last Church of God in Malawi, but also for many years of the entire church even outside Malawi. Whenever a church has been established we expect it to grow or expand from its starting point. From Msondozi the Last Church of God spread to many other areas.

.

---

[80] Int. Rev Chiuli Manda, retired Reverend, Kamsita, 31.8.2012.

Chapter 3: The Growth of the Last Church of God from 1935 to 1962

The growth of the Last Church of God in Malawi is much attributed to those members that were left behind after Msumba had left for Tanzania in 1928. Msumba established the church in Karonga and at Msondozi. The leaders that he ordained and left behind continued the work of extending the church to many other areas.[1]

Msumba left the church in the hands of Isaac Mkhuta. He also appointed Luka Nyirenda as District Principal, and Katongo Mphande and Mutepelera Ng'oma were ordained as pastors.[2] These are the leaders who facilitated the expansion of the church. As the church was expanding it encountered challenges, one of which was a division of the church, which led to the starting of another headquarters at Kazando. Polygamy played a key role as a factor in the rapid growth of the church during its formative years, but with time it became less and less important as a tool for attracting new members to the church. The church had to concentrate on other ways of bringing new members into the church for its continuity.

Basically, there were three main ways by which the church was spread: first, it was the deliberate effort from the headquarters to introduce the church into new areas.[3] In this way some leaders from the headquarters were sent to several places and planted the church there. When these leaders arrived in a new place they would first go to the chief and introduce themselves and their mission. If permission was granted, they would speak to those interested.

If they found any followers or converts, they would baptize them and choose leaders to take care of the church while they moved on to other places. Later they would report these new churches to the headquarters which then sent someone to officially open the church and ordain the

---

[1] Int. Bishop Chiuli Manda, retired Area Bishop, Munkhokwe, 19.2.2012.
[2] Ibid. 19.2.2012.
[3] Ibid. 19.2.2012.

residing pastor. This is how the church came to areas like Mzimba and Kasungu.[4]

Another way was when members moved from one area to another for personal reasons. If they found that in that new place there was no Last Church of God, they would start one if the people were interested and report to the headquarters.[5]

Similar to the above factors was the initiative of those who went outside the country to look for jobs. When those members found that there were many of them that belonged to this church, they usually requested the headquarters to send them some leader to establish the church there. Once the church was established, it would be left in the hands of selected leaders to continue the work.[6]

Thus, in the years of its formation, the Last Church of God experienced rapid growth to the extent that the provincial commissioner in Karonga deferred granting the church's request to build churches. He feared that members would become too numerous and that would mean many more applications for churches.[7]

This rapid growth was attributed among other factors to the church's stand on polygamy.[8] Those Christians who would not be accepted in other churches on the grounds of polygamy found acceptance in the Last Church of God. For this reason, it was popularly called *"church la mitala"* (church for polygamists).[9] Besides that, the church did not demand much from its members, especially in terms of monetary contributions or special teachings for them to be regarded as confirmed members. For instance, no special instructions were required for one to join the church, as the Last Church of God was less strict in its rules compared to other

---

[4] Int. Bishop Chiuli Manda, retired Area Bishop, Munkhokwe, 19.2.2012.

[5] Ibid. 19.2.2012.

[6] Int. Bishop Chiuli Manda, retired Area Bishop, Kamsita, 19.2.2012.

[7] The Provincial Commissioner Northern Province, Nkata – The Chief Secretary of the State, 18.10.1927.

[8] Ibid.

[9] Int. Bishop Chiuli Manda, retired Area Bishop, Kamsita, 19.2.2012.

churches. Thus, it also attracted a lot of members from the Watch Tower Society, which had strict rules for its members.[10]

It is interesting to note that even though the church was growing fast, many of its members were adults and old people. The church did not appeal much to the youth.[11] From the time of its establishment many who joined the church were elderly people and adults who could not find acceptance in other churches. Even as the church expanded people had the mentality that the Last Church of God was for the elderly people.

Besides that, some of its practices were not appealing to the youths.[12] For example, the clerical regalia for pastors turned the interest of many youths away from the church. Pastors used to put on a lot of headgear and long robes and used to carry rods in their hands.[13] Here one would be right to conclude that Msumba borrowed from the Zionist way of dressing, only that he modified it to involve pastors only. All Zionist denominations in Malawi use robes or uniforms during worship, taking after Dowie's style.[14] This kind of dressing contributed to putting the youths off the church.[15]

Lastly, the Last Church did not accept choirs, drums, dancing and not even clapping of hands during the worship service.[16] We know that these are some of the things which attract many youths to the church. Thus, for a long time the Last Church of God was regarded as a church for

---

[10] The Provincial Commissioner Northern Province, Nkata - The Chief Secretary of the State, 18.10.1927.

[11] Int. Bishop Joseph Sibale, District Bishop – Chitipa, Chitipa Boma, 26.4.2013.

[12] Int. Rev Kaundama, Kamsita, 12.7.2011.

[13] Int. Rev Kaundama, Kamsita, 12.7.2011.

[14] Ulf Strohbehn, *The Zionist Churches in Malawi. History - Theology - Anthropology*, Mzuzu: Mzuni Press, 2016, p. 175.

[15] The original Christian Apostolic Church in Zion, Illinois, though proud of the Dowie heritage and offering healing prayers every Sunday, has long given up on ritual dressing etc and has become a regular Evangelical church. There were many young people. (Information from Klaus Fiedler from his visit there in the late 1980s.)

[16] Ibid. 12.7.2011.

elderly people. However, things have changed these days. One will find youths in the Last Church of God. The reasons for this change shall be discussed later.

The Spread of the Church from Msondozi

The Last Church of God is today found in many districts in Malawi. Some of these districts include: Kasungu, Mzimba, Rumphi, Chitipa, Dowa, Ntchisi, Nkhotakota, Salima, Blantyre and Karonga.[17] The issue of "which is the original Last Church of God" is not yet resolved, however.

Nkhatabay

In Nkhatabay district the first and thus earliest church was the one at Msondozi (1925), started by Jordan Msumba himself. It was first built close to the lake and because of this they oftentimes experienced problems in connection to the water. The members, under the leadership of Rev Mkhuta, decided to look for a better site in 1967. This second site was far from the first one but it is close to the MI road. This is where the headquarters stands to this day. Before they built the present church, the members had built a temporary shelter for worship.[18]

From Msondozi the church extended to Dwambazi and Lweya areas. The one that brought the church to Dwambazi area was Rev Chigawinga. These churches included: Mgodi (village headman Mutepelera), Chifira (village headman Chiweyu), Mbamba (Traditional Authority Fuka), Kalowa (village headman Nkholozo) and two more churches, one at Makwenda and the other one at Kuwirwi. However, not much is known about Rev Chigawinga.[19]

The earliest churches in Lweya area were, Chiwole, Chigwiti, Chizi, Phiri, Lwazi, Kaulambwi and Kajiriwi.[20] Luka Nyirenda and Katongo Mphande were the ones responsible for starting these churches. Many of these

---

[17] Int. Bishop Chiuli Manda, retired Bishop, Munkhokwe, 19.2.2012.
[18] Ibid. 19.2.2012.
[19] Ibid. 19.2.2012.
[20] Ibid. 19.2.2012.

churches were started between 1925 and the 1940s. Over the years other churches were added in these areas.[21]

The church came to Munkhokwe in 1969 through Mr Chibanzi. He was a Tumbuka and he came from Mzimba, but he had married a Tonga wife. Mr Chilibwanji brought this church from Mlowe (Sanga), where he was a member. He died in 1974 and was succeeded by Mr Chiuli Manda, who was ordained as pastor in 1976. He moved the church from the site where Rev Chilibwanji established the first church to another site within the same Munkhokwe. The church was built in Chilibwanji's village. However, later on the members of the church started having problems with the community who were not happy with the establishment of the church. This caused members to look for a better site for the church. They left and found a temporary place for worship along the Ml road at Kamsita, where they used to worship under a tree.[22]

The moving of the church to Kamsita coincided with the retirement of Rev Chiuli Manda in 1998. He was succeeded by Rev Kaundama, who was ordained on 8th August 1999. After his ordination, he mobilized the members to construct a new church. Members raised the money through what is locally called *Fandi* (these are activities that members engage in order to raise funds). Finally, the church at Munkhokwe was completed and they moved from Kamsita to the new church and demolished the church that was built in the village of Rev Chiuli Manda. The construction of the church took them six months.[23]

Karonga

Karonga is one of the districts in which the Last Church of God was introduced quite early. The church was brought there by Jordan Msumba himself. Some state that the church was started there in 1916 while others say that it was started in 1924.[24] In the beginning the members in various places used to meet under a tree. The first church that is

---

[21] Int. Bishop Chiuli Manda, retired Bishop, Munkhokwe, 19.2.2012.
[22] Int. Bishop Chiuli Manda, retired Bishop, Kamsita, 25.10.2012.
[23] Int. Rev Kaundama, Kamsita, 12.7.2011.
[24] See discussion about the early dates in Msumba's life in chapter 3 section 3.2

mentioned in 1927 was the one at Mwangasi village. By that time, the members numbered between 700 to 800.[25] It was Ben Ngemela who did much of the spreading of the church in Karonga and beyond to Rungwe in Tanzania.[26] The church in Karonga faced some big challenges in its early years. It is mentioned that Chief Kyungu Peter was suspicious of the Last Church.[27] He had been a teacher and apparently also had educated advisers.[28] Kyungu Peter petitioned the government to ban the church. He expelled Ngemela from Karonga and even arranged the burning of some prayer houses. It is stated that "He saw the Last Church as retrogressive and as a threat to his authority over the masses."[29]

Ben Ngemela

The history of the Last Church in Karonga is incomplete without Ben Ngemela. He was originally from Mwaya in Tanzania. He came to Karonga *boma* but later on he settled in Ngerenge. Ngemela had one sister called Tuyowepo and she came to Karonga with him. She was married to Mr Mwalilino of Karonga and died in 1994. Ngemela married two wives.

The first wife was NyaUhango (Dalapalapa) from Mwenilondo (Karonga).[30] NyaDalapalapa had two sons namely, John and William. Both sons became pastors in the church. John was the pastor of the church at Isaki in Tanzania for Ngemela sent him there to maintain his family land. John had six children, all girls, of whom three are alive at the time of writing. One of them is the wife of Rev Mwakalenga of Chibavi Last Church of God. On the other hand, William was pastor of the church at Wilole in

---

[25] Godfrey A. Banda and Peter G. Forster, "The Last Church of God and His Christ" in *Journal of Religion in Africa*, vol. 29, pp. 455-456.

[26] Terence O. Ranger, *The African Churches of Tanzania*, Historical Association of Tanzania Paper No. 5, Nairobi: East African Publishing House, 1972, p. 21.

[27] Godfrey A. Banda and Peter G. Forster, "The Last Church of God and His Christ" in *Journal of Religion in Africa*, vol. 29, pp. 455-456.

[28] Ibid. p. 447.

[29] Ibid. p. 447.

[30] Int. Rev Mwakalenga, Chibavi Last Church of God, Chibavi, 5.11.2013.

Karonga. He had five children, three daughters and two sons, but all of them have died.[31]

The second wife was NyaMchimba from Kasantha (Ngerenge). It is said that Ngemela sent this wife away while she was pregnant, because he thought that he was not the one responsible for the pregnancy. The woman gave birth to a son at her parents' home and the child was named Burton. Ngemela never took her again as his wife.[32]

Ngemela became very popular in Karonga and Tanzania, more than the founder of the church. This is explained partly by the fact that Ngemela had the gift of prophecy. It is said that he prophesied many things which came to pass. For instance, he prophesied that on the Ngerenge hill there will come whites in the future who will bring development. Years later, the Chinese came and opened the rice scheme on the hill. He also prophesied about the tarred road between Malawi and Tanzania and indeed, many years after his prophecy, the tarred road was constructed. It is further said that when someone came to do him harm through magic he would know and even say it. Ngemela finally died around 1964.[33] By that time the members of the Last Church in Karonga and Tanzania were called BaNgemela (people of Ngemela).

Chitipa

The church was introduced in Chitipa in 1935 by Phillip Kameme from Kameme, who brought the church from Karonga to Mwamukumba village in Kameme (Chitipa). It should be noted that by 1935 the Last Church of God was already in Tanzania. Some members from Kameme were congregating in the Last Church in Tanzania. When Phillip Kameme established the Last Church of God they started church meetings and worked towards bringing those members, who were worshiping in Tanzania, to join the church in Kameme. Once the church was

---

[31] Int. Rev Mwakalenga, Chibavi Last Church of God, Chibavi, 5.11.2013.
[32] Ibid. 5.11.2013.
[33] Ibid. 5.11.2013.

established, Phillip Kameme became the Bishop, while Sichula and Sichinga were presiding pastors.[34]

From Kameme the church spread to Nthalire and Wenya, mainly by Phillip Kameme, in the same year 1935. However, the church was left in the hands of Bishop Mughogho. The church was also brought to Misuku by a man named Daniel Mlenga who became the presiding pastor.[35]

Today, the main congregations in Chitipa are as follows: two congregations in Kameme, four congregations in Ulambia, and four congregations in Misuku, two congregations in Wenya and two congregations in Nthalire. These congregations have presiding pastors. However, these are not the only congregations in Chitipa. Besides these main churches there are 139 prayer houses in Chitipa with 97 pastors. By 2007 there were around 30,000 members of the Last Church of God in Chitipa district.[36]

Mzimba

The earliest church in Mzimba was Elangeni and it is said that it was started by Msumba, who left it in the hands of Principal Agillipa Shaba. However, Luka Nyirenda, one of the leaders left by Msumba, also played a major role in the planting of the church in Mzimba district.[37] Nyirenda first came to Mkhasyeni in 1938 where he was welcomed by Bandawe Longwe (a Tonga).[38] At first there were only nine converts at Mkhasyeni. From Mkhasyeni the church reached Euthini and there they also baptized some people. Later the church reached Ethinzini and Susa, where some people were baptized too. After Nyirenda returned to Nkhatabay, Agillipa Shaba continued the work not only in Mzimba but he also went to other districts.[39]

---

[34] Unfortunately, I could not find their first names.
[35] Int. Rev Mwakalenga, Chibavi Last Church of God, Chibavi, 4.4.2013.
[36] Ibid. 4.4.2013.
[37] Int. Rev Chiuli Manda, retired Bishop, Munkhokwe, 30.7.2012.
[38] Int. Mr G.D. Mvula, church member, Maulawo, 28.8.2012.
[39] Ibid. 28.8.2012.

Dowa

In Dowa, the church first came to a place called Galileya in 1938. Some reports say that Agillipa Shaba from Mzimba brought the church to Dowa.[40] Yet others believe that the church was brought there by a certain Mr Kaunga who had married at Chilowamatambe. The church was welcomed by Ashoti (village headman Shoti) together with Achimbudzi (village headman Chimbudzi) in 1940.[41]

From Galileya the church reached Mponela, where it was welcomed by Mtukula (village headman Chinguwo) and Kayaza (village headman Kayaza) and Debadeba (village headman Tembo).[42] The church also reached Bowe, where it was welcomed by Masoakakula (village headman Mphamba). From Bowe, the church went to Mtengowanthenga and there the church was welcomed by Baitoni Thotho.[43] However, Principal Chimchele also played a major role in spreading the church in Dowa and Mponela areas.

Ntchisi

The church was brought to Ntchisi in June 1964 by principal Mkangali and principal Chiwirira.[44] The first churches were at Ntchisi boma, Maloma, Kasakula and then it spread to other areas within the district.

Salima

It is believed that the church was started in Salima by Bishop Mbuna in July 1956.[45] However, not much is known about Mbuna, especially where he came from and where the first church in Salima was. In 1982 Rev Chikhasu from Dowa started the church at Khombeza trading centre. The other early congregations included Nakondwa in Gwengwe and Pitchayi.

---

[40] Int. K.V.N. Katsache Bvula, Church General Chairman, Kasamba, 28.8.2012.
[41] Ibid. 28.8.2012.
[42] Ibid. 28.8.2012.
[43] Ibid. 28.8.2012.
[44] Ibid. 19.2.2012.
[45] Int. Bishop Chiuli Manda, retired Area Bishop, Munkhokwe, 19.2.2012.

The other people who contributed to the spread of the church in Salima were Rev Kalulu, Rev Kamende and Mr Alifa (secretary to Rev Chikhasu). There are about 40 congregations today in Salima.[46]

Blantyre

In Blantyre, the church was brought by Rev Pengapenga, who was ordained by Rev O. Masinda.[47] The church started there in 1983.[48] The first church was established in Lunzu. The church has registered little success in Blantyre, for even today there are not many churches there. The leaders mentioned five congregations, two in Ndirande Township, another two in Mbayani and the one in Lunzu.[49]

Conclusion

By 1983 the Last Church of God had been introduced into all the districts where the church is present today. The only difference was the rate at which the church was spreading in each district. The church continued to expand at a fast rate in Nkhatabay, Karonga, Dowa, Kasungu and Mzimba districts. Generally, the Last Church thrives better in rural areas than in urban areas. This probably is due to the fact that many members of the church have little or no education and usually reside in rural areas.

The Last Church of God did not only spread within Malawi but it also spread to neighbouring countries. These countries include: Tanzania, Mozambique, Zambia, Zimbabwe and South Africa.[50] The church went there mainly with those who went to work in the mines. There are various versions in certain places over how the church got there.[51] But the church as of today has not yet reached Europe or Asia.

---

[46] Int. Rev Kaziyendele, Salima, 22.07.2015.
[47] Int. O. Masinda, General Principal, Kazando, Munkhokwe, 21.9.2011.
[48] Int. Bishop Chiuli Manda, retired Area Bishop, Munkhokwe, 21.9.2011.
[49] Int. O. Masinda, General Principal, Kazando, Munkhokwe, 21.9.2011.
[50] Int. Bishop Chiuli Manda, retired Area Bishop, Munkhokwe, 21.9.2011.
[51] On the countries outside Malawi I include the information I received, but I had no opportunity to independently study the Last Church of God outside Malawi.

The Spread of the Last Church of God outside Malawi

Zambia

Some members state that the church was started by Rev Mutepelera (village headman), who was sent together with Kaphinya Banda to Mufulira in the Copperbelt in 1934.[52] It is said that these went there in response to the call by the members of the Last Church of God who went to work in the mines namely, Muzguri and Changombo Mphande.[53] Thus Rev Mutepelera and Rev Kaphinya Banda assisted Muzguri and Mphande to register the church in Zambia. It is believed that from Mufulira the church went to Kitwe. In 1959 Rev Chiuli Manda started the church at Chibuluma.

Zimbabwe

There are two versions on how the church came to Zimbabwe. The first version states that the church was brought there by Rev Agrippa Mugomo in the 1960s. He was sent there by the church in Malawi to follow the Tonga working in the mines. But when he got there he wanted a good life, especially to have tea with milk every day.[54] The members were not happy with his demands; therefore, he was sent back home and was succeeded by Mtegama Mphande. It should be noted that the pastors that were sent in these countries from Malawi were paid a salary by the members since it was not their country. The first churches in Zimbabwe were at Moria, Jombo and Kamonimota.[55]

The other version says that the church was started in 1940. The church in Malawi sent Mwasoni Longwe from Mzenga, Maxson Mvula from Mzimba and Barness Lowokani Mwale from Kande. These men were sent in response to the appeals of Mr Nkholozo Chirwa from Kalowa, who used to write letters calling for someone to come and start the church

---

[52] Int. Bishop Chiuli Manda, retired Area Bishop, Munkhokwe, 21.9.2011.
[53] Ibid. 21.9.2011.
[54] Int. Bishop Chiuli Manda, retired Area Bishop, Munkhokwe, 19.2.2012.
[55] Ibid. 19.2.2012.

there.[56] From the two versions above it is possible that both groups actually went to Zimbabwe and started the church in their different areas at different times.

Mozambique

Rev Pengapenga from Blantyre brought the church to Mozambique in the mid-1980s. Pengapenga too was sent by the church in Malawi. It is not known with whom he left the church there when he returned to Malawi.[57]

South Africa

The church is said to have been established in South Africa a bit late in the 1990s. A man named Alexander Banda from Nkhatabay went to work in Johannesburg; before that he had been working in Tanzania.[58] While in South Africa he found that there were some members of the Last Church of God who were congregating together with members of the African National Church and those from Emanuel Church. Banda decided to organize the members so that they could worship separately as Last Church of God. When he came back in 2004 he reported this church to the headquarters and he was ordained as Pastor, so that he could be the presiding pastor of this congregation in South Africa.[59]

However, another account shows that the church was introduced to South Africa in the 1930s and not in the 1990s as the version above states. This is possible, taking into account that many people from Nkhatabay had been going to South Africa to seek jobs as early as the 1920s. For instance, in September 1932, Timothy K. Mwanjisi wrote from Kapako Native Mission, Rungwe to the District Officer in Mbeya;

> That we are the Last Church of God and His Christ in three trinity. This native mission has been extended from Karonga Nyasaland and South Africa and Uganda Protectorate and it is already known

---

[56] Int. Rev O. Masinda, General Principal, Kazando, 21.9.2011.
[57] Int. Rev Muguvu Phiri, Church's General Secretary, Kazando, 11.3.2011.
[58] Int. Rev Chiuli Manda, retired Bishop, Munkhokwe, 19.2.2012.
[59] Int. Rev O. Masinda, General Principal, Kazando, 21.9.2011.

by the Government of Tanganyika Territory and Kenya Colony and Nyasaland and to the Union of South Africa and Rhodesia North and South.[60]

This account implies that the church was already in South Africa by 1932. And not only was the church in South Africa by that time, but also in Zimbabwe. An explanation would therefore be that when it came to Johannesburg the church was started there in the 1990s. However, by this time the church had already been introduced into some parts of South Africa.

Tanzania

Jordan Msumba went to Mwanza (northern part of Tanzania, on the southern shore of Lake Victoria) in 1935; however, by that time the Last Church of God had already been started. In fact, the church was first introduced in the Rungwe area in the 1920s by Ben Ngemela, who extended the church from Karonga to Rungwe.[61] Ngemela became one of the important leaders of the church, not only in Karonga but also in Rungwe in Tanzania.

In September 1932 Timothy K. Mwanjasi, a representative of the Last Church of God in Rungwe, wrote to the District Officer in Mbeya that they were about 325 men already converted and that he was asking for permission to start the church in Mbeya.[62] By 1954, the church claimed over 10,000 adherents in Rungwe.[63] Again by 1972 there were branches of the Last Church in Mbeya, Mbozi, Ukinga and other places.[64] But it was not until the 1980s that the church managed to reach Dar es Salaam, with two people from Nkhatabay who went to work there, one of whom was Rev Walter Mwale.[65]

---

[60] Terence O. Rangers, *The African Churches of Tanzania*, Historical Association of Tanzania Paper No. 5, Nairobi: East African Publishing House, 1972, p. 21.
[61] Ibid.
[62] Ibid.
[63] Ibid.
[64] Ibid.
[65] Int. Rev O. Masinda, General Principal, Kazando, 28.8.2012.

The church continued to progress and today there are many branches of the church in many parts of Tanzania. The current Archbishop of the church is Mchungaji (Pastor) Japhet Wanzagi Nyerere, the firstborn son of Julius Nyerere, the former president of Tanzania.[66]

Growth Patterns

Looking at the story of the spread of the Last Church of God above one observes two growth points, namely Karonga and Msondozi. It is interesting to note that from Karonga Ngemela took the church to Tanzania bypassing Chitipa. Later on, the church came to Chitipa from both Karonga and Tanzania. On the other hand, from Msondozi the church spread within Nkhatabay and then to Mzimba, Dowa, Kasungu, and Nkhotakota, and later on to Blantyre. It is not known why the church did not come to Rumphi at this time.

When it comes to the spread of the church beyond Malawi, Msondozi played a major role. Because even in Tanzania, where Ngemela played a big role, we also saw that Msumba went there and planted a church at Mwanza. It was from Msondozi that leaders sent people to various places to establish churches.

Even though the church spread to other countries outside Malawi, the headquarters of the church remained at Msondozi. However, the recent years have seen Tanzania and Zambia electing their own Archbishops. As far as the leadership of the entire church is concerned it is no longer based at Msondozi. It is difficult to know the membership in various places over the years as the church was expanding.

From 1962 onwards there started leadership conflicts in the church that eventually led to the split of the church.

The Last Church of God and His Christ between 1962 and 1979

From the time of its formation until the 1960s the church seems to have had no serious problems as far as its running was concerned. However,

---

[66] Int. Bishop Joseph Sibale, District Bishop Chitipa, Chitipa, 6.4.2013.

the period between 1962 and 1979 is characterized by the division of the church and by open conflicts between the two resultant churches (African Last Church of God and Reformed Last Church of God). Until 1963 the General Principal was Rev Mkhuta Banda, but then he was old in age.[67] This presented the need for someone to take over his place. This resulted in a leadership conflict in the church that eventually led to the split.

White Longwe had joined the church in April 1953 from African Church and became the personal secretary of Mkhuta Banda.[68] When the question of leadership arose in 1962, Rev Kaphinya Banda, who was then the General Secretary of the whole church, expected to be the successor. However, it was Longwe that took over the place of Mkhuta Banda. This did not go well with Rev Kaphinya Banda and problems started in the church.[69]

It is difficult to deduce exactly what happened as each side blames the other for the split. However, the truth in this matter is important as it determines the answer to the question "which one is the main Last Church of God?" as both sides claim to be the 'original' Last Church of God and not the breakaway. Some preliminary studies on the church have made quick conclusions on this question and have ended up in the trap of leaving aside one church from a history of the Last Church of God which I think does not present a balanced and correct history of the church.[70] It is therefore important to give both versions of the split so that, maybe through analysis, one may determine which church would be regarded as the original Last Church of God. I believe that the correct

---

[67] Minutes, Reformed Last Church of God, Kazando Synod, 19.10., nd.

[68] Minutes, Reformed Last Church of God, Kazando Synod, 19.10., nd.

[69] Minutes, Reformed Last Church of God, Kazando Synod, 19.10., nd.

[70] Godfrey A. Banda and Peter G. Forster, "The Last Church of God and His Christ" in *Journal of Religion in Africa,* vol. 29, pp. 455-456. Godfrey Banda and Peter Forster fail to highlight the schism and quickly treat the Reformed Last Church as the main Last Church of God and the African Last as a breakaway without proper justification for their choice. The question is: what if the evidence shows that African Last is the main Last Church?

answer to the above question might also affect the course of the study of the history of the church.

The Version Held by the Reformed Last Church of God

It should be mentioned from the beginning that the members of this church, especially the leaders, refuse to be called the "Reformed," claiming that the name was just imposed on them by the other group.[71] But for the sake of differentiation between the two churches I will refer to them by that name.

This group claims that one year after Isaac Mkhuta retired, White Longwe began to boast that he was going to succeed Mkhuta Banda.[72] However, all the members in the district (Nkhatabay) rejected him and instead chose James Kaphinya Banda to take the place of Mkhuta Banda. The story continues that Longwe, not being satisfied with the results, summoned late Kaphinya to the District Council, where they were advised to vote near the *"boma"*. The elections took place at Phiri in Singu village. No one voted for White Longwe, while 9,032 members voted for Kaphinya. The report was sent to the District Commissioner of Nkhatabay. This happened in 1964.[73]

Longwe, not convinced, again summoned Kaphinya Banda to the District Commissioner's office. The DC at that time was Keliment Mvula (probably Clement). The other people that were present included two Members of Parliament, Mr Katenga and Mr Tambalaweku and the clerk, Mr Mphande.[74] However, we are not told in the report how this meeting ended.

The account continues that Kaphinya Banda thought that Longwe organized to spoil the church and that the government might therefore think of stopping the church. Kaphinya Banda therefore arranged to

---

[71] Int. Gogo Chimbaza, retired Rev, Munkhokwe, 16.7.2012.
[72] Minutes, Reformed Last Church of God, Kazando Synod, 19.10, nd.
[73] Ibid.
[74] Ibid.

separate himself from the church. He made his own church known as Reformed Last Church of God and His Christ.[75]

The above version has, however, some loopholes that are worth pointing out. Firstly, the claim that during the voting process Longwe literally had no followers is absurd. We all know that where there are people fighting for positions, usually each one has followers, even if they are few. This kind of bias raises up more questions than it is able to answer.

Apart from that, the number of people claimed to have cast the votes seems to be exaggerated (9,032). If today the number of people that attend the big meetings is usually around 5,000 to 6,000, what about then in the 1960s when the church was still small?

Another drawback to the above version is that it lacks some important details like the exact dates when the case was taken to the DC. The report again does not indicate the decision of the DC when the case went there for the second time.

It is interesting to note that, while they claim that the name "Reformed" was never given by themselves, in one of the letters the General Principal himself states so. He clearly states that "Kaphinya arranged to separate the church so he made his own church, Reformed Last Church of God and His Christ."[76] When I first asked the General Principal (Rev Masinda) together with other leaders who were with him about this, they quickly agreed that indeed the name "Reformed" was just imposed on them.

However, when I showed them the letter by Rev Masinda himself, they were all surprised that I possessed such a letter. They started giving different explanations, but then the truth could not be denied as they all agreed that the hand writing and the signature on the letter really belonged to Rev Masinda. It was therefore my impression from the interviews with these leaders that they were hiding some information.

On the same issue one questions the decision of Kaphinya. If Longwe was a "nuisance" and the church really did not choose him, why was he not just excommunicated from the church?

---

[75] Minutes, Reformed Last Church of God, Kazando Synod, 19.10, nd.
[76] Rev P.G.O. Masinda - Wilson and Morgan Legal Practitioners, 4.11.1992.

Finally, it is very unusual in church history that the main church with its rightful leadership would leave the headquarters to the "confusionists" in the name of making peace. This is what the Reformed Last Church of God claims to have happened.

It is also important to look at what the African Last Church of God (also called "Last White") has to say pertaining to the division of the church before any conclusions can be drawn. The story will be presented as written by White Longwe himself.

The Version according to the African Last Church of God (Last White)

According to this side's report, Kaphinya Banda was the General Secretary of the entire church and Longwe was the personal secretary of the General Principal. In 1956, there was a church meeting at Dwasulo.[77] It was at that meeting that a suggestion came up of the need to choose a new General Principal who was energetic, since Mkhuta Banda was old. Later there was another meeting at Mbamba. At this meeting, a letter was written to the General Principal presenting the request for a new General Principal.[78]

The General Principal accepted the request, and he called all the regions to a meeting at the headquarters in Msondozi. The meeting was opened with the Tonga hymn no. 172.[79] Afterwards the General Principal thanked the people for their timely request and asked them to suggest the name of the person to replace him. White Longwe was chosen and there was no other name given.[80]

The General Principal thanked the people for choosing Longwe and told the people that he was going to call all the regions to witness the ordination of Longwe at the Synod to be held at Phiri on 7th September

---

[77] Minutes, African Last Church of God and His Christ, Msondozi Synod, nd.
[78] Ibid.
[79] Ibid.
[80] Ibid.

1962.[81] However, Kaphinya Banda was not happy with the decision. On the appointed day members from different areas came. Among those who came were members from Elangeni, Dowa, Nkhotakota, Euthini and Nkhunga. It is said that Kaphinya Banda organized the people from the region of Malisawo to spread the news around the whole area that Longwe was rejected and that they were not going to ordain him as General Principal. The situation got worse and members from the central region, namely Debadeba Kasewe and Rotani Makeseni Vula, told the people that all the Tongas should go outside and leave the visitors to decide. After their meeting, they called back all the other members to hear their decision.[82]

Late Kasewe from Dowa stood up and told the congregation that they were going to ordain the Principal that was already chosen, otherwise they were going to be like Ham who insulted his father (Genesis 9:22). Longwe was ordained the following morning, Sunday, 7th September, 1962. Kaphinya Banda and his group left and took away the books that contained the minutes.[83]

When Kaphinya and the others returned home they called the members from the area of Nkhunga and told them that they too should ordain their own principal. Those Christians, without really understanding what had happened and without asking from the headquarters for details, accepted the decision. Mr Kaphinya Banda was chosen and went to Mr Mulowoka to ask him to ordain him. It is said that Mulowoka himself was not an ordained pastor. Nevertheless, the meeting for the ordination ceremony was called to take place at Dambo, village headman Kang'oma.[84]

When Longwe heard that there was a meeting at Dambo, him together with Mr Katongo Mphande and Mr Mugomo, went to attend the meeting. They found that the region of Malisawo was present but the other regions were absent. Late Kaphinya Banda came with late Chipo-

---

[81] Minutes, African Last Church of God and His Christ, Msondozi Synod, nd.
[82] Ibid.
[83] Ibid.
[84] Ibid.

lopolo and one member from Dwambazi. Longwe and his team called the Amalisawo and Kaphinya with his two colleagues to a meeting in the house of Mulowoka.[85] The question that Longwe asked was "what kind of meeting was it that they did not invite others?" Confusion broke out on this question.

The late Chipolopolo, Katongo and Mulowoka pleaded with Longwe to ordain Kaphinya as he wanted to be the vice to Longwe. Longwe, not wanting further quarrels, forgave Kaphinya and ordained him in the morning of 9th December 1962 as his Vice General Principal. Longwe claims that from Kazando to Nkhunga there is no one who can point the place where Kaphinya was ordained as Vice Principal. At that meeting, there were only fifty people from the Malisao region. Longwe told Kaphinya to go to the former General Principal to get the certificate that he was now the Vice Principal. But Kaphinya never went to the General Principal, instead when he arrived at his home he started organizing his own meetings.[86]

Late Mkhuta heard about Kaphinya's activities and was not happy. He wrote a letter to Kaphinya inviting him to a meeting but Kaphinya did not come. He wrote Kaphinya a second letter and again Kaphinya never showed up for the meeting. The third letter that Mkhuta wrote to Kaphinya was to inform him that he was excommunicated from the Last Church of God and therefore he should find his own name for his church. When Mkhuta died, the conflicts increased and Longwe summoned Kaphinya to the District Commissioner in 1963. The DC advised them to go and discuss the issue together amicably.[87]

The "reconciliatory" meeting was scheduled at Phiri. They also invited Chipangano Church and Nechenala (probably African National Church) so that they should facilitate the discussions. But Kaphinya's group refused saying they were going to the DC to present their candidate Kaphinya. The DC sent them back as he said that he already had the name of James Longwe as Principal that was given to him by Mr Luka Nyirenda. In

---

[85] Minutes, African Last Church of God and His Christ, Msondozi Synod, nd.
[86] Ibid.
[87] Ibid.

response Kaphinya's group said that Longwe was already excommunicated from the church. The DC insisted that they should bring Longwe with them. They did not go further with it. In 1965, the DC called Longwe. He went, but Kaphinya's group refused to go.[88]

In 1967, the DC again called all the churches that were having disputes, including Blackman's Church and the Last Church of God. The meeting took place on 24th January, 1967. The first case to be handled was that of the Last Church of God and the judges were the DC, Mr A.J. Mvula, Members of Parliament, Mr Katenga Kaunda and Mr Tambalaweku. The first to speak was Kaphinya, followed by Malisao Nyirenda. When it was time for the side of Longwe to speak, the first to speak was Luka Nyirenda, followed by Longwe who had written down his speech and was reading it. Longwe first explained how some churches had split without fights like the Blackman's Church and raised the concern that this was not the case with the Last Church.[89]

The DC then asked Kaphinya's group as to the way forward. The group said that they did not want to continue together and that they were now out of the Last Church. They opted to have their own name. The DC asked them to mention their name and Kaphinya mentioned "Reformed Last Church." The DC finally dismissed the meeting, warning them that now that the case was over he should not hear of any conflicts again.[90]

In March the same year of 1967 the Last Church had a synod meeting at Kawalazi. They sent messengers to various areas to announce the meeting. When the messengers arrived at Kazando, village headman Malenga Sanga, they were beaten up by Kaphinya's group and the case was taken to court. On the 18th of September 1967, the Magistrate ruled that the Reformed Last Church should pay £37.10 to the African Last Church for the injuries that had been caused. Apart from the fine they were warned that if they were going to repeat the violence, they would be put into prison.[91]

---

[88] Minutes, African Last Church of God and His Christ, Msondozi Synod, nd.
[89] Ibid.
[90] Ibid.
[91] Ibid.

There is a reference to the ruling of the magistrate above from the DC's report of January 1979 which reads "Furthermore it was stated that in the same year (1967) an open conflict erupted and it was settled by the magistrate."[92] One would think that after the 1967 ordeal the conflicts would have ceased. On the contrary, the conflicts between the two churches continued as evidenced by the report.

> The meeting was opened with a short prayer. Thereafter the District Commissioner introduced the subject of the meeting which was church dispute involving the two religious groups, the African Last Church of God and the Reformed Last Church of God and His Christ. The District Commissioner pointed out that disputes between the two groups seem to persist despite the effort taken by his predecessors to settle them.[93]

By that time (1979) these two churches were already known by their names as affirmed by the above report, even though the Reformed Last Church of God negates its name. The report states that:

> Both sides confirmed that their church was one at first but they separated in 1967 when the conflict came to the climax. Since that time two groups emerged and have been known as the African Last Church of God and the Reformed Last Church of God and His Christ.[94]

This version contains more specific details of people, dates and places, giving it more weight and credibility. However, one cannot rule out the possibility of bias, as it was written by Longwe himself.

One interesting thing from both the versions is the lack of mention of prayer at a time when the church was going through a crisis. Prayer is central in the life of the church. One would expect that at a time of crisis like the one described above both leaders would call for members to pray hard for God's intervention. But nothing is mentioned in both accounts. Prayer was one of the "marks" of the early church besides devotion to instruction, fellowship and the breaking of bread (Acts 2:42). The same should be the case as Christians gather together today, devotion to these things above must be evident. One can of course argue that probably individually the members were devoted to praying over

---

[92] Minutes from DC's office Ref. No. 15/3/169, 22.1.1979.
[93] Ibid. 22.1.1979.
[94] Ibid. 22.1.1979.

the issue at the time. But corporately, also, their zeal for the word and prayer is to be expected.[95] Devotion to the word of God and prayer or the lack of it affects the credibility of their profession as Christians, both individually and corporately. This was probably one of the reasons why the conflict got worse over the years.

From the above versions, one cannot be wrong to conclude that Rev Kaphinya did separate from the African Last Church over leadership conflicts and started his own church. However, he still wanted to maintain the name of Last Church of God. It seems that for some time he and his followers were still using the same name "African Last Church of God and His Christ," until when the open conflicts erupted between the two groups (one of the reasons was the use of the church's name) and Kaphinya was forced to give a different name to his church at the DC. Thus, the name "Reformed Last Church of God" came up. Hence this name was not imposed on them.

It seems, however, that Kaphinya and his followers later realized the implication of the new name; it meant that they were the secessionists. This might have brought the fear that probably many members were not going to follow them. The way out was for them to insist that they were not the "Reformed" and that the name was just imposed on them by the other group.

It is interesting that some of the members I interviewed rejected the name "Reformed" and boldly stated that they belonged to the original Last Church of God. On the other hand, some members freely called themselves "Reformed". One other thing that was clear was that many members do not really know up to now what exactly happened and all they believe is what their leaders have told them.

As of today, both these churches are separately registered officially with the government. The African Last Church got its common seal in 2011 under the name "The Last Church of God and His Christ International" leaving out "African." On the other hand, the Reformed Last Church got their common seal in 2010 and they are registered under the name "The

---

[95] R.E.H. Uprichard, *What Presbyterians Believe*, Ahoghill: The Oaks, 2011, p. 118.

Last Church of God and His Christ" leaving out the "International." In short, both are called the Last Church of God and His Christ and both left out "African".

My conclusion is that the Last Church that was founded by Msumba is the one that is now registered as the Last Church of God and His Christ International (Msondozi headquarters) and that the Last Church of God and His Christ (Kazando headquarters), which was referred to earlier as the Reformed Last Church is a breakaway. However, they may not agree with this. I base my conclusion mainly on the issue of the headquarters. Msumba left Msondozi as the headquarters of the church. So, any other headquarters besides Msondozi is questionable. However, the history of both these two churches is worth studying as being heirs to the same origins.

The Last Church of God and His Christ after the Split

Soon after the split the leaders in both churches were busy going to various places and notifying people of the division. Each side tried to convince the members that they were the "original" Last Church of God. Members in many places, not knowing exactly the events at the headquarters, were easily convinced by anyone who went there first. This eventually caused confusion in many places. Gogo Chimbizi of the Reformed Last Church of God claims that White Longwe went to Lusaka in Zambia to win over the already existing Last Church of God to their side, but Gogo Chimbizi sent him back telling him not to cause confusion.[96]

There were some cases where the entire congregation and not only individuals would switch from belonging to either African Last or Reformed Last Church. This meant that they took with them even the church building. A good example is what happened at Kazando, when Kaphinya started the "Reformed Last Church of God." What actually changed was the name but he had the same members and the same church building.

---

[96] Int. Gogo Chimbaza, retired Reverend, Reformed Last, Munkhokwe, 8.7.2012.

Another example happened at Balachander in Mzimba. During the church conflicts the whole congregation had moved to Reformed Last.[97] However, the entire congregation later came back to African Last and the Synod meeting of 2011 took place at this congregation.[98] In the same year the congregation at Elangeni led by Bishop Beza also made a switch, Bishop Beza and his entire congregation had previously claimed to belong to the Reformed Last Church (during the split) but later they returned to the African Last Church of God.[99]

What became the distinguishing feature even up to now was the headquarters. While some would say, they belong to the Last Church of God Kazando Headquarters, others would say they belong to the Last Church of God Msondozi Headquarters.

Because of this confusion some leaders, especially Pastors from Dowa, led by Rev Chimcheli, Ntchisi; Rev Mkwezalamba, Nkhotakota, Rev Madondolo, Mponela, and Rev Kanyalumwala dragged Longwe and Kaphinya to court.[100] These congregation leaders wanted the two leaders to tell them which church between the two was the "original" Last Church of God, since both sides were claiming to be the main church and this was causing confusion at grass root congregations.

It is said that the DC asked the two leaders (Longwe and Kaphinya) to tell the concerned parties the truth. From Longwe's side it was Rev Chiuli Manda who spoke. He said that it was the DC who caused this problem by not making a clear statement on the issue ever since the problem was presented to his office, hence allowing the Reformed Last Church to continue with the use of the name Last Church.[101]

Manda further stated that if the DC had earlier on told the Reformed Church to stop the use of the name Last Church, these problems could have been eliminated at the very beginning. To this the DC did not respond. The DC then asked Kaphinya's group to tell the concerned

---

[97] Int. Rev Chiuli Manda, retired Bishop, Munkhokwe, 30.7.2012.
[98] Ibid. 31.8.2012.
[99] Int. Rev Chiuli Manda, retired Bishop, Munkhokwe, 31.8.2012.
[100] Ibid. 31.8.2012.
[101] Ibid. 31.8.2012.

members the truth. They remained silent for some time. This made the DC angry and when they realized that the DC was about to ban them, Kaphinya told the gathered audience that they were the Reformed Last Church and that they had broken away from the Last Church.[102]

The DC told everybody present that they had heard it themselves and therefore the matter was resolved. However, the leaders that brought the issue to the DC asked for a letter from the DC to carry to their various congregations as a proof of the discussions. The DC granted them the letter.[103] Unfortunately I have not seen this letter.

The Reformed Last Church of God had many members in Nkhatabay after the split, claiming about three quarters of the members in the district. They also claimed many members in Nkhotakota, Ntchisi and Dowa districts. On the other hand, many churches in Karonga and Chitipa remained in the African Last Church.[104]

It is also important to note that while the division was taking place some places were not affected. Even up to now it's just news to them that such a division took place. Good examples of such places are Karonga and Chitipa districts and the churches outside the country. I asked one member at Chitipa whether she knew that the church was divided, her response was that she just hears about it and does not even know the name of the other church.[105]

The Relationship between the African Last Church and the Reformed Last Church after the Split

Bitter relationships between these two churches continued manifesting themselves in open conflicts, especially among churches close to the Kazando headquarters. In one extreme case, it even involved the burning of a church. This happened in Mponela. Apparently after the return of the pastors from the discussion at the DC many members realized that they had actually joined the Reformed Last Church, hence they decided

---

[102] Int. Rev Chiuli Manda, retired Bishop, Munkhokwe, 31.8.2012.
[103] Ibid. 31.8.2012.
[104] Ibid. 31.8.2012.
[105] Int. Mama Nyondo, church member, Chitipa Boma, 6.4.2013.

to go back to the African Last Church. This angered some of the members left in the Reformed Last Church, and one of them decided to burn the church that belonged to the African Last Church.[106]

This erupted into conflicts with the African Last blaming the Reformed Last Church for the act, while the Reformed Last refused the blame. Longwe and Kaphinya were summoned to the DC's office in Dowa. Before Longwe actually went to the DC's office, he visited the burnt church. It is stated that he stationed four District Principals on the four corners of the church while he stood in the middle and started preaching.[107]

As he was preaching there came slowly a man walking as if he were drunk and fell at Longwe's feet and confessed that it was him who had burnt the church. Bishop Chiuli Manda was not very sure of the name but mentioned "Debadeba." After the confession Longwe commanded seventeen pastors to ride bicycles in front, the one who burnt the church in the middle and Longwe himself came behind.[108] They were on their way to the DC's office.

At the DC, the issue was discussed and Longwe explained that someone had already confessed the act and that the person was right there to make a confession. The DC then asked Longwe to say what he wanted the office to do with the man. Longwe's reply was: "Who am I to pass judgement after God has already shown the one who had sinned?" The DC then referred the man to the court.[109]

The conflicts between these two churches were intense around Kazando headquarters. However, in many other places today the members of both churches co-exist cordially. Members of both churches are free to worship together and they support each other during funerals or church meetings. Although these two churches do not share Holy Communion,

---

[106] Int. Rev Chiuli Manda, retired Bishop, Munkhokwe, 31.8.2012.
[107] Ibid. 31.8.2012.
[108] Ibid. 31.8.2012.
[109] Ibid. 31.8.2012.

both churches can share Holy Communion with other churches that broke away from the Last Church of God.[110]

Further Splits from the Last Church of God

After the division between the Reformed Last Church of God and the African Last Church of God there have been further splits in the church. However, these took place peacefully. These churches include the Old Last Church of God and His Christ, the New Last Church of God and His Christ and the Last Church of Malawi.

The Old Last Church of God and His Christ

The Old Last Church of God was started at Mgodi in Chintheche around the year 2000 by a man known as Chisonga, due to leadership conflicts involving him and another person. Apparently Chisonga wanted a certain position in the church. And when he did not get it he started his own church. Chisonga belonged to the Last Church of God and His Christ (Kazando headquarters). Chisonga died around the year 2006 and so did the church.

The New Last Church of God and His Christ

This church was started by a man known as Rev Kulinji, who was a General Principal in Liwalazi in Nkhotakota. He was involved in a leadership struggle with the church secretary called Kasambala (now passed on). Rev Kulinji too came from the Reformed Last Church of God and His Christ (Kazando headquarters). The church is still there in Nkhotakota.

Having looked at the above churches which seceded from the Last Church of God and His Christ, there is also one more church which split from the Last Church of God in Tanzania. This is called the Last Church of Malawi.

---

[110] Int. Rev Chiuli Manda, retired Area Bishop, Munkhokwe, 31.8.2012.

The Last Church of Malawi

This church split from the Last Church of God in Tanzania. The church came to Malawi in around 1995 and was brought by a man known as Sichoni at Kasisi in Chitipa. So far, this church is only found in Chitipa district. From this Last Church of Malawi sprouted another church known as the New Last Church of God. This is different from the New Last Church of God in Nkhatabay mentioned above.

The main cause of these divisions seems to have been the struggle for leadership and the conflicts that are happening today within the Last Church of God and His Christ International as we are going to see, if not amicably dealt with, might again result in a further split of the church.

Conclusion

Msumba had indeed started the church and left it in the hands of the leadership that was there. But Msumba did not leave behind an organized way or a structure of running the church like how to choose leaders to various positions and for how long someone should stay in office. As the church was expanding, these issues eventually arose and the leaders had to do what they thought was best in the situation. But where there are no clearly stipulated rules nor a constitution, conflicts are bound to happen. In my opinion, the split of the church was partly due to the fact that from the beginning the church did not clearly put in place a procedure for electing leaders for such a big office as General Principal. The two churches in question continued as different entities after the split. One church was in short called African Last while the other was called Reformed Last. I believe that the African Last is the "original" Last Church with its headquarters at Msondozi.

Chapter 4: The Last Church of God and His Christ ("Reformed Last")

After the split in 1962 Rev Kaphinya established the headquarters at Kazando with the support of those who did not want Longwe to be the leader of the Last Church of God. There were no changes in terms of doctrine, structure, life etc from that of the African Last Church. The only thing that actually changed was the headquarters.

Kaphinya became the General Principal of the church until his death in 1974. Kaphinya was succeeded by Rev Chipolopolo Isaac Nkhata in 1975, who served until his death in 1979. From 1979 to 1982 there was no General Principal and the General Secretary acted for the General Principal until 1982, when Rev J.B. Phonji Nyirenda became the General Principal. Phonji Nyirenda did not serve long in that position as he died in 1984. After the death of Phonji Nyirenda, Rev O. Masinda was chosen to succeed him and is still the General Principal of the church. So far, all these General Principals have been from Nkhatabay district.

Figure 1: The current General Principal Rev O. Masinda

The Reformed Last Church is currently found in the following districts: Nkhatabay, Nkhotakota, Mzimba, Dowa, Kasungu, Mchinji, Lilongwe, Salima and Blantyre, while the Reformed Last Church of God and His Christ has many of its members in Kasungu, Nkhatabay and Dowa districts.

In an attempt to describe the life and piety of the Reformed Last Church an account of one congregation (Munkhokwe) gives a picture of many if not all congregations under the Reformed Last Church of God and His Christ.

Munkhokwe Last Church of God and His Christ (Kazando Headquarters)

The Beginning of the Church at Munkhokwe

At first members of the Reformed Last Church of God in Munkhokwe were under the pastoral care of Rev Mutepelera, who was the pastor of Mgodi Church at Chintheche. However, due to the long distance from Munkhokwe to Mgodi, Rev Mutepelera agreed to the request of members in Munkhokwe to have another prayer house built there. So, Rev Mvula, who was originally from Mzimba district but had settled at Kapeska, was chosen to be the pastor of this new church in Munkhokwe. This was in the 1960s.[1]

At first the members used to worship under a tree, but later on they found a site and built a church that was grass roofed. Unfortunately, in the same 1960s the government declared that the land where the church had been built, including all neighbouring land, was under the government. They therefore found another site where the current church is built and with the compensation money they bought iron sheets and bags of cement. The new church was built in the early 1970s. After Rev Mvula there came Rev Chimbaza in 1984, and he was succeeded by Rev Chimgogu Chirwa. The current Reverend is Mboya Banda.[2]

Buildings

The church at Munkhokwe was built with burnt bricks. They used iron sheets for the roof and it has a cement floor. The front is a bit

Figure 2: Kazando Reformed Last Church (Headquarters), 2010

---

[1] Int. Rev Mboya Banda, Munkhokwe, 12.7.2010.
[2] Ibid. 12.7.2010.

elevated and has a small wall that separates it from the rest of the church. There is a wooden pulpit in the front and wooden chairs, both in front and the rest of the church. The church is surrounded by village houses.

There is a remarkable difference in terms of church buildings between Reformed Last and African Last at least in Nkhatabay district. The five churches of the Reformed Last Church of God were all roofed with iron sheets, while the four African Last churches I visited were grass roofed. This is also true with the headquarters; the church at Kazando is in a much better shape than the headquarters at Msondozi (African Last).

Leadership in the Reformed Last Church of God

Leadership at the national level is as follows. At the very top is the General Principal, currently Rev O. Masinda Phiri from Kazando. He is followed by the General Chairman, currently Mr Behappy Macley Mwale from Kasungu. He is responsible for settling disputes in the church. Then there is the General Secretary, who is currently Rev Guvu Phiri from Nkhatabay. He is followed by the General Treasurer, currently Rev Idress Phiri from Mchinji.

Figure 3: Some of the pastors of the Reformed Last Church of God during the 2010 women's conference at Phiri. Third from right is the current General Secretary Rev Guvu Phiri.

Then there is the Senior Moderator, currently Rev Yokamu from Mpamba who is followed by Moderators and then Principals (Pastors).[3]

At the congregational level, the highest office is that of pastor followed by preachers, then church elders (male). Like African Abraham Church, the Last Church has a separate women's hierarchy which is independent

---

[3] Int. Rev O. Masinda, General Principal, Kazando, 6.11.2011.

but within the church. The women's hierarchy does not equate to the maximum level of the men's hierarchy.[4] This is a similar phenomenon to the African Abraham Church which has Mai Mkulu as the women's highest office.[5] The women's highest office in Last Church is that of *Amayi Mariya* followed by *Alalakazi*. These are followed by deacons who can either be men or women. So, from deacon a woman is promoted to *Alalakazi* and then to *Amayi Mariya*.[6] The difference in hierarchical heights prevents women's participation in the executive committee which is the decision-making organ of the entire church.[7]

Election of a Pastor for the Congregation

Last Church does not demand its pastors to go for pastoral training. When there is a need for a pastor the members choose from among themselves someone who is a good preacher. The members are supposed to nominate three preachers and they have to give good reasons for their choice. Then the three chosen members are asked to go outside, while the remaining members vote in the church. They call a name one by one and those who want that person have to raise their hands and are counted.[8]

A person is supposed to raise a hand only once. When the voting exercise is over, the one with the highest votes becomes the pastor. If, at that time, the church has no secretary, the person with the second highest

---

[4] Jemiter Mwale, "The Establishment and Development of African Abraham Church in Malawi (1929-2000): A Case Study on the Major Changes in Doctrine and their Impact (Chamchere Mission Station)," BA, University of Malawi, 2000, p. 3.

[5] Ibid. p. 8.

[6] *Alalakazi* are women who have stopped menstruating; they assist in preparing and serving Holy Communion. *Amayi Mariya* are older than *Alalakazi*.

[7] Jemiter Mwale, The Establishment and Development of African Abraham Church in Malawi (1929-2000): A Case Study on the Major Changes in Doctrine and their Impact (Chamchere Mission Station), BA, University of Malawi, 2000, p. 8.

[8] Int. Rev Mboya Banda, Munkhokwe, 12.7.2010.

votes becomes the secretary. However, the headquarters have to arrange for the ordination of the pastor.

The pastor does not receive a salary as they believe that God and his Son Jesus Christ shall pay them in the life to come. The pastors have their own attire that they put on whenever they are ministering.

Women Participation in the Church

Women in the church take part in preaching during the Sunday service or during the women's Sunday. They also participate in fundraising activities for the church, and of course, the general cleanliness of the church is left in their hands. The women have their own women's group known as *Amayi Achikondi*.[9] Sometimes women are given opportunity to organize a big conference which is usually patronized by members from different areas like shown in the picture:

Figure 4: (front line) are some of the women from Nkhotakota who participated in the preaching during the 2010 women conference that took place at Phiri in Nkhatabay district.

Figure 5: Part of the gathering during 2010 women's conference at Phiri. Close to 6,000 people attended this conference.

During such big conferences women are supposed to lead the entire service, including preaching. According to the church's tradition there are supposed to be three preachers for one sermon. The woman with the highest rank is the last one to preach.

---

[9] Int. Mama Buwani NyaManda, Chairperson *Amayi Achikondi*, Munkhokwe, 12.7.2010.

Amayi Achikondi

The *Amayi Achikondi* in Munkhokwe congregation started around 2005 and since that time the chairperson has been Mama Buwani NyaManda. The ministry of *Amayi Achikondi* involves visitation of the sick and ministering during the funeral of a fellow church member. The *Amayi Achikondi* can also be either *alalakazi* or *Amayi Mariya*.

The activities of *Amayi Mariya* include preparing the elements for the Holy Communion. The *Alalakazi* assist in counselling couples if there are family conflicts.[10] The *Amayi Mariya* have their own uniform, a black dress with a white collar and a black head dress. The *Amayi Achikondi* usually meet on Fridays. Their meeting involves prayer, preaching or Bible sharing and singing. They also visit backsliding members to encourage them.

Figure 6: Amayi Achikondi at Phiri (2010)

Leadership in Amayi Achikondi

The leadership of *Amayi Achikondi* comprises the chairlady; at Munkhokwe she is currently Mama Buwani NyaManda. She is seconded by the vice. These are followed by the secretary and her vice and the treasurer and her vice. These leaders stay in office for a period of one year after which they are replaced (or re-

Figure 7: Amayi Achikondi from Kasitu Last Church ministering through singing at Phiri (Nkhatabay) during 2010 women's conference.

---

[10] Int. Mrs Rev O. Masinda, Kazando, 6.11.2011.

elected as has been the case with Mama Buwani NyaManda).[11]

The Uniform of Amayi Achikondi

Their uniform is different from that of *Amayi Achikondi* in the African Last Church of God (Msondozi). It is composed of a white dress and black shoes. However, *Amayi Maria* put on a black dress. The *Amayi Achikondi* members put on the uniform during the funeral of a church member, during church meetings or conferences and when visiting the sick.[12] In other churches like CCAP a member of *Umanyano* does also put on the uniform when she is going to preach on a Sunday. However, this is not the case here because preachers usually are chosen on the same day while they have already come for the service.

Figure 8: Standing behind the Amayi Mariya is a youth choir from Nkhafu (Nkhatabay) during the 2010 women's

The Youth in the Reformed Last Church of God

The youth between thirteen and thirty-five years of age also have their role to play in the church. They take part in preaching during the Sunday service and also during youth Sundays. Apart from that, they are given opportunity to organize a conference where they invite members from other congregations and they are the ones who lead the services during such meetings. They also fundraise for the church. Further to that, they have a youth choir. At Munkhokwe the youth choir is led by the pastor himself, Joseph M. Banda. They meet on Wednesday and Saturday afternoons for Bible sharing and choir practice.[13] The youths also sing during the church conferences.

---

[11] Int. Mama Buwani NyaManda, *Amayi Achikondi* Chair Person Munkhokwe, 12.7.2010.

[12] Ibid. 12.7.2010.

[13] Int. Wales Mahemani, youth, Munkhokwe, 13.7.2010.

Sometimes a youth choir may even comprise of some youths from other churches. For example, the choir at Nkhatabay *boma* comprises of members from different churches like the Assemblies of God and African Church. This choir also attended the 2010 women's conference at Phiri.

Figure 9: A choir with members from different churches including the Last Church from Nkhatabay boma performing at Phiri during the 2010 women's conference

I observed that most of the youths in the church were around the age of 15. This is true even for the African Last Church. It shows that a good number of the older youths leave the church. This experience is also true for youths in Zionist Churches where 20% of children born into Zion discontinue with the faith of their parents.[14] This proves that "the biological reason for being a member of a church is no safeguard for the church's future."[15]

Sunday School in the Reformed Last Church of God

Sunday school is allowed in the Reformed Last Church, but some congregations do not have it. This is the case at Munkhokwe. Pastor Mboya Banda explained that the absence of Sunday school at his church was simply due to the lack of initiative on his part and the leadership of the church. Therefore, children learn about the beliefs of their church from the main service they attend with their parents on Sundays. There are no immediate plans for starting a Sunday school at Munkhokwe Reformed Last Church.[16]

---

[14] Ulf Strohbehn, *The Zionist Churches in Malawi. History - Theology - Anthropology*, Mzuzu: Mzuni Press, 2016, Ibid. p. 301.

[15] Ibid. p. 103.

[16] Int. Rev Mboya Banda, Munkhokwe, 12.7.2010.

Membership in the Reformed Last Church of God

Rev Mboya Banda stated that there are 500 registered members at Munkhokwe. However, those who are active in the church are about 200. Some of the members were born in the church while others came from other churches and joined the church for different reasons. For instance, out of the eight members I interviewed six were born in the church. These were Mr and Mrs Kinna, *Mama* Gutamu, Zifa Nkhana, Michael Kampetewu and Frida Banda. On the other hand, Sarai Kaunda joined the church following her husband and Gogo Reverend Chimbaza at first belonged to African Church before he joined the Last Church. The pastor himself, Mr Joseph Mboya Banda, was born in the church while his wife joined the church following her husband.[17]

The number of new members who join the church may reach up to eight in a year. Some of these follow their partners into the church. Others are attracted by the message and the choirs in the church. However, before they can be registered the pastor asks the person why she or he would like to join the church. The church also sometimes loses some of its members through death or by choice. The number of those members that leave the church can go up to five in a year. It is true that the traditional Malawian concept of marriage adds to and subtracts from the membership.[18] Many of the new members who join the Last Church are women following their husbands. At the same time, it is the women again, who leave in bigger numbers due to the traditional Malawian understanding of marriage - that a wife should join her husband's faith and congregation.[19]

A member is supposed to follow the Ten Commandments in the Bible, has to be baptized and is expected to partake in Holy Communion. A member is supposed to give an offering on Sunday. In the very past members were expected to give an offering of one tambala during church meetings. Pledges or tithes are not demanded from the members

---

[17] Int. Rev Mboya Banda, Munkhokwe, 12.7.2010.
[18] Ulf Strohbehn, *The Zionist Churches in Malawi. History - Theology - Anthropology*, Mzuzu: Mzuni Press, 2016, p. 304.
[19] Ibid., p. 304.

but they are not prohibited. Nevertheless, members are expected to participate in fundraising activities of the church to meet the expenses of the church. The church and its members are encouraged to support government's efforts in raising the living standards of the people in the community, for instance, if there is community work such as moulding bricks for school blocks.

The Reformed Last Church of God and His Christ is so far present in six countries; Zimbabwe, Zambia, Mozambique, South Africa, Malawi and Tanzania. They claim to have almost 3.5 million members in these six countries.[20] However, this figure may be quite exaggerated. In fact, the figure may represent membership of both Reformed and African Last Church. In Malawi membership may roughly be around 300,000 and 400,000.[21]

Sacraments in the Reformed Last Church

Baptism

The Reformed Last Church administers baptism by immersion. The baptism can happen at any time and any day, whenever the one who wants to be baptized is ready. The pastor baptizes the person in the name of God the Father, the Son and the Holy Spirit. Generally, the church allows only adult baptism and not children's baptism. But in Munkhokwe congregation children are also baptized. The pastor argues that even children are sinners due to the fall of Adam and Eve, hence the need for them to be baptized too. Babies are brought to the pastor and together with their parents they go to the Jordan (river) where the body of the baby is immersed in the water leaving the head above, while he

---

[20] Int. Rev O. Masinda, General Principal, Kazando, 6.11.2011.

[21] The leaders say the districts with the most members are four, Kasungu, Dowa, Nkhatabay, and Ntchisi with 50 to 100 congregations each having about 500 members. With these kinds of figures membership should be between 30,000 and 40,000.

just pours water over the head. In addition, children are also blessed by the Reverend taking it from Jesus who used to bless little children.[22]

Adults, however, must answer positively to questions from the pastor before being baptized at the "Jordan."[23] For example they are asked "do you agree to give little by little thanksgiving offering for the growth of the church," "do you promise God to always read his word, to pray in his Church and to partake in Holy Communion?"[24] The pastor may also read some of the following texts: Mathew 3:13 [As soon as Jesus was baptized, he came up out of the water. The heaven was opened to him, and he saw the Spirit of God coming down like a dove and alighting on him."], Ephesians 4: 22 ["So get rid of your old self, which made you live as you used to the old self that was being destroyed by its deceitful desires."], Galatians 5:19 ["What human nature does is quite plain. It shows itself in immoral, filthy, and indecent actions."]. He then explains the scripture to those being baptized.[25] Then the person is baptized.

Holy Communion

The *Amayi Maria* are given the responsibility to prepare the elements for the Holy Communion. A house close to the church belonging to one of the members of the church is chosen where the preparations take place. Before *Amayi Mariya* and *Alalakazi* can light the fire the preacher and *gogo mliska* (retired preacher and pastor) prays to dedicate the whole process to God. The bread and wine (*vinyo ndi mkate*) are prepared. After the preparations, it is left to the deacons, *Amayi Mariya* and *Alalakazi* to carry the wine and the bread to the church. However, it is the preachers who serve the Holy Communion to the people after it has been blessed by the Reverend. Holy Communion is administered during

---

[22] Int. Rev Mboya Banda, Munkhokwe, 12.7.2010.

[23] It is not clear when and how the idea of calling the river "Jordan" came up. But this is a Zionist expression, which Providence Industrial Mission also uses (Allan Anderson, *An Introduction to Pentecostalism: Global Charismatic Christianity*, Cambridge University Press, 2004, p. 103).

[24] Ibid. 12.7.2010.

[25] I think the point throughout these scriptures is for the person to leave his or her old life and become a new creature as a symbol of baptism.

big conferences (usually three times a year). Even members of other churches are welcome to partake in the Holy Communion.

Marriage

Rachel NyaGondwe Banda [Fiedler] writes about three types of weddings present in a matrilineal society: the *chinkhoswe* wedding, the blessed wedding (*ukwati wodalitsa*) and the church wedding.[26] She writes that church weddings are unattainable for the rural majority.[27] In many cases couples in the Last Church of God prefer to have their marriage to be just prayed for at their home on the day when traditionally the woman is escorted to her husband's home. This is regarded as a church wedding, but its practice is unique to the Last Church and probably to other Independent Churches as well. Church weddings as conducted in mainline churches are not common in the Last Church of God. The Last Church does also recognize *ukwati wodalitsa,* especially for those that eloped, only that it does it differently. After being disciplined by the church the pastor prays for the couple.

When the couple would like to bless their marriage either traditionally or in the church, they are first required to fulfill their traditional obligations, especially of the man towards the girl's family. He has to first pay whatever they had agreed on with the woman's side. Only then can the couple register their marriage with the church. On the agreed date and time, the marriage is blessed by the pastor at the church. And the pastor counsels the couple with regard to what the Bible says concerning marriage. This is done before he actually blesses the two in church. Rev Mboya said that after the church ceremony is over the church does not send any counselling team to the couple. Whoever goes to the home of the newly wedded couple goes there in his or her own capacity and not in the church's name.[28]

---

[26] Rachel NyaGondwe Banda, *Women of Bible and Culture: Baptist Convention Women in Southern Malawi,* Zomba: Kachere, 2005, p. 172.

[27] Ibid. p. 172

[28] Int. Rev Mboya Banda, Last Church Kazando, Munkhokwe, 12.7.2010.

The Reformed Last Church of God and Culture

Members of the Reformed Last Church of God and His Christ are allowed to seek assistance from traditional doctors when they are sick. Rev Mboya gave an example of the "school" of Moses and the bitter water in the desert.[29] Mboya argued that Moses used a piece of wood to make the water sweet. Mboya also referred to Proverbs 18:18 where it says "casting lots will put a stop to arguing". However, the application of this quotation is debatable because in Israel behind the casting of lots was God Himself and the question is, who is behind divination or *kuombeza*?

Nevertheless, members are encouraged to seek traditional medicine mainly for their sickness and not divination (*kuombeza*). If a person is suspected of being a witch, she or he is temporarily removed from the church according to Numbers 15:30.[30] The Last Church believes in the power of Jesus, but the members and many in the society believe that illness and death are rarely due to natural causes but to spirits or enemies. Culturally the people believe that the diviner can tell whether an enemy or a witch has caused the misfortune.[31] So, when a member is accused by his relatives or in his/her village, the church allows the person to consult a diviner. The report from the diviner is accepted by the church. But here one questions how the church believes the report from the traditional doctors as truth and hence as evidence against the accused, for usually when diviners are consulted, innocent people suffer.[32] An ordinary member is temporarily removed for six months while those in leadership positions are suspended for one year and six months.

---

[29] Actually, there was nothing like a "school of Moses" during the time of Moses. The point to be taken from Mboya's example is the fact that Moses threw the stick into the water at Marah to make it sweet (Ex. 15:22).

[30] Numbers 15:30 referred above states that "But suppose one sins on purpose. It does not matter whether he is an Israelite or outsider. He speaks evil against the Lord. He must be cut off from his people."

[31] J.W.M. van Breugel, *Chewa Traditional Religion*, Blantyre: CLAIM-Kachere, 2001, p. 233.

[32] Handwell Yotamu Hara, *Reformed Soteriology and the Malawian Context*, Zomba: Kachere, 2008, p. 136.

In the past polygamy was allowed by the church but things have now changed. Due to cultural changes as well as to social economic factors polygamy has been forbidden. Those in polygamous marriages are allowed to remain like that and keep their wives. But anyone who marries two wives now must be excommunicated.[33] This development is not unique to Last Church alone as other Independent Churches like African Abraham Church have also banned polygamy over the years. The main explanation given for the banning in AAC is that polygamy caused a lot of problems to wives, which included lack of care and commitment.[34] However, as much as this is a contributing factor, the banning of polygamy in the Last Church has to do mainly with the society's change in attitude towards it.[35]

In the Reformed Last Church beer drinking is allowed but one should not get drunk. Mboya referred to Romans 14:14 where Paul was saying that no food is "unclean" in itself. The church continues to face challenges from some members who over drink and in so doing continue to tarnish the image of the church. The Reformed Last Church differs here from the African Last Church which has prohibited beer drinking for its members.

Headquarters' Visitation

The General Principal usually visits a church only when there is a conference at that particular church. Usually this is once in a year. However, the Munkhokwe congregation is visited often by the Area Moderator and the District Principal. The current Moderator is Rev Chimgogu Chirwa and since he worships in the same congregation it is to their advantage. The General Principal O. Masinda did visit Munkhokwe congregation in 2012.[36] There is usually a gap between the headquarters

---

[33] Int. Rev Mboya Banda, Munkhokwe, 12.7.2010.

[34] Jemiter Mwale, The Establishment and Development of African Abraham Church in Malawi (1929-2000): A Case Study on the Major Changes in Doctrines and their Impact (Chamchere Mission Station), BA, University of Malawi, 2000, p. 9.

[35] For a further discussion on polygamy in the Last Church see chapter 7.

[36] Int. Rev Mboya Banda, Munkhokwe, 12.7.2010.

and the grass root congregations as far as visitation from the top is concerned.

Relationships of the Reformed Last Church beyond the Country

The church's relationship with other Last Church congregations outside the country is different from that found in the African Last Church. This is the case because the General Principal of the church in the country is not the General Principal for all the six countries in which the Reformed Last Church (Kazando) is found.[37] As such the Synod meetings do not rotate in these countries in terms of venue as it used to be the case with the Last Church of God (Msondozi) before the situation there changed.

However, members of the church in the six countries sometimes do invite each other at the congregational level. But this year (2012) the members of this congregation (Munkhokwe) have not visited any church outside the country nor have they received visitors from other congregations abroad.[38]

Sunday Worship in the Reformed Last Church of God and His Christ

The Sunday services as conducted by the Last Church of God have some distinctive features. The service is usually characterized by three preachers. These are required to read at least three biblical passages or verses each during preaching. The preaching is usually done verse by verse as the reader reads the passages.[39] As is the case in Zionist Churches, the preaching proceeds according to ranks. Usually, the Pastor and the highest office holder present give the last address while the youngest preacher is the first to preach.[40] If the preachers include both men and women, then women are the first to preach. The ascending

---

[37] Int. Rev O. Masinda, General Principal, Kazando, 6.11.2011.

[38] Int. Rev Mboya Banda, Munkhokwe, 12.7.2010.

[39] The preaching of verse by verse is also a Zionist practice.

[40] Ulf Strohbehn, *The Zionist Churches in Malawi: History – Theology – Anthropology*, Mzuzu: Mzuni Press, 2016, p. 180.

authority of the speakers has been explained by some to be in line with African oral traditions.[41] The example given is that of the traditional council where different advisors and representatives speak, but the chief concludes the meeting with his address, which is a reflection of different opinions and aspects presented.[42] One will not hear choruses in the course of the service. But choirs are there and drums are allowed. This pattern is the same as the one found in the African Last Church of God.[43]

I will present a description of the service as observed on 19th September, 2010. I arrived at the church around 10:00 a.m. and I found one member (a man), who was arranging the chairs in the church. Later other members started coming in and some church leaders sat outside discussing with Rev Mboya Banda. Meanwhile in the church the youth choir started singing and they were joined by Rev Mboya Banda, who was beating the drums.[44] Around 10:30 a.m. the leaders entered the church and took their seats in front. The chairperson of the service that day addressed the congregation, which was not yet settled in terms of noise and he asked one leader in front to pray.

After the opening prayer, the chairperson asked the congregation to rise and sing a hymn from their own Tumbuka hymn book. This was led by Rev Banda. Then the chairperson announced the theme for that day which was *kulimbikisa* (encouragement). In relation to that he asked one person from the front to read in Tonga Psalms 148:7 ["Praise the LORD from the earth, you great sea creatures and all the deepest parts of the ocean."] After the reading the chairperson commented to the audience that they should give God praise according to His word. He asked the youth choir to sing one song. They sang about "*umasiye*" or the bitterness of orphan hood.[45]

---

[41] Ulf Strohbehn, *The Zionist Churches in Malawi: History – Theology – Anthropology*, Mzuzu: Mzuni Press, 2016, p. 159.

[42] Ibid., p. 157.

[43] On singing of choruses and general worship in the church, we are going to see that there are now changes in the African Last, especially in Mzuzu, Chitipa and Karonga districts.

[44] Their songs and hymns are also accompanied with a lot of dancing.

[45] Youth Choir, Last Church, Kazando, Munkhokwe, 19.9.2012.

The youth choir was followed by *Amayi Achikondi* with one song. The message in the song was that, when going to heaven, a person will not carry anything, neither children nor wealth nor anything else but Christ. Then the first preacher (male) asked the reader to be reading scriptures for him as he was preaching verse by verse. As usual three Bible texts were given to the reader by the preacher.

The first text was Amos 3:2 ["Out of all the families on earth I have chosen only you. So, I will punish you because you have committed so many sins."] He explained that God has chosen them at Munkhokwe as His own, but unfortunately, they have turned away from God. So, He will punish them. The preacher also asked the reader to read Jeremiah 23:20-24 where God declares that His anger will not turn back against false prophets. He warned the audience that God's anger will not turn back from them if they keep on sinning. Finally, he read 1 Timothy 5:24 ["The sins of some people are plain to see, and their sins go ahead of them to judgement; but the sins of others are seen only later"]. He explained that both sins and good works are easy to see in a person. Therefore, one cannot hide his or her sins forever.

When the first preacher was through with the preaching, the chairperson asked the *Amayi Achikondi* to sing a second song. After the song, the second preacher was called (a man again). He also gave three texts to the reader to be read at his instruction as he explained the scriptures. The first text was Acts 10:33 about Cornelius and Peter. He explained that like Cornelius they were in the house of God to listen to what He has to say. Then he gave I Corinthians 2:11 where Paul said that he had made up his mind to pay attention to only one thing, Jesus Christ and His death on the cross. He told the audience that the one thing that is needed in their lives is Christ. The third text was Mathew 7:2 where Jesus said that it was not everyone who said to Him "Lord, Lord" that will enter the kingdom of God, but only those that do His will. The second preacher finished his message. The second hymn was sung by the whole congregation.

The third preacher commented on the first and second preaching before he too gave one text to be read, Proverbs 18:24 ["Even a man who has many companions can be destroyed. But there is a friend who sticks closer than a brother"]. As he finished preaching offerings were collected and a prayer for them was offered. It should be noted that even though the theme was given the preachers did not preach on that theme.

The chairperson asked the congregation to sing the last hymn and a final prayer was offered. The church secretary then made the announcements and the clerk welcomed the visitors. Before the members dispersed the clerk called the names of three people and asked them to come forward. Two women and one man came in front. The pastor asked the congregation if they knew the wrongs committed by those three people. The congregation collectively answered "yes". Then one sitting next to me explained that the three had married outside the church (eloped), so after their six months of church discipline they wanted to be reincorporated into the church.[46]

The pastor then asked the reader to read the Bible story of the woman caught in adultery. The pastor explained that just like Jesus did not condemn that woman so he too did not condemn them but that they should go and sin no more.[47] Afterwards he prayed for them.

Conclusion

The Reformed Last Church also continued to expand in various areas after the split. However, in terms of its organization, structure, beliefs and practices it did not depart from the African Last. A major difference as of today is the fact that the Reformed Last has not so far absorbed Charismatic/Pentecostal influences which is the case with the African Last.

---

[46] Int. Mama Banda, church member, Munkhokwe, 19.9.2012.
[47] Int. Rev Mboya Banda, Last Church Kazando, Munkhokwe, 12.7.2010.

Chapter 5: The Last Church of God and His Christ International ("African Last")

Longwe and the African Last Church of God after the Split

The headquarters of the African Last Church of God remained at Msondozi. The explanation is that Longwe was from Msondozi, hence had the support of many members from that area. This made it difficult for Kaphinya and his group to claim Msondozi as their headquarters.[1] White Longwe became the Archbishop of the church after Mkhuta. One will notice that beginning in the 1960s significant changes started taking place in the church and that after the split in 1967, the church began manifesting some mainline characteristics which Msumba had originally repudiated.

Longwe had three wives, namely, Akwachauheni, Achimbowolu and Akaviboku who did not have any children. It is said that Longwe was not just an ordinary leader. But rather he was a charismatic leader and this was the reason why Mkhuta had chosen Longwe to succeed him. It is told that when Longwe was in the African Church (before he joined Last Church) he was second in leadership to Yesaya Zerenji Mwasi from whom he learned the leadership management style.[2] Concerning Mwasi it is said, among other things, that he had a reputation for outstanding intellectual ability and formidable gifts of leadership.[3] Among the Tonga of Bandawe, Mwasi became known as a rainmaker and miracle-worker and places where he conducted services came to be regarded as sacred.[4] Likewise, it is said about Longwe that he had some of the gifts that Mwasi possessed.

It is reported by his admirers that Longwe was well respected because of his charisma. For instance, it is said that sometimes when it was time for

---

[1] Int. Rev Chiuli Manda, retired Bishop, Munkhokwe, 31.8.2012.

[2] Ibid. 31.8.2012.

[3] Yesaya Zerenji Mwasi, *Essential and Paramount Reasons for Working Independently*, Blantyre: CLAIM-Kachere, 1999, p. 7.

[4] Ibid. p. 7.

prayers and it was raining, Longwe could point his rod to heaven and pray to God to hold the rain so that His children could pray peacefully. It would happen that there would be no rain at the place of worship while all around the place heavy rains were pouring down (in those days most meetings used to take place under a tree).[5] This is the only reference I came across in the Last Church where a rod was used as a transmitter of prayer as done in Zionist Churches.[6] Otherwise, the carrying of rods by pastors in the Last Church seems to have served more as a symbol of authority and leadership identity. This is different from the Zionist practice (from where Msumba might have borrowed the tradition), where the Bishop's staff is used as an extension of the man himself. People are touched with it when direct contact is not possible or appropriate.[7]

It is also said that sometimes, when there was a church meeting and someone planned to do some harm to him (through magic), Longwe would perceive it and would just delegate someone to carry on with the meeting, and give an excuse that he was not feeling well. This of course might have been a misinterpretation by outsiders who were "known to accuse the Last Church of witches."[8]

Longwe was also a visionary leader. He was one of the people who saw the need for the members to start giving to the church in order for the church to grow. He suggested this in 1957 during one of the church meetings at Nkhunga. This was even before he became the Archbishop of the church. He suggested that each member should be giving at least 6 pence (6 tambala) per year.[9]

Longwe's suggestion, however, did not go down well with many members that were present, including Luka Nyirenda, who, with some

---

[5] Int. Rev Chiuli Manda, retired Bishop, Munkhokwe, 31.8.2012.

[6] Ulf Strohbehn, *The Zionist Churches in Malawi, History-Theology-Anthropology*, Mzuzu: Mzuni Press, 2016, p. 180.

[7] Ibid. p. 180.

[8] Godfrey Banda and Peter Forster, "The Last Church of God and His Christ" in *Journal of Religion in Africa*, vol. 29, 1999, pp. 455-456.

[9] Int. Rev Chiuli Manda, retired Bishop, Munkhokwe, 31.8.2012.

others in the meeting, walked out to show their disapproval.[10] Their argument was that this had never happened in the church since its establishment. However, there seemed to have been another reason why Longwe met such resistance namely, that he was just a new member and the people thought that a new member could not dictate to them what to do. However, if Longwe's suggestion had been adopted, it would have benefited the church much in terms of its finances.[11] Longwe finally died on 14th May 1997 and Stanwell Mhone replaced him.[12]

Achievements during Longwe's Term (1962 to 1997)

It is important to highlight some of the achievements during Longwe's term. He led the church for 35 years. It was during this time that there came a change in the leadership structure. Some positions were introduced in the church like Senior Bishops, Area Bishops and Missionaries. Missionaries in the Last Church of God are pastors in charge of other pastors in an area. They are sometimes also called head pastors.[13] This was an attempt to bridge the gap between the headquarters and the grass roots congregations.

Apart from the change in the leadership structure, Longwe was the one who initiated the change of the dressing gear of pastors. Pastors now started to put on clerical shirts and a white collar instead of long robes and head gears. And the carrying of rods was stopped. The pastor's regalia was one of the things that is believed to have made many youths not to be attracted to the church.[14] So probably Longwe wanted to attract even the youths to the church which at that time was regarded as a church for elderly people and polygamists. But was the attraction of the youths to the church the main reason for the change of the pastor's regalia? This will be discussed in chapter ten.

---

[10] Int. Rev Chiuli Manda, retired Bishop, Munkhokwe, 31.8.2012.

[11] Ibid. 31.8.2012.

[12] Ibid. 31.8.2012.

[13] Int. Rev Kaundama, Kamsita, 8.10.2010.

[14] Ibid. 8.10.2010.

Longwe also accepted that choirs should be singing in the church and that they could use drums in their singing. Before this time choirs were forbidden in the church. Also, it was during Longwe's time that women really started meeting as *Amayi Achikondi* in the 1970s. Even though there was a provision for this organization within the constitution, it was only later that the group actually came into being in the church.[15] There are no clear reasons for this but it seems it had to do with culture, where women were not allowed to stand before men. One of the activities of *Amayi Achikondi* is singing in the church. And they have to stand in front to sing. It seems many men at that time could not stand it.

Women were also now allowed to preach in the church. This started in the 1990s, the later years of Longwe's term. Today these women also organize their own women's conferences in their various districts at least once in a year where they even invite colleagues from other districts.

These above changes were just a beginning of the transformation of the church. With time, several other changes took place and they continue to happen. There should be many factors that contributed to these changes.

Districts where the Last Church of God and His Christ International (Msondozi) is Found

Today the church is found in the following districts: Nkhatabay which has around forty congregations and about 30,000 members.[16] One of these congregations is Munkhokwe Last Church.[17] The Church came to Munkhokwe in 1969 through Mr Chilibwanji.[18] He was a Tumbuka from Mzimba who married a Tonga wife. Mr Chilibwanji brought this Church from Mlowe (Sanga) where he was a member. He died in 1974 and was

---

[15] Int. Rev Kaundama, Kamsita, 8.10.2010.

[16] Int. Rev Chikosera Phiri, Archbishop African Last, 24.6.2011.

[17] This Munkhokwe Last Church belongs to African Last Church (Msondozi headquarters) and is different from Munkhokwe Reformed Last Church that was discussed in chapter five. They are two different congregations within the same area but under different headquarters.

[18] Int. Rev Kaundama, Kamsita, 10.8.2012.

succeeded by Rev Chiuli Manda. In 1998 Rev Kaundama took over from Chiuli Manda. One of the things Kaundama did was that he facilitated the building of the church (Fig. 10).

The other churches in Nkhatabay include Katoto Last Church.[19] This was started by Rev Matola in 2003. Before this time members were worshipping at Chikumba congregation (Chihame). Due to the long distance to Chikumba they decided to have a prayer house at Katoto.[20]

Figure 10: Munkhokwe Last Church of God, 2010

Rev Chimuliu started the Last Church at Matete and Nkhafu in 1995 and 2009 respectively. He is also the one who opened the church at Sanga in Traditional Authority Mankhambira. On the other hand, Bishop Jali Phiri started the Chigwiri Last Church in Tukombo (1995) and Kamwali Last Church.[21]

In Nkhotakota, there are twelve congregations with about 3,600 members. Some of the churches there include Kalowa and Dema congregations that were started by Philimon Chirwa.[22] However, it was Rev Madondolo who held the church together during the time of the division. After Madondolo's death the church was left in the hands of Rev Chande, who is still the District Principal.[23] In Ntchisi there are eight congregations with about 2,500 members.[24]

---

[19] This Katoto is different from the one in Mzuzu.
[20] Int. Rev Matola, Katoto Last Church, Chintheche, 12.9.2010.
[21] Int. Bishop Chikosera Phiri, Archbishop, Mzuzu, 12.10.2011.
[22] Int. Rev Chiuli Manda, retired Bishop, Munkhokwe, 31.8.2012.
[23] Int. Rev Kaundama, Kamsita, 10.8.2012.
[24] Int. Bishop Chikosera Phiri, Archbishop, Mzuzu, 12.10.2011.

There are only two congregations in Rumphi and Lilongwe. The church in Lilongwe was started in 2004 by Mr Mughogho.[25] In Kasungu there are five congregations with about 1,600 members.

The African Last Church of God is also found in Mzimba District in places such as Elangeni, Mbalachanda, Euthini and Ekwendeni. The church in Ekwendeni was opened recently in 2010. The church is also found in Mzuzu in the following places: Masasa, started in 1983; Khwechi, started in 1987; and Chibavi, opened in 1992.[26] The one at Msongwe was started in 2004 by Rev Chikosera Phiri and the church is also found in Mchengautuwa and Kaviwale areas. The present Head Pastor for Mzuzu congregations is Rev Z. Ngulube.

The African Last Church has many of its members from Karonga and Chitipa districts which were not affected by the division. In Chitipa by 1997 there were about 30,000 members. Today there are 139 prayer houses and fourteen big congregations, two in Kameme, four in Ulambia, four in Misuku, two in Wenya and two in Nthalire. There are 97 Pastors and about 50,000 members. In Karonga there are 155 congregations with about 56,000 members.[27]

Sacraments in the African Last Church of God and His Christ

Baptism

The church does not organize a special day or classes or teaching for baptism of its members. So, any member who thinks that he or she is ready for baptism just comes to the pastor who baptizes the person the very same day.[28] They baptize by immersion in a river which they refer to as the "Jordan."[29] The person is baptized in the name of the Father, the Son and the Holy Spirit. As for members who come from other churches,

---

[25] Int. Bishop Alex Sibale, Principal Chitipa, Chitipa Boma, 6.4.2013.
[26] Int. Rev Chikosera Phiri, Archbishop, Mzuzu, 1.1.2012.
[27] Int. Bishop Alex Sibale, Principal Chitipa, Chitipa Boma, 6.4.2013.
[28] Int. Rev Kaundama, Kamsita, 12.10.2012.
[29] The naming of the river as "Jordan" is common with Reformed Last, Zionist Churches and PIM.

if they were baptized already the church does not demand another baptism for them.[30]

There is also a clause in the constitution of the Last Church that states that if there is a conference, things like baptism, blessing of children, and reinstatement of those who were temporary removed from the church, should be done on Saturday because there is not enough time on Sunday; and besides that, God finished all his work on Saturday and rested on Sunday.[31] Little children are not baptized but instead they are blessed. Rev Kaundama stated that they take this from Jesus who used to bless little children.[32]

When parents bring children to be blessed the pastor reads scriptures either from Luke 18:15 ["people were also bringing babies to Jesus to have him touch them. When the disciples saw this, they rebuked them."], or Mathew 19:13 ["Then little children were brought to Jesus for him to place his hands on them and pray for them. But the disciples rebuked those who brought them."], where Jesus blessed little children. After preaching, the pastor takes the child in his arms, lays his hand on him or her and then prays. The children that are blessed are those that cannot make their own decisions (from one month to eight years of age).[33]

Marriage

The African Last Church of God recognizes both church weddings as well as blessed marriages. But the common type of marriage is whereby the pastor prays for the couple on the day when traditionally the girl is escorted to her husband's home.[34] Elopement (*kusomphora*) is not accepted in the church, and anyone who marries through eloping is

---

[30] Int. Rev Kaundama, Kamsita, 12.10.2012

[31] Constitution of the Last Church of God and His Christ, clause no. 23, nd.

[32] Int. Rev Kaundama, Kamsita, 12.10.2012.

[33] Ibid. 12.10.2012.

[34] This practice is echoed in Klaus Fiedler, "For the Sake of Christian Marriage, Abolish Church Weddings," in: *Religion in Malawi,* 1995, p. 20.

disciplined.[35] Changing rules on marriage, including the prohibition of polygamy, are significant changes that have happened in the church.

Holy Communion

Holy Communion is usually celebrated when there is a conference (*ungano*) and in many cases, it is administered by the people from the headquarters. The elements for the communion are locally made. The leaders choose two *alalakazi* (women who have stopped menstruating) and one church elder (male) to prepare the elements for the Holy Communion. The church elder serves as the supervisor. These people go to the house of one of the members that has been selected, usually because it is close to the church.[36] First a prayer is offered and the women prepare bread without yeast and "wine;" the ingredients used for wine include sugar and tea leaves. When everything is ready, they invite the pastor and other church leaders to bless the elements.[37]

Once in the church the service starts with a prayer followed by a first song from the Tonga/Tumbuka hymn book. Then Bible reading, after which the pastor preaches the word of God. The preaching is followed by a second hymn, and then Holy Communion is served. Anyone is free to partake in the Holy Communion after evaluating their hearts as apostle Paul advised in 1 Corinthians 11:27-28 ["If anyone eats the Lord's bread or drinks from his cup in a way that dishonours him, he or she is guilty of sin against the Lord's body and blood. So, then you should all examine yourselves first, and then eat the bread and drink from the cup"]. Church leaders including *alalakazi* assist in serving the Holy Communion to the people.[38]

Funerals

If a church member dies the pastor is informed, who in turn tells the secretary to send the message to other church leaders. Then they go to the house of the bereaved and some members spend the night there

---

[35] Mrs Rev Kaundama, Kamsita, 12.10.2012.
[36] Ibid. 12.10.2012.
[37] Ibid. 12.10.2012.
[38] Ibid. 12.10.2012.

with the mourners. The pastor prepares the programme which includes three preachers.

On the burial day, the members go into the funeral house while singing. A prayer is offered followed by preaching and then a closing prayer. Once they come outside, the second preacher takes over and she or he preaches to the people outside.[39]

After the outside preaching is over, an offering is collected and after blessing, it is given to those responsible for it. As they leave for the graveyard male church members carry the coffin while the people are singing. At the graveyard, a prayer is offered and the body is lowered into the grave. Before the *adzukulu* put the soil into the grave there is the third preaching. After that the *adzukulu* are instructed to fill the grave as choirs are singing. Finally, a closing prayer is offered.[40]

Rev Matola of Katoto congregation stated that some pastors like himself do not preach at the funeral of a church member because he is also a mourner. Therefore, he asks a pastor or preacher from another branch to preach on his behalf. However, he gives *malonje* when it is time for the church to speak about the deceased.

In some congregations, when a member dies and was without blame, it is the pastor of the congregation who preaches at the funeral. On the other hand, if the deceased was with blame and died before being fully re-incorporated in the church, the pastor does not preach, instead a preacher does. Likewise, the *Amayi Achikondi* do not wear uniform at such a funeral. On the death of the pastor, the area bishop is supposed to lead and preach at the funeral. If it is the area bishop who has died, then the senior bishop preaches.[41]

When asked about laying of flowers or wreaths on the grave, Rev Matola said that they do not put wreaths on the tombs because beginning with Genesis through Revelation there is no mention of putting wreaths on people's tombs. He also said that since flowers are a token of love, then

---

[39] Int. Rev Matola, Pastor Katoto Last Church, Chintheche, 26.10.2010.
[40] Ibid.
[41] Ibid.

they should be given to the person while still alive. However, when a relative of the deceased insists on laying wreaths they are allowed to do so but not as a church.[42] In this practice African Last shares a similarity with the Watchman Healing Mission and African Abraham Church which also views this practice as a deviation from the real meaning of death. For them death is a sorrowful occasion and not a joyous one. The wreath, which is usually decorated with flowers, is interpreted as an indication of joy. They argue that there is no way joy and sorrow can be found on the same occasion.[43] Of course, here one can argue that on the cross joy (love) and sorrow mingled together, but this was Jesus.

Buildings in the African Last Church of God

Many churches of the African Last Church of God are built with burnt bricks. The majority of them are grass thatched. For instance, out of the five churches that I visited in Nkhatabay district only one had used iron sheets for roofing. The windows are usually without frames and without window

Figure 11: Katoto African Last Church of God (Chintheche, 2010)

panes. The pews are sometimes made from bricks plastered with clay. In some cases, the front of the Church is a bit elevated and a small "wall" made of bricks with passable space on both sides demarcates the front from the rest of the church. The front of the church usually contains the wooden pulpit, and some wooden chairs. Many of these churches have no door shatters. Such church buildings characterize many of the African Last churches in various districts in the country, including the church at

---

[42] Int. Rev Matola, Pastor Katoto Last Church, Chintheche, 26.10.2010.

[43] Nelson Chikometsa, "Death Rites in African Instituted Churches: The Watchman Healing Mission and the Restoration Church," BA, University of Malawi, p. 8.

the headquarters, which can accommodate 200 members. The explanation for this is simple; the Last Church is one of the churches which does not emphasize giving on the part of its members. For instance, today members are asked to give K100 per member per year and even Sunday offerings are not very much emphasized. This makes members to construct such low-cost buildings. Many of the Last Church buildings look like the church in the picture.

However, there is an exception to this in Chitipa. Sibale, Principal for Chitipa, proudly states that many churches in Chitipa are roofed with iron sheets. For instance, he states that in Kameme out of the 22 churches only five are grass thatched.[44]

Likewise, in Ulambia, out of the 50 congregations only seven still have grass thatched roofs. They are currently constructing a very big church at Chitipa *boma*, which will seat about 1,000 people. Sibale also mentioned that there is a very beautiful church at Chipwele in Misuku, which has just been completed and is yet to be dedicated to God. When I asked him

Figure 12: The African Last Church Msondozi headquarters and the foundation of the new headquarters

---

[44] Int. Rev Matola, Pastor Katoto Last Church, Chintheche, 26.10.2010.

about the secret behind such success he said it is due to the leadership that is currently in place in the district.[45]

Sibale mentioned that when he took over the position of District Principal in 2003 from Bishop Ridwell Nyondo he found only two churches in Chitipa that were iron roofed. So, he started teaching the pastors and congregations on the importance of giving as well as of dedicated service to God and His work. And the members responded positively.[46] This was also supported by Mrs Dube, a Seventh-day Adventist. She commented that the Last Church is today indeed a church that one may consider to join.[47] She said that Bishop Sibale has contributed a lot in transforming the church in terms of both seriousness of worship and development.[48] Unlike with other denominations, the pastor of the African Last Church resides in his own house right in his village. So usually there is no Pastor's house on the Church premises. However, there is an exception to this at Chibavi church, where they have the pastor's house close to the church.

There are plans to build a better church at the headquarters. It was agreed that each congregation within Nkhatabay should contribute 2,000 Kwacha for bricks for the construction of the church.[49] So far, the foundation of this church has been completed. However, there are also plans that all congregations within the country should assist with contributions towards the building of this church at headquarters. The sad report on the matter was that churches within and outside Malawi started to contribute towards the building of the headquarters' church but the money was misappropriated. The people were disappointed and stopped the contributions.[50]

---

[45] Int. Bishop Alex Sibale, Bishop Chitipa, Chitipa Boma, 6.4.2013.
[46] Ibid. 6.4.2013.
[47] Int. Mrs Dube, former member of Last Church, Chitipa, 5.4.2013.
[48] Int. Mrs Dube, former member of Last Church, Chitipa, 5.4.2013.
[49] Int. Rev Chimuliu, Area Bishop, Msondozi, 10.10.2010.
[50] Int. Bishop Alex Sibale, Chitipa Boma, 6.4.2013.

Leadership in the African Last Church of God

Leadership in the African Last Church in Malawi in Relation to the Last Church outside Malawi

As the African Last Church spread from Malawi to other countries, all the members were under the overall leadership of the church in Malawi (the Archbishop). The Archbishop would visit these countries especially during the Synod meetings. At first the venue for the Synod meeting would rotate between Malawi, Zambia and Tanzania. But due to the rise in transport costs things changed. And, with time, the church, especially in Tanzania and Zambia, expanded fast and there was need for the top leadership to reside within their respective countries. Probably the members in these two countries realized that if they were going to depend on the leadership from Malawi, the church was not going to move effectively. This did not happen just at once. And it seems there was no discussion about it, but it happened gradually and by 2010 Tanzania and Zambia had their own top leadership.[51]

In Zambia, the leader is called the Archbishop, while in Tanzania he is called the General Principal. In countries like Mozambique and Kenya, where the church is still small, they do not have national church leaders, but rather they are led by the bishops assisted by Archbishops from neighbouring countries.[52]

Leadership of the African Last Church of God in Malawi

In Malawi, at the top of the hierarchy there is the Archbishop (at first called General Principal), who is the overseer of the church. After Jordan Msumba there came Rev Isaac Mkhuta in 1936.[53] However, Mkhuta went to South Africa for work and during his absence George Makwenda was chosen to act in his place. Mkhuta returned in 1942 and he took back the position of General Principal. He served until his death in 1964.[54] After

---

[51] Int. Bishop Alex Sibale, Chitipa Boma, 6.4.2013.
[52] Int. Bishop Alex Sibale, Chitipa Boma, 6.4.2013.
[53] Int. Rev Chimuliu, Area Bishop, Msondozi, 10.10.2010.
[54] Int. Rev Chiuli Manda, retired Reverend, Munkhokwe, 25.10.2010.

Mkhuta died, White Longwe took over in 1962 (ordained on 7th September, 1962). Longwe served as Archbishop until his death on 14th May 1997. Longwe was followed by Stanwell Mhone, who was ordained on 28th August 1997. Mhone served as Archbishop until his death on 7th June 2008. The current Archbishop, Rev Chikosera Phiri, was ordained on 23rd August 2002 and resides in Masasa in Mzuzu.[55]

Below the Archbishop is the General Chairman (currently Bishop Chande). He is responsible for settling church disputes, especially at the national level. He is followed by the General Secretary, who is currently Rev L.M. Longwe (from Nkhatabay). Another important position on the national level is that of General Treasurer. After these positions come the Senior Bishops, who supervise the Area Bishops. Usually each district is supposed to have one Senior Bishop. There are, however, two Senior Bishops in Nkhatabay, namely Rev Kaswamphande and Rev Chimwalira, and in Karonga they are Rev A.G. Mkandawire and Rev J.F. Makwakwa. These two districts decided by themselves to have two Senior Bishops instead of one, probably because there are many congregations in the districts.

Then come the Area Bishops, there can be several of these within a district, depending on the size of the area. They oversee the Missionaries. For example, there are four Area Bishops in Nkhatabay district namely, Bishop Ulala (from Kaiya to Dwambazi area) who was ordained on 18th December 2010, Bishop Chimuliu (from Lweya to Thotho) who was ordained on 6th April 2002, and Bishop Chimwalira (from Kawalazi to Chikunga). The fourth Bishop, Henry K. Mwasi, was ordained on 28th August 1997.[56]

The Area Bishops are followed by Missionaries (Head Pastors). These are responsible for judging cases in churches as well as planting churches in new areas. Usually Missionaries are many, since they supervise pastors of congregations. There are currently seven Missionaries in Nkhatabay alone: Mselu Manda ordained on 18th December 2010 (from Kande to Kaiya), Chiuli Manda ordained on 21.6.1978, Bruno Muluzi (Dwambazi to

---

[55] Int. Rev Chiuli Manda, retired Reverend, Munkhokwe, 25.10.2010.
[56] Ibid. 25.10.2010.

Kande), Kananga Banda (Thotho to Nkhatabay), Kubema Banda (from Kabiya to Chihame), Matridi (he came from Chipangano Church) and Kamukungu (Kahenga to Kavuzi).[57]

Below the missionaries are pastors in various congregations, who are followed by preachers (only men). After preachers come elders, and in many congregations, they are only men. However, at Munkhokwe congregation (Nkhatabay) there are both men and women elders (but this is a rare case). The elders are followed by the deacons (both men and women). Women can only be promoted from eldership to *alalakazi* while men can be promoted from elder to preacher.[58] Thus, there are no women pastors nor preachers and the constitution is silent on this.[59]

Choosing Leaders in the African Last Church of God

When there is a shortage of leaders for a certain position in the church the Pastor informs the members, who choose new leaders. They choose through voting and for every position members are requested to nominate at least three people who are to compete for the position. Those who have been nominated are then asked to go and stand outside and close their eyes. The members in the church are then requested to go and stand behind the person they want for a particular position. The one with most people takes the position. Once the leaders (elders and deacons) have been chosen, they are prayed for by the pastor before they start discharging their duties.[60]

Likewise, if there is need for a pastor in the church, it is the responsibility of the church members to choose one of the members as their pastor. The difference is that with pastors, on the day of election some delegates from the headquarters are in attendance. But if they are far from the headquarters then they invite the District Principal or Bishop to ordain the pastor. The one to be chosen as pastor should have the following characteristics: must relate well with others; should have knowledge and

---

[57] Int. Rev Chiuli Manda, retired Reverend, Munkhokwe, 25.10.2010.
[58] Int. Fanny Chirwa, Chairperson *Amayi Achikondi*, Munkhokwe, 16.9.2010.
[59] I have not heard of demands for the ordination of women.
[60] Int. Rev Kaundama, Kamsita, 10.10.2010.

understanding of the Bible (be able to preach); should be dedicated to the church. In addition, their general behaviour should be good.[61]

Any ====male who is holding a position in the church is fit to contest for the position of pastor. The procedure used for choosing a pastor is the same one used in choosing other leaders in the church. The one with most people behind him becomes the pastor. After the pastor has been chosen it is now left to those at the headquarters to arrange a meeting for his ordination. It is there where the new pastor is advised on how to live with people for the betterment of the church. The pastor is responsible for the general welfare of the church, but in particular he is involved in preaching, administering of baptisms, Holy Communion, blessing of little children and marriages among other things.[62] The constitution of the church is silent on whether a woman can be pastor in the church. So far there has never been a woman pastor in the church and I have not heard of proposals or demands for them.

The main duty of the preachers is preaching during church services, funerals and wherever necessary. On the other hand, the church elders are regarded as the "owners" of the church. They make sure that everything in the church is running smoothly. For instance, they check whether the church has enough money for its activities or not. If not, they have to call for some fundraising activities. They also look at the welfare of the members; if some are backsliding or suffering, they visit and encourage them.[63]

The deacons are the *"asilikali"* (soldiers) of the church. They are usually the ones sent out on church errands such as delivering letters to other congregations. They identify the members who are backslidden or are suffering and then reach out to them before the church elders do so. It is also the duty of the deacons to make sure that there is order and no

---

[61] Int. Mrs Fanny Chirwa, Chairperson *Amayi Achikondi*, Munkhokwe, 25.10.2010.
[62] Int. Rev Kaundama, Kamsita, 10.10.2010.
[63] Int. Rev Kaundama, Kamsita, 10.10.2010.

noise during the service or conferences. The elders and deacons also assist in preaching in the church together with the *alalakazi*.[64]

Leadership Training in the African Last Church of God and His Christ

Unlike many other churches that require their pastors to go for a theological training course before starting their duties, this is not the case with the pastors in the Last Church of God. Rev Kaundama explained that the church views theological training as not necessary because God does not look at that but looks for people who do His will. However, those who desire to become pastors are encouraged to know at least spoken English.[65]

However, the church is currently opening up to the issue of pastoral training. In its revised constitution, the church agreed that pastors can go for pastoral training, even though modalities like how and who will pay for their courses are not covered. Nevertheless, this is a step further to positive change. Some pastors like Rev Mwakalenga and Rev Mwambughi have undergone some pastoral training at their own expense.[66]

As much as the Bible indeed is the source of inspiration for the church, one cannot rule out that further understanding and knowledge about the Bible, people and other issues can make an effective pastor who in turn can have an enlightened and effective congregation.

Bishop Sibale in Chitipa saw the need for such training, so at least once every year he organizes one week of training for pastors within Chitipa.[67]

Relationships of the African Last Church beyond the Country

The Last Church in Malawi continues to relate to the Last Church outside the country, but with a decline in the interactions. For instance, in 2009

---

[64] Int. Rev Kaundama, Kamsita, 10.10.2010.
[65] Int. Rev Kaundama, Kamsita, 10.10.2010.
[66] There is more on the two Pastors in chapter 9.
[67] Int. Bishop Sibale, Chitipa Boma, 6.4.2013.

the Synod meeting was held in Fonkha in Zambia, while in 2010 it was held at Masasani in Tanzania. The Archbishop then was from Malawi. Each congregation was supposed to send at least four members and their pastor to attend the Synod meeting wherever it was held. The Synod meeting is usually held between 8th and 12th August once a year. But nowadays, due to the rise in travelling costs only those who can afford do go and attend the Synod meetings in other countries. For instance, in Nkhatabay in 2010 only one representative managed to go to Tanzania and that was Rev Mselu Manda, missionary responsible from Kawiya to Kande in Nkhatabay district.[68]

The Archbishop, in many cases, is supposed to source his own transport money if he is to attend such meetings outside the country. In 2010, when there was the ordination of the Archbishop and the General Secretary in Zambia, Archbishop Chikosera Phiri failed to go due to the challenge of travelling costs. Instead it was Bishop Sibale from Chitipa who went there and ordained those two leaders.[69] Again the fact that Msondozi is no longer the headquarters of all these countries has also reduced the interaction the church in Malawi used to have with the church outside the country.

In order to maintain relationships of the church among these countries the International Board of Trustees was created in 2006. Among other things, this board was to look into the issue of registering the church in all these countries. This board was to be assisted by the National or Local Boards of Trustees. There is also a bond of agreement that the church, though operating in different countries, is still one, but under the leadership of their respective Archbishop or General Principal. They agreed to have the same laws and the same constitution to run the church although practically the countries act independently.[70]

---

[68] Int. Rev Chimuliu, Area Bishop, Msondozi, 20.10.2010.
[69] Int. Bishop Sibale, Chitipa Boma, 6.4.2013.
[70] Int. Bishop Sibale, Chitipa Boma, 6.4.2013.

Women in the African Last Church of God and His Christ International

Women play a big role in the church and like anywhere else women make up the majority of the church. They are active and participate in many activities in the church. For instance, they participate in the leadership of the church as deacons and sometimes also as church elders. Women also look after the general cleanliness of the church in terms of sweeping and smearing the floor. During church repairing they assist in cutting grass and bringing it to the church for use. [71]

It is also the duty of the women to contribute food stuffs and cook for the people when the church is hosting a big meeting (*ungano*). On Sunday, they take part in preaching during the service and at least twice every year they are given the chance to organize a big meeting in which they lead the whole programme. Apart from that they are also given some Sundays called Women's Sunday where they lead the whole service. Women are also given a chance to organize a conference once every year where they lead the entire conference.[72]

Some of the women in the church belong to a women's group known as *Amayi Achikondi* and through this group they also participate in the church.

Amayi Achikondi

The specific date as to when this group started in the African Last Church of God is not known. However, some suggest that the group started around 1979. It was born in Msondozi during one of the big meetings when members from var-

Figure 13: Amayi Achikondi at Munkhokwe doing a choir practice during a Thursday meeting (2010).

---

[71] Int. Mrs Fanny Chirwa, Chairperson *Amayi Achikondi*, Munkhokwe, 25.10.2010.
[72] Ibid. 25.10.2010.

ious congregations in the country assembled at Msondozi. Since then the leaders of the congregations were asked to go and introduce this group to their various congregations. In some congregations, the group was introduced earlier than in others.[73]

Unlike the women's organizations in other churches such as *Umanyano* of Livingstonia Synod, *Amayi Achikondi* does not have any specific written aims or rules. It can, however, be said that *Amayi Achikondi* as an organization "follows the wind of women's organizations locally."[74] Often *Amayi Achikondi* is referred to by other names such as *Umanyano.* This is because by the time the organization was formed, there were already other women's organizations operational in churches such as Livingstonia Synod.[75] The *Amayi Achikondi* also has a leadership structure at district level.[76] The current chairperson for Nkhata-Bay District is Mrs Njikho.

Ministry of Amayi Achikondi

The group first and foremost provides a platform for women to come together and fellowship. They usually meet on Thursday afternoons for prayers and choir practice. They also visit sick church members in their communities and even lazy members to encourage them. They also do fundraising activities to raise funds for the church and their group.[77]

Leadership in Amayi Achikondi

The *Amayi Achikondi* are led by the chairperson, seconded by her vice chairperson. Then the secretary and her vice and lastly, the treasurer and her vice. The term of this leadership is for one year. However, the out-

---

[73] Int. Rev Kaundama, Kamsita, 10.10.2010.
[74] Cf. Rachel NyaGondwe Banda, *Women of Bible and Culture: Baptist Convention Women in Southern Malawi*, Zomba: Kachere, 2005, p. 92.
[75] Ibid. p. 92.
[76] Int. Rev Kaundama, Kamsita, 10.10.2010.
[77] Int. Mrs Fanny Chirwa, Chairperson *Amayi Achikondi*, Munkhokwe, 25.10.2010.

going members can be re-elected, but with the approval of the Reverend. Sometimes the Reverend has the mandate to choose the chairperson.[78]

Membership in Amayi Achikondi

Any lady member of the church who is above seventeen years of age can join *Amayi Achikondi,* whether married or single. There are no special teachings or classes for one to qualify for membership. However, after one has joined she is encouraged to buy the uniform and bring it to the deacon who in turn takes it to the pastor to bless it before she can use it.[79] A member is not expected to memorize any prescribed aims is being as done with *Umanyano* in Livingstonia or *Umodzi* Women of the Baptist Convention of Malawi, since there are no such aims.[80]

The Uniform

The *Amayi Achikondi* have a uniform just like other women organizations in various Christian denominations in the country. The uniform produces a common identity and is a bridge between women from different regions and social economic backgrounds.[81] Their uniform consists of a long black skirt, white long-sleeved blouse, black collar, white belt and black shoes. This seems to be the same as that of *Amayi a Umanyano* in CCAP (Livingstonia Synod). They put on uniform during the funeral of a church member (however, if it is a baby that was not blessed by the pastor they do not wear uniform); during conferences (*ungano*); and whenever they visit the sick. However, those women in monthly period do not put on uniform as they are considered to be impure. This is an instance where we see the influence of culture on the life of the church members.

---

[78] Int. Mrs Fanny Chirwa, Chairperson *Amayi Achikondi*, Munkhokwe, 25.10.2010.
[79] Ibid. 25.10.2010.
[80] Cf. Rachel NyaGondwe Banda, *Women of Bible and Culture: Baptist Convention Women in Southern Malawi*, Zomba: Kachere, 2005, p. 92.
[81] Cf. Rachel NyaGondwe Banda, *Women of Bible and Culture: Baptist Convention Women in Southern Malawi*, Zomba: Kachere, 2005, p. 114.

Mama Fanny NyaChirwa explained, to the surprise of some members at Munkhokwe, the meaning of the five buttons found on the blouses of their uniform. She said the top button stands for the woman's respect for marriage. The second one stands for the woman's knowledge about God. The third button stands for the woman teaching the children in the home about God, whereas the fourth button stands for dedication to the things of God. And lastly the fifth button stands for the woman's responsibility to welcome visitors in her home.[82]

Past Influential Women in African Last Church of God (Nkhatabay)

Many women had dedicated themselves to the work and growth of the church in the past. However, four women (Azikonda Manda, Donifasi NyaSaka, Nkhulambwi Longwe and Mrs Buleya) are still very much alive in the minds of many members who knew them. They have left their foot prints in people's hearts.

Mama Azikonda NyaManda (Mrs Chilibwanji)

NyaManda was a Tonga from Munkhokwe in Nkhatabay and she was married to Rev Chilibwanji who was a Tumbuka. She was one of the people who made it possible for the African Last Church of God to start at Munkhokwe in Nkhatabay. At first, she and her husband were living at Mlowe (Sanga), where the husband was Pastor of the church. They later moved from Mlowe to Munkhokwe (NyaManda's village) and her husband Rev Chilibwanji decided to start the church at Munkhokwe and she supported him. She encouraged other people in the village to join the church. The church was started in 1969. She also assisted much after the church was split into Reformed Last Church of God and the African Last Church of God (Last White). She did a lot of evangelization, mainly door to door, encouraging members not to move out of the church and also

---

[82] Int. Mrs Fanny Chirwa, Chairperson *Amayi Achikondi*, Munkhokwe, 25.10.2010.

encouraging those that had joined the Reformed Last Church to return. In that way, the church at Munkhokwe was greatly strengthened.[83]

Mama Donifasi NyaSaka

Donifasi NyaSaka too comes from Munkhokwe village. She did a lot for young people in the church, encouraging them and counselling them on Christian living. Like *Mama* Azikonda, NyaSaka urged others to come and join the church. She assisted many who were in need by giving them flour, fetching firewood and where necessary even drawing water for them. Through her works of charity many, it is said, joined the Last Church. She is still alive only that now she is very old.[84]

Mrs Nkhulambwi Longwe

She was one of the wives of Bishop White Longwe. She was from Watayachanga village (Nkhatabay). She is remembered for her gift of teaching. She used to teach women who were given leadership positions in the *Amayi Achikondi*. She taught them on how best to perform their jobs. She passed on.[85]

Mrs Buleya

Mrs Buleya was from Chalaundi (Nkhatabay) and was the first Chairperson of *Amayi Achikondi* at district level in Nkhatabay. She was talented in singing, so she would compose songs and sing in the church. She used to lead the singing of songs in the church. Usually it is men that lead the singing in the church, but because she was talented she was given that role. Apart from that she also used to teach others how to sing. Mrs Buleya died in 2009.[86]

---

[83] Int. Mrs Fanny Chirwa, Chairperson *Amayi Achikondi*, Munkhokwe, 25.10.2010.
[84] Int. Rev Kaundama, Kamsita, 10.10.2010.
[85] Int. Rev Kaundama, Kamsita, 10.10.2010.
[86] Ibid. 10.10.2010.

Women in the Church at Chitipa

There are also some women in Chitipa who fought against the return of polygamy and beer drinking in the church. This was especially during the time when some group, which is against the revised constitution, started causing trouble in Chitipa in 2009. These women stood their ground even when they were accused of destroying the church and threatened by the group in question. They argued that when polygamy and beer drinking was allowed, it was the women who suffered much in homes due to those practices and now that the church has forbidden them it is a relief to many women, so there is no going back.[87] The women were determined to maintain their stand on the issues in question. These women included; Alesi NaMkoko, Enesiya NaKalonge, Eunice NaMsongole, Ivy NaKalagho, Ellen NaKamba, Rose NaKalumbi, Sofia NaMtowe and NaKayange (Mrs Kanthonga).[88]

The Youth in the African Last Church of God

The youth play an important role in the church. Second to the women it is the youths who are in large numbers in the church. By the youth, I mean anyone between thirteen and thirty-five years. They participate in the leadership of the church, but this is only for the youth who are married. They can serve as deacons. On Sundays, they sometimes take part in preaching the word of God. Like *Amayi Achikondi* they are also given Youth Sundays in which they lead the entire service. And again, once every year, they are put on the church programme to call or host a big conference in which members from other congregations from various districts come and attend. The youth lead the service.[89]

The youth also have a choir that ministers during the Sunday service. They also take part in any work that may arise at the church such as brick

---

[87] This experience that in most cases the women suffer under polygamy is supported by the findings of Moses Mlenga, *Polygamy in Northern Malawi. A Christian Reassessment,* Mzuzu: Mzuni Press, 2016, esp., pp. 121-142.

[88] Int. Bishop Sibale, Chitipa Boma, 6.4.2013.

[89] Int. Rev Kaundama, Kamsita, 10.10.2010.

moulding and fundraising activities. The youth usually meet on Friday afternoons for choir practice.

Sunday School

It is a necessity for any group to develop a process of training and educating new members.[90] Every group is faced with the challenge to continually teach the norms, beliefs and practices of the group to new members and children. This is important if the group is to preserve the group's beliefs and practices and to hand them down to succeeding generations of followers.[91] This is also true for religious organizations. Various churches organize children in various classes where they are taught the beliefs and doctrines of their church and the Bible. These churches may have confirmation classes, Sunday or Sabbath schools. The Last Church is no exception. However, there are some congregations which do not have Sunday school like Katoto Church (Chintheche). Rev Matola confessed that since the starting of the church in 2008 they have never had Sunday school. However, he said that there are plans to introduce it.[92]

In some congregations, they do have Sunday school but it is not strong in the sense that it depends on whether somebody has volunteered to teach the children or not. If such a person moves away or is occupied, even the Sunday school goes on holiday. This is what happened at Munkhokwe. At the time, I visited the church the Sunday school had been temporarily closed for two months because the one who had volunteered to teach the children was sick.[93] No one had volunteered to take his place and the pastor had not yet found a replacement. Children therefore just come to the main service with their parents. This is, however, to the disadvantage of children as usually preachers target only the grownups in their messages.

---

[90] Ronald L. Johnstone, *Religion in Society: A Sociology of Religion*, Upper Saddle River, New Jersey: Roberts, 2004, p. 41.
[91] Ibid.
[92] Int. Rev Matola, Pastor, Katoto Last Church, Chintheche, 27.10.2010.
[93] Int. Rev Kaundama, Kamsita, 10.10.2010.

In some congregations, however, they have a vibrant Sunday school. For instance, Bishop Sibale states that in Chitipa they do have an active Sunday school and among other things the children memorize verses and are taught Bible stories. In 2012, the Bible Society of Malawi conducted a competition for children to memorize 200 verses from the Bible. Out of the six winners of the competition in Chitipa, three were from the Last Church of God at Chitipa *boma*.[94]

It is clear that the presence of the Sunday school in the Last Church of God depends on the pastor of the church. If the pastor is committed to train the children he takes Sunday school seriously and the opposite is equally true. It does not seem to be a concern for many parents as well as the leadership of the church at the national level, whether congregations have Sunday school or not. But one wonders if the children are not properly trained, what kind of a church would be there tomorrow? For the Bible commands parents to train a child in the way he/she should go so that even when he/she is old will not depart from it (Prov 22:6). This is, however, a bit different from the practice of other "African Instituted Churches" like the African Abraham Church, where it is a must for children to go to Sunday school for a period of six months and the youth undergo a Bible Study of another period of six months and thereafter they are baptized.[95]

Membership in the Church

The African Last Church of God recognizes two kinds of "members" associated with the church. There are those who attend services, sing in a choir, send their children to Sunday school and financially give to the church.[96] But, though interested, they have not yet come to a personal faith in Christ. The other kind of membership is a "full" or "communicant

---

[94] Int. Bishop Sibale, Chitipa Bishop, Chitipa Boma, 6.10.2013.

[95] Jemiter Mwale, "The Establishment and Development of African Abraham Church in Malawi (1929-2000): A Case Study on the Major Changes in Doctrines and their Impact," BA, University of Malawi, p. 3.

[96] R.E.H. Uprichard, *What Presbyterians Believe*, Ahoghill: The Oaks, 2011, p. 103.

member."[97] They have come to faith in Christ. In the commonly used language today, they have become born-again. Anyone is welcome to join the church, whether born-again or not.

Ten of the congregations I visited in Nkhatabay have between 200 and 300 registered members. However, the members that were active were between sixty and eighty. And the majority were women; for instance, at Munkhokwe church there were 230 registered members of which about sixty were active members (thirty-five women, fifteen men, and the remaining are children).[98]

From the interviews, I had with fifteen members (ten women and five men) at Munkhokwe church it was clear that there were two groups of members found in the church. Those who were born in the church and those that joined later from other churches for various reasons. Four out of the five men (Mr Msadala, Mr Mgombola, Mr Ngwira and Mr Mazawamba) were born in the church. However, Rev Kaundama was at first a member of the Assemblies of God and later of CCAP, before he joined the Last Church of God.

On the other hand, only two out of the ten women were born in the church and these are Mama NyaChirwa and *Mama* NyaChirwa. The rest came from other churches. Mrs Mahemani was from CAP (Church of Africa Presbyterian);[99] Mrs Mabungo from CCAP; Mrs Mskalu Longwe from Anglican; Mrs Mazawamba from Anglican; Mrs Msadala from Last Reformed; Mrs Sala Kamanga from Last Reformed; and Mrs Mahemani from African International Church. All these women followed their husbands into the Last Church of God.

It is clear that some people join this church because they are following their husbands or, in some cases, their wives. Rev Kaundama also stated

---

[97] R.E.H. Uprichard, *What Presbyterians Believe*, Ahoghill: The Oaks, 2011, p. 103.
[98] Int. Rev Kaundama, Kamsita, 10.10.2010.
[99] Formerly known as Blackman's Church.

that some people are drawn to the church because of the assistance the church renders to them during difficult times like funerals or sickness.[100]

Bishop Chimuliu agreed with Rev Kaundama, although he added other reasons. He stated that some members claim that their previous churches demanded too much money from their members through activities like paper Sundays. So, to run away from this "burden" they leave their church and join the Last Church of God, where there are no such demands. Mr Chimuliu also stated that their youth sing very well in the church so that girls from other churches admire them and would like to get married to them, so they join the church. And thirdly some join the church just because they like the preaching and the message offered in the church.[101]

Like the other churches, the Last Church of God congregations also lose members due to death or by choice of an individual. For instance, Rev Kaundama said that in 2010 in his congregation at Munkhokwe one lady got married outside the church, she did not want to be disciplined, so she joined a Pentecostal Church. Six youths also left for a Pentecostal church because they heard that white people in that church were distributing bicycles to its members. However, five returned when they realized that there were no such donations.[102] However, the Pastors I interviewed were quick to point out that the number of members they lose in a year is less compared to the number of new members whom they receive.

Upon joining the church members are expected among other things to give offerings during the church service (Exodus 28:1). They are also expected to give *vuna* (harvest offering) according to Deuteronomy 14:22. Apart from that, they are supposed to give *mapangano* (pledges, K100 per year). A member is supposed to be baptized and partake in Holy Communion. If members have children, they are supposed to bring them for the Reverend to bless them.[103]

---

[100] Int. Rev Kaundama, Kamsita, 10.10.2010.
[101] Int. Rev Chimuliu, Area Bishop, Msondozi, 20.10.2010.
[102] Int. Rev Kaundama, Kamsita, 10.10.2010.
[103] Int. Rev Matola, Pastor, Katoto Last Church, Chintheche, 27.10.2010.

Members are advised to cooperate with the government of the day in terms of development activities. For example, during the one-party rule members were told to buy MCP cards and were also encouraged to participate in self-help projects authorized by the party and the government.[104] Likewise today, if there are community projects taking place in the community, members are supposed to take part.

A member can be disciplined by the church upon breaking the rules of the church. For instance, if a member is found drunk or committing adultery; marrying outside the church; or is confirmed by the traditional doctor to be a witch; he or she is disciplined. Ordinary members are removed from the church for six months after which they are advised and re-incorporated fully into the church. Those in leadership are removed for a period of one year and six months and they automatically lose their leadership positions.[105]

Generally, most members in the African Last Church like those in the Reformed Last Church have little or no education. Very few have gone beyond secondary school level. The church is found mainly in rural areas. But things are now changing as people recognize the importance of education. The problem is, however, that when some youths in the church get educated, they tend to leave the church for other churches. They look at the church as the "last" of the churches.[106]

The African Last Church of God and Culture

Different churches respond differently to various aspects of culture. Some churches allow their members to participate in certain aspects of their culture while others do not. We have already seen that polygamy in this church was in the beginning allowed just like beer drinking was, but both are now forbidden in the church. Anyone found engaging in any of them is temporarily removed from the church for a period of six months

---

[104] Int. Rev Matola, Pastor, Katoto Last Church, Chintheche, 27.10.2010.
[105] Ibid. 27.10.2010.
[106] Int. Rev Kaundama, Kamsita, 10.10.2010.

(for discipline) if they are just members and a period of one year and six months for leaders.[107]

On the other hand, members are allowed to seek help from traditional healers if they are sick, because, according to Rev Kaundama, the traditional doctor's knowledge of medicine comes from God. But members are not allowed to go for divination or *maula* (to find out who caused the suffering or had bewitched somebody). However, there is an exception to this when a member is being accused in the family or village of being a witch. In this case, he/she has to get permission from the church first before visiting a diviner. It is a must for church leaders to get permission from the church before going to the traditional doctor.[108]

Once a member has been confirmed by the traditional doctor as being a witch, he or she is excommunicated from the church. But the problem with this is: on what basis does the church prove that indeed the accused is a witch? By intervening in this way, is the church not also responsible for bitter relationships between the accuser and the accused? By excommunicating the person, the church agrees that indeed the person is a witch. The church, however, is supposed to be the salt, mending bad relationships and not widening them.

Headquarters' Visitation

How often do the leaders from the headquarters visit congregations at the grass root level and what is the relationship between the headquarters and the congregations? The national executive leadership is made up of forty members. These include the Archbishop, Senior Bishops, Area Bishops and other pastors and church leaders. The executive meets whenever there is need, for instance, if there is a big conflict in a certain congregation.[109]

It is at such executive or Synod meetings that members draw up the programme for big conferences. The Archbishop has to plan for at least three conferences, which are usually referred to as the Archbishop's

---

[107] Int. Rev Kaundama, Kamsita, 10.10.2010.
[108] Ibid. 10.10.2010.
[109] Ibid. 10.10.2010.

conferences (*ungano wa* Bishop) indicating time, venue and dates of the conferences. Likewise, the Senior Bishops and Area Bishops do the same. At the congregation level, the Pastors are also expected to come up with their own conferences. Usually all these conferences end in November, that is, at the end of the dry season.[110] With such schedules the pastors do not often worship in their own congregations as they have to attend these meetings in different congregations.

In a year, the Archbishop may visit a lucky congregation once, especially when the congregation is hosting a big conference. However, the congregations are often visited by Area Bishops and Missionaries. Usually these too may visit a particular congregation once or twice a year if the congregations are close to the home of the Area Bishop or Missionary. In short, the interaction between the headquarters and congregations at grass root level is limited.

Dedication of a New Church Building (*Koura Tchalitchi*)

It is common practice in many churches to dedicate a new church building to God before the members can start using it. Even King Solomon in the Old Testament dedicated the temple to God after its completion amidst sacrifices and a great ceremony (1 Kings 8). The difference lies in the way the dedication is done. Whereas some churches would have a "simple" ceremony, others would have a much more complicated ceremony like that of the Last Church.

When members have completed the building of a church, it may take some time before it is dedicated, sometimes even one year or more (while using the building). This is because members have to find enough money first for the dedication ceremony. They invite a lot of people, including members from other areas, traditional chiefs surrounding the church and even some members from other churches. The money is used to buy cattle and other food stuffs to be used during this time. Some of the meat is given to the chiefs around the church to share in their celebration. When they get the required amount of money the members

---

[110] Int. Rev Kaundama, Kamsita, 10.10.2010.

notify the Headquarters that they are now ready and the day for this occasion is fixed.[111]

What happens at the church during the dedication is interesting. On the day of dedication, the new church is closed with traditional mats (*mphasa*), especially the windows and the doors. Behind the mats stand some people who are well concealed, so that they cannot be seen by anyone entering the church. In the front of the church are three women who are also well concealed with mats and the one in the middle (who stands at the pulpit) is *Mayi Maria.* They stand so still that one cannot know that they are actually people standing there. It is said that in the past they used to have "Joseph" also but with time they decided to let only the *Mayi Mariya* remain.[112]

In the meantime, all the people are gathered at a chosen place close by and when everything at the church is ready, they all start out towards the new church. Members are let in through one door while Pastors and leaders stay outside. When members have finished entering the church this door too is closed with a mat (at this time there is darkness in the church). As the leaders approach the church, at every five steps of the way, they stop while a verse is read and they sing until they reach the door of the church. They have to ask for permission to enter the church in a dramatic way. Inside and behind the closed door stands a person who is already knows what he is going to answer the people outside. The one leading the people outside starts reading the chosen verses and the one inside responds until he opens the door by removing the mat.[113]

After opening the door, he loudly beats on the mat and the people who were standing behind the mats on windows and on the other doors, including those in front remove the mats, roll them and together they throw them down causing a big noise. This is the time that members see that there were actually people inside. The three women in front continue to stand until the leaders enter the church and take their position. The entering of these leaders in the church signifies that now

---

[111] Int. Rev Chimuliu, Area Bishop, Msondozi, 20.10.2010.
[112] Ibid. 20.10.2010.
[113] Int. Rev Chimuliu, Area Bishop, Msondozi, 20.10.2010

the church is officially opened. The service begins with a prayer and songs are sung and choirs perform. These are followed by preaching from three Pastors, usually from the headquarters. A dedication prayer is offered before the closing hymn and prayer.

When I asked about the significance of the three women in front Rev Kaundama said that it was just a tradition, adding colour to the whole function. Probably that is why "Joseph" was later omitted.

African Last Church of God and Reformed Last Church of God compared

When one looks at these two churches one notices that they are different mainly in their names. They share a lot of similarities and there are few differences. For instance, the office of leadership at the congregation level is the same, including the women office of *Alalakazi*. In addition, they share a common way of electing leaders into various church offices. And again, the pastors in both churches are not paid a salary as they believe that God is the one who will reward their work in heaven.

The Sunday service is likewise similar with both churches demanding three preachers, and three Bible readings from each preacher. The two churches also use the same hymns and do not demand offerings from their members.

There are, however, some minor differences between the two churches. For instance, whereas women in some congregations of the African Last Church of God (Msondozi) are free to sit together with church elders in front and preach from the pulpit, in the Reformed Last Church of God women are not allowed to preach from the pulpit but they have to stand just in front of the congregation. Rev Banda explained that this is so because Paul said that women should not stand before men.[114] However, one questions whether the "standing before men" is only applicable with regard to the woman preaching from the pulpit.

---

[114] Int. Rev Mboya Banda, Last Church Kazando, Munkhokwe, 12.7.2010.

Another difference is the concept of *Amayi Maria* and *Alalakazi*. In the African Last Church of God these two terms are used interchangeably, and there seems to be no difference between the two. In the Reformed Last Church of God, one moves from *Alalakazi* to *Amayi Mariya*. *Alalakazi* are those women who have reached menopause and the *Amayi Mariya* are more elderly than the *Alalakazi*.

Also in the Reformed Last Church of God alcohol is still not forbidden, though drunkenness is, while in the African Last Church members are now forbidden to take beer. Again, in the Reformed Last Church of God infant baptism is practiced in certain congregations like Munkhokwe, while this is not the case in the African Last Church of God. From these observations, it is clear that these two churches are different mainly in the name and one would say that even the names of these two churches today are not that different. When I asked the two sides whether there was any hope of them becoming one again they stated that, if the other group would be willing to be under their headquarters, then there is no problem. From this it is clear that no group would want to be subject to the other. But members are free to worship in any of these two.

However, the recent years have seen Pentecostal and Charismatic tendencies reaching some congregations within the African Last Church of God, thereby changing the nature of worship in those congregations. This does not seem to be the case with the Reformed Last Church. Probably this will be a major point of departure between these two denominations if the Reformed Last Church does not move in the same direction.

Chapter 6: Marriage and Polygamy in the Last Church of God and His Christ

Marriage is one of the "sacraments" in the Last Church of God. For a long time, the church had been recognizing monogamous as well as polygamous marriages. In fact, the church was based on polygamy. But with time this very basis of the church has been removed. However, even though polygamy was officially prohibited in 2008, the forbidding was a slow process, brewing itself up over the years. Also, its prohibition was not necessarily due to biblical interpretation but rather due to the interplay between the ever-changing nature of culture that has been fueled by socio-economic factors. This, however, does not mean that the prohibition of polygamy has gone smoothly without challenges. Two case studies will highlight some of the challenges within polygamy in the church after its prohibition.

Marriage and Weddings in the Last Church of God and His Christ International

The church recognizes blessed marriages only. This means marriages that are blessed at the church (church weddings) and marriages which the pastor or church leader prays for at home after all the traditional obligations have been fulfilled. Those who marry outside the church (through elopement) are temporarily removed from the church and put on discipline for six months before they can fully re-join the church. When a couple wants to have, their marriage blessed, the man should first fulfill his traditional obligations to the woman's side such as payment of *lobola*.[115] Once that is settled he and the girl with witnesses from both sides, are allowed to register the wedding at the church. When the date for the wedding is set, the church announces the wedding for at least three consecutive weeks. This gives room for those with valid objections to the marriage to come forward, before the pastor blesses the two.[116]

---

[115] Int. Fanny Chirwa, Chairperson, *Amayi Achikondi*, Munkhokwe, 16.9.2010.
[116] Ibid. 16.9.2010.

On the day of officiation, the couple, accompanied by relatives from both sides and friends, comes to the church. The ceremony starts with a prayer followed by a song and a Bible reading. The pastor gives advice to the couple based on the scripture that was read. The couple then repeats after the pastor as they make vows of commitment to each other. This is followed by putting the rings on each other's finger, after which the couple and the witnesses sign the marriage certificate.

After the officiating ceremony at the church some few deacons, both men and women, accompany the couple to their home to give them more biblical advice concerning marriage. The common passage that is used at such a time is Ephesians 5:22-33 where husbands are commanded to love their wives as Christ loves the church and wives are to submit to their husbands in the family.

Mama NyaChirwa, who is also a member of *Amayi Achikondi,* said that the difference between the advice given by the church leaders and that given by aunties is that the aunties' interest is to check if the man is fertile and that the girl is a virgin.[117] The aunties carry many things that are used in the bedroom such as a white cloth etc, but the church advisors do not.[118] In the traditional set up the bedroom instructions are referred to as *zakumphasa* and are regarded as pillars of marriage. If not carefully adhered to by the couple they may result in problems in marriage and even in the end of it.[119] The bedroom instructions are usually carried out at night by the groom's and bride's aunties.[120]

In Chitipa for quite a long time, from the 1930s to 2003, the common practice of marriage was *winga*. *Winga* was a practice where, after the man had fulfilled all the required traditional requirements to the family of the girl he intended to marry, he would inform the pastor. A day would then be arranged when the girl's side would escort the girl to the man's side amidst singing. Upon arrival, the pastor would read the

---

[117] Int. Fanny Chirwa, Chairperson *Amayi Achikondi*, Munkhokwe, 16.9.2010.

[118] Ibid. 16.9.2010.

[119] Towera Mwase, "The Marriage Instructions for Girls and Women in Mzuzu Churches," MA, Mzuzu University, 2012, p. 100.

[120] Ibid.

relevant scripture passages to them and pray for the couple and then leave the two families to continue with their ceremony.[121] Such a blessing of marriage is similar to the "marriage prayer" practiced in some other churches.[122] In theological terms such a wedding contains everything required and the cost factor is small. But the fact that this "marriage prayer" takes place in a home, not in the church, mates it seems as second class.[123]

From 2003, the practice of *winga* has been discouraged among church members; instead couples are urged to have their marriage blessed at the church. Bishop Alex Sibale said that a good number of members now officiate their marriages at the church. On average, Sibale said, he blesses at least one marriage in a month in his congregation. Of course, sometimes a month passes without officiating any marriage.[124]

It should be mentioned that the issue of having marriages blessed at the church is not very common in many Last Church congregations. Many couples prefer to just have their marriages blessed at home because it is not expensive as compared to those who have their marriage blessed at the church and then a wedding celebration afterwards.[125] This practice of blessing the marriage at the couple's home is not done by mainline churches. However, in my opinion it is a good and convenient practice for many couples considering the fact that church weddings are not common even in mainline churches. Instead of this practice being discouraged (like in Chitipa), it should be encouraged. Apart from offering prayer

---

[121] Int. Bishop Alex Sibale, Chitipa Boma, 6.4.2013.

[122] Klaus Fiedler, *Conflicted Power in Malawian Christianity: Essays Missionary and Evangelical from Malawi*, Mzuzu: Mzuni Press, 2015.

[123] This is why Klaus Fiedler advocates the abolition of church weddings. Klaus Fiedler, "For the Sake of Christian Marriage, Abolish Church Weddings" in: James L. Cox (ed), *Rites of Passage in Contemporary Africa. Interaction between Christian and African Traditional Religions*, Cardiff: Cardiff University Press, 1998, pp. 46-60 and also: Klaus Fiedler, "For the Sake of Christian Marriage, Abolish Church Weddings," in: *Religion in Malawi*, 1995, pp. 22-27.

[124] Ibid. 6.4.2013.

[125] Int. Fanny Chirwa, Chairperson *Amayi Achikondi*, Munkhokwe, 16.9.2010

alone the making of required vows and promises between the couple should also be part and parcel of the ceremony.[126]

Polygamy in the Last Church of God and His Christ International

The Beginning of Polygamy in the Last Church

Msumba made it clear from the beginning that the church was aimed at accepting those that were being rejected by other churches because of polygamy. During that time polygamy as a cultural practice appealed to many people. In fact, one would not be wrong to say that it was "fashionable" at least in those communities where it was practiced. Msumba is quoted to have said that:

> The desire of the establishment of this church is, she is pity for the people of Africa. Many brethren from Europe and America came here to help us believe God and to be a husband of one woman. We believed but many of us failed. It is not our law. It is not God's law. Therefore, this church is coming out from every sect which rejects to Worship God with one husband and many wives; she believes and co-operates with the faith of Abraham, the father of us all.[127]

Thus, many of the first members in the church were polygamous. In fact, the outsiders saw the Last Church of God as a church for polygamous people (*tchalitchi la mitala*). The argument was simple, God did not forbid polygamy and men in the Bible which were mightily used by God were polygamous. When the church began, it may have appealed to many mainly as a social rather than a spiritual issue. The earliest members in the church had one thing in common, rejection by other churches. Deprived of "religious" status in mission churches on polygamous grounds they found comfort and oneness in the Last Church. Celebrating their newly found "social" status in the church became

---

[126] Klaus Fiedler, "For the Sake of Christian Marriage, Abolish Church Weddings," in: *Religion in Malawi*, 1995, pp. 22-27; revised as: Fiedler, Klaus, *Conflicted Power in Malawian Christianity: Essays Missionary and Evangelical from Malawi*, Mzuni Press, 2015.

[127] Terence O. Ranger, *The African Churches of Tanzania*, Historical Association of Tanzania Paper No. 5, Nairobi: East Africa Publishing House, 1972, p. 21.

almost a custom for members to bring beer to the church and drink together during church services.[128] In this case membership in the church provided the members more with equality and status as compared to spiritual fulfillment.

However, it did not mean that men were allowed to marry anyhow. They had to follow the necessary traditional obligations and then the pastor would pray for the couple to start their married life. Those that just married through elopement were disciplined by the church.[129] With this kind of arrangement usually the husband and the second or other wives would become members in the Last Church, while the first wife remained in her church (mostly because the first wife did not see the need to get out of the church where she was a member, since in mainline churches the first wife is not excommunicated). And again, because she would not be happy to worship with the other wives who had robbed her of her husband.[130]

Causes of Polygamy

There are many causes of polygamy such as bareness on the part of the wife, or the desire to have many children, especially in cultures where they value children very much. Some men marry to have *nsima yinandi* "to eat more nsima."[131] From Msumba's statement members were involved in polygamy because of culture. Polygamy was one of the prevailing cultural practices at that time. So, of the many reasons that are given why men marry more wives the main reasons were men's desire to have sex with different wives, and that to have many children meant more wealth according to the cultural understanding at least of that time.[132]

---

[128] Int. Rev Kaundama, Kamsita, 10.10.2012.

[129] Int. Rev Chiuli Manda, retired Area Bishop, Munkhokwe, 10.10.2012.

[130] Moses Mlenga, *Polygamy in Northern Malawi. A Christian Reassessment*, Mzuzu: Mzuni Press, 2016, p. 73ff.

[131] Ibid. 2013, p. 78.

[132] Ibid. p. 82.

Polygamy in the Last Church of God after Msumba's Death

With time, the generation that had joined the church mainly on polygamy grounds started phasing out. The church started being filled with new members that were either born in the church or those that continued to join the church. As the church was growing it meant increased membership, and is it not often true that "new members will not share precisely the same experiences of the original core group, and some will have significantly different personal objectives that they expect the group to achieve?"[133] It was now up to the members that had been born in the church to marry more than one wife just because the church allowed it or to choose to live differently from their parents before them. Faced with this challenge the foundation was unconsciously laid early in the life of the church for a modification of the acceptance of polygamy in the church in the future.

The seed for future change on polygamy had been sown but it was far from being noticed. Many of the members that were born in the church continued to be polygamous although there were some who chose not to be polygamous.[134] This, however, varied from place to place depending also on the prevailing culture of the area as far as polygamy was concerned. For instance, many members in Karonga and Mzimba districts continued with polygamy mainly because polygamy was a common cultural practice in these districts. This was unlike the case in Nkhatabay where the common kind of polygamy is *mbulu, a* version of polygamy where a married person continues to have sexual relations with a girl or boy friend of their childhood.[135] Therefore, members that were born in the church in areas like Nkhatabay started being interested in the church not because of its acceptance of polygamy but for worship.

---

[133] Ronald L. Johnstone, *Religion in Society: A Sociology of Religion*, Upper Saddle River, New Jersey: Roberts, 2004, p. 93.

[134] Int. Rev Kaundama, Kamsita, 10.10.2012.

[135] Int. Rev Chiuli Manda, retired Area Bishop, Munkhokwe, 10.10.2012. For *mubulu* among the Tonga see Moses Mlenga, *Polygamy in Northern Malawi. A Christian Reassessment*, Mzuzu: Mzuni Press, 2016, p. 116-118.

One may therefore conclude that it was mainly the youthful members that, from the early times, tried to behave differently from the established customs. This had to do with the general trend that in most cases it is the youth that easily embrace change as they do not have anything to lose from the past.[136] However, with time some adults started to join this youthful group. Whereas in the past polygamy offered social status to those involved, this seemed to change with time since these days having more than one wife may be quite expensive.

The trend continued through the years with members looking at the church as a place where everyone was free to worship. On the other hand, outsiders were looking at it as a church for polygamous people. Those that were removed from other churches on polygamy grounds continued to join the church. But slowly and unconsciously change had begun to take place. The Last Church was no longer there to mainly welcome polygamous people but started to be a house of prayer in its own right.

It has been observed that generally due to religious and socio-economic factors polygamous families in all five districts in the northern region have greatly reduced in number.[137] Some people have further argued that contemporary men are not ready for polygamous marriages due to socio-economic factors. This also became true for the Last Church of God. By the early 1990s the number of polygamous members had eventually declined even without any intervention from the church. Thus, in the 1990s one would not find more than five polygamous families in a congregation.[138] During this time there were some pastors who took an individual stand against polygamy. For instance, Rev Kaundama would not bless a polygamous marriage in his church, instead

---

[136] Rhodian Munyenyembe, *Christianity and Socio-Cultural Issues: The Charismatic Movement and Contextualization in Malawi*, Zomba: Kachere; Mzuzu: Mzuni Press, 2011, p. 29.

[137] Moses Mlenga, *Polygamy in Northern Malawi. A Christian Reassessment*, Mzuzu: Mzuni Press, 2016, p. 101.

[138] Int. Rev Chiuli Manda, retired Area Bishop, Munkhokwe, 10.10.2012.

he would ask a preacher or a church elder to do so. He argued that the Bible forbade polygamy, so why should he bless such a marriage? [139]

With many monogamous members taking up leading positions it was inevitable that sooner or later the issue of whether polygamy should be allowed to continue or not would arise. This happened in 2008 when the church underwent a constitutional review and polygamy was finally forbidden.[140] It was agreed that those who were already in polygamous marriages should keep their wives and if they had positions in the church they should continue serving in those positions. However, anyone who was going to marry several wives after this law was passed should be disciplined and should never be given any position in the church. It should be mentioned here that there seems to be a gap between the headquarters or top leadership of the church and the grass root congregations.

Thus, sometimes some decisions made at the Synod level do not seem to reach the congregations or if they do reach them, those congregations are not willing to accept them. One example is this forbidding of polygamy. Some members, when asked about it, were not sure whether it is forbidden or not, and others still say that polygamy is allowed. While it is the case that polygamy is officially forbidden, it is also true that there are some members who are still for it. There are challenges with regard to the church's current stand on polygamy as the two case studies below reveal.

Interpretations of the Decline and Prohibition of Polygamy

Various reasons have been suggested as to the causes of the decline of polygamy in general. The reasons range from religious and sociological to economical causes. Is it possible to deduce a single cause for the decline of polygamy in the Last Church? Polygamy in the Last Church was prohibited while its practice had already significantly declined in the church.

---

[139] Int. Rev Kaundama, Kamsita, 24.9.2012.
[140] Int. Bishop Alex Sibale, Chitipa, 5.4.2013.

Would the decline and later prohibition of polygamy in the church be explained by religious factors? Of course, some pastors like Mr Kaundama and Mr Sibale mentioned that the Bible forbids polygamy and that is why they personally do not support it.[141] While it is true that some members were not involved in polygamy because they understood that the Bible forbade it, this does not seem to have been the main reason why many started shunning polygamy. Even when interviewing the Archbishop on the issue, the reasons that he gave had mainly to do with the HIV/AIDS pandemic and economic challenges and not with the members' understanding of the Bible on the issue.[142] Besides that, the grass roots' understanding of marriage in the Bible seems mainly to be based on their interpretation of stories found in the Bible, especially stories of persons such as Abraham, Jacob, and others. Therefore, I think religious factors would not best explain the decline and prohibition of polygamy in the Last Church.

Those who observe that economic factors have contributed to the decline of polygamous marriages are right. For time has shown a continued rise in prices of basic necessities, making it a challenge to support big families.[143] The rising cost of living alludes to the fact that traditionally in the past it was the responsibility of the wives to produce food and care for their children, the husband and themselves. In this way, the husband did not feel the "burden" of looking after a big family; in fact, an additional wife was an asset. But today wives and children are looking up to the husband for their upkeep, and any additional wife is a liability. This factor is true, but taken alone, it is inadequate as an explanation for the decline of polygamy, for it suggests that given all the resources needed monogamous people would actually marry more than one wife, which I think is not true.

Sometimes sociological explanations have also been given by some of the members in trying to account for the decline. The emphasis here has

---

[141] Polygamy in the Bible is not directly forbidden. Its prohibition is deduced indirectly.
[142] Int. Rev Chikosera Phiri, Archbishop, Mzuzu, 12.10.2012.
[143] Moses Mlenga, *Polygamy in Northern Malawi. A Christian Reassessment*, Mzuzu: Mzuni Press, 2016, p. 82, 96.

been on the challenges that have hit the society, especially HIV and AIDS. But this does not explain the preference of people when it comes to substitutes of "traditional" polygamy like having other sexual partners outside marriage.[144] While polygamy has declined, people (some even in the church) are opting for its substitutes like being legally married to one wife but at the same time having secret partners. One should also bear in mind that HIV and AIDS became a serious threat in the 1990s in Malawi and by then polygamy had already started to decline in the Last Church.

In my opinion, the decline in polygamy in the Last Church can best be explained by its cultural implication, which has been fuelled by the other factors mentioned above. By this I take it that the changes taking place in the Last Church are a reflection of what has been or is going on in the wider society as far as polygamy as a cultural practice is concerned. We all know that culture is dynamic. As time changes so do the people's choices and tastes.[145] The relevance that polygamy had during the time of the establishment of the church has with time been reduced if not largely washed away. What seemed to have been the people's taste in 1925 has proved to be changing with the generations down the line. This I think explains why polygamy has been declining slowly over the years. Not only in the Last Church but also in some African Independent Churches where polygamy has also been prohibited.[146] When I asked some men in the church whether they would marry more than one wife, their answer was "no". To my surprise the first reason given for their decision had nothing to do with economic or HIV/AIDS factors but rather that polygamy is outdated. For many polygamy is now "old fashioned." However, I am aware that polygamy continues to be practiced by some in various areas, but this is to be expected in any cultural change.

---

[144] Moses Mlenga, *Polygamy in Northern Malawi. A Christian Reassessment*, Mzuzu: Mzuni Press, 2016, p. 140.

[145] Rhodian Munyenyembe, *Christianity and Socio-Cultural Issues: The Charismatic Movement and Contextualization in Malawi*, Zomba: Kachere; Mzuzu: Mzuni Press, 2011, p. 29.

[146] Jemiter Mwale, "The Establishment and Development of African Abraham Church in Malawi (1929-2000): A Case Study on the Major Changes in Doctrines and their Impact (Chamchere Mission Station)," BA, University of Malawi, 2000, p. 8.

It should be mentioned that polygamy is now also prohibited in the Reformed Last Church of God and in other churches which had embraced the practice for a long time like the African Abraham Church. I believe that the prohibition even in these churches has to do with the fact that culture is changing all the time and so are the people's tastes.

The prohibition of polygamy in 2008 by the church was actually just a confirmation of what the members themselves had chosen and was not an imposition by their leaders. Why should the members continue to stick to something that does not seem to be relevant to them anymore? The challenges that have accompanied the prohibition of polygamy in the church are to be expected, for what change does not meet any resistance?

Chibavi Last Church of God and His Christ International

Chibavi congregation is within Mzuzu city and was started in 1992. At first the members used to pray at Masasa congregation, but due to long distance and because there were several of them in Chibavi, they decided to open a church there. This was facilitated by three people namely: Mr Zowani (from Nkhotakota), Mr Msiska (from Karonga) and Mr Mwambughi and their families. Mr Zowani became the first pastor of this church up to 1996, when he returned to his home in Nkhotakota. He was succeeded by Mr Msiska, who pastored the church until 2002, when he was promoted to Head Pastor for the three congregations of Masasa, Chibavi and Ekwendeni. Mr Mwambughi took over up to 2007, when he was promoted to Bishop and was succeeded by the current pastor Mr Mwakalenga.[147]

Chibavi congregation grew over the years. In 2007, there were 60 to 65 members. By now, there are 300 registered members, but only 150 are active members.[148]

---

[147] Int. Rev Mwakalenga, Chibavi, 5.11.2013.
[148] Int. Rev Mwakalenga, Chibavi, 5.11.2013.

Polygamous Members in Chibavi Last Church of God

When the church was just started, there was only one polygamous family, that of Mr Msiska. By then he had two wives. However, Mr Msiska married a third wife in 2005 and he was stripped of his position as head pastor. What happened was that his brother was involved in a family conflict with his wife, and Mr Msiska as an elder brother was called to assist in resolving the conflict. Mr Msiska, in the process of assisting his brother, ended up marrying his brother's wife. When the news reached the church, he was removed from his position as head pastor.

Msiska was removed not because he had married another wife (this was before polygamy was forbidden), but because he had married his brother's wife, which is against the Bible. Mr Msiska is back in his home village in Karonga but it is also rumoured that he has been involved in another case with women and he has been stopped as a pastor altogether.[149]

When Mr Mwakalenga became the pastor of the church in 2007 he found only two polygamous families in the church, those of Mr Msiska and Mr Kambalila. Mr Kambalila is still a member in the church but he was stripped of his position as preacher upon marrying a third wife. Mwakalenga recalls that before he became pastor there were other four polygamous members in the church apart from Mr Msiska. Unfortunately, they passed on. He further explained that when polygamy was finally forbidden by the church the town congregations were not affected much since it was already phasing out.[150]

Mchengautuwa Last Church of God and His Christ International

Mchengautuwa is a new congregation and a branch of Chibavi congregation. It was started by Mr Elias Msukwa, Mr Rombani Kaonga and Rhoda Lola in 2012. These members decided to branch out of Chibavi due to long distance. On their first day of meeting separately from

---

[149] Int. Rev Mwakalenga, Chibavi, 5.11.2013.
[150] Ibid. 5.11.2013.

Chibavi they were 24 members. Some members came from Kavilala and Sonda areas. The main leadership of the church continues to be from Chibavi but the members are allowed to choose the acting Reverend. The first acting Reverend was Mr Kaonga, but he went to South Africa, therefore he was succeeded by Mr Chibaka in April 2013. The congregation has 45 to 50 active members.[151]

Polygamous Members in Mchengautuwa Last Church of God

There has not been a polygamous case since the church was brought from Chibavi in 2012. However, there is an interesting case concerning the present Rev Chibaka. He was initially a member of Last Church in Salima, but when he came to his home village in Enukweni he joined CCAP, because there was no Last Church there. From Enukweni he came to Zolozolo and together with two others, namely Mr Nyirenda and Chibaka's brother, they started the Zoe Harvest Ministry.[152]

However, the three men soon parted ways, Nyirenda went to Blantyre and Chibaka went back to Enukweni where he joined Holy Christian Church and was ordained pastor in 2010. He came to Mzuzu again to Mchengautuwa and discovered that there was a Last Church of God congregation which he joined. In 2013, he was chosen the acting pastor for the church.[153] It is Chibaka's marriage experience that is of interest.

Chibaka's Marriage Story and His Leadership Appointment

On my first day to observe the Sunday service at Mchengautuwa Last Church a woman stood up at the end of the service and addressed the church secretary that her case was already presented to the church, so she was waiting for the leaders' action. The leaders (excluding the pastor) quickly agreed and told her that they will meet her at the end of everything that day. I didn't know that she was Mr Chibaka's wife and that at that time there were issues going on in their marriage. I later

---

[151] Int. Mr Chibaka, Acting Reverend, Mchengautuwa, 27.11.2013.

[152] The church was based on what Zacchaeus in the Bible did by giving back what he had stolen from the people.

[153] Int. Mr Chibaka, Acting Reverend, Mchengautuwa, 27.11.2013.

learnt that Mr Chibaka had officially left the woman and was planning to get back his first wife with whom he had two children.[154]

I asked the head bishop Mr Mwambughi, who is also overseeing Mchengautuwa congregation, why they had allowed Mr Chibaka to be acting pastor when the constitution now clearly forbids electing a polygamous person to any leadership position. He explained that they did not know his personal story until someone from Enukweni was surprised that the Last Church would accept a polygamous man to be Reverend. Apparently, this man knew Mr Chibaka. That was when the leaders decided to look into the matter in order to find the truth.[155] I decided to ask Mr Chibaka himself about the matter.

Mr Chibaka stated that he had a wife and two children, but he had not paid *lobola* for her. This marriage, according to him, ended, and the children went with their mother. Then he married a second wife (from Dowa), with whom he stayed eight months and he again did not fulfill his traditional marriage obligations. According to Chibaka at the time these things were happening, he had backslidden in his faith. Then he became a real born again Christian and he started feeling that he had not done right and that in fact the first wife was the real wife.[156]

One night he had a dream in which someone told him that his wife (first wife) was in prison. He went to see her. Her name was called out and she came crying while closing her eyes with her hand. She told him that in order for her to be released he had to pay MK 2,000. She went back to her cell crying. Chibaka interpreted the dream to mean that God wanted him to go and get back his first wife. He explained the dream to his new wife and told her that theirs was an adulterous relationship.[157]

He began arrangements for separation from her and he also explained his situation to the church leadership, who welcomed the idea. He further said that he called the wife's relatives and explained to them that he had been living in darkness, but now he had decided to put things

---

[154] Int. Mr Chibaka, Acting Reverend, Mchengautuwa, 27.11.2013.
[155] Int. Rev Mwambughi, Bishop, Chibavi, 15.10.2013.
[156] Int. Mr Chibaka, Acting Reverend, Mchengautuwa, 27.11.2013.
[157] Ibid. 27.11.2013.

right. They divided everything in the house including the money that was in the bank and the woman went away. Mr Chibaka then started negotiating for his first wife to come back. During my last Sunday visitation at the church Chibaka told the congregation that the wife was coming that week.[158] The church secretary asked the members to give a special offering as a welcoming gesture to the *mama busa*. It is not known yet what the decision from above will be, whether he will be allowed to continue in his position as acting pastor and later on be ordained as pastor. But Chibaka continues at the moment to preach and lead the activities of the church.

Even though Mr Chibaka insists that he was not involved in polygamy because he had ended his marriage with his first wife before marrying the second wife, his own story shows that it is not true. They had just separated. His argument that he did not pay any *lobola* hence there was no marriage is again not satisfying. How could he stay with a woman for over two years and bear two children, with the full knowledge of parents from both sides and yet claiming that he was not married? Interestingly he stated that in his dream he was instructed to go and get back his first wife, which wife was he going to get since he claims there was no marriage? The case of Mr Chibaka was one of polygamy, even if he did not want to accept it.

Polygamy, for whatever (justifiable) reasons, tends to negatively affect children and the women, especially the first wife. The attitude of women towards polygamy is generally not good.[159] For what woman can in earnest rejoice over other women sharing her husband? The story of the Banda family at Bandawe is an illustration of how polygamy works in some families in the Last Church of God.

---

[158] Int. Mr Chibaka, Acting Reverend, Mchengautuwa, 27.11.2013.

[159] Moses Mlenga, *Polygamy in Northern Malawi. A Christian Reassessment*, Mzuzu: Mzuni Press, 2016, p. 120ff (Chapter 6: "Polygamy as a Feminist Challenge.")

Mr Banda's Polygamous Family in Nkhatabay District

Mr Banda (not his real name) is a Tonga and works at a local clinic. He has three wives and eight children. His first wife (NyaChilausipa) has four children, his second wife (NyaMunyirenda) has three children and his third wife (NyaZgambo) has one child. At first Mr Banda belonged to the CCAP, but upon marrying his second and later his third wife he joined the Last Church of God. His first wife still remains in the CCAP, while the younger wives have joined the Last Church following their husband.[160]

Family Life

The first wife lives in her own house, while the younger wives share a house. The male children share a room in the extended kitchen, preferring independence, while the girls put up with their mothers in the houses. Each wife has got her own piece of land for cultivation and each one looks after the welfare of her own children. They give each other turns to prepare meals for their husband. Sometimes the children do share the meals together, for example when one wife is away. The husband prefers to sleep at the house of his first wife.[161]

The younger wives are very close to each other. They are usually found together, even when going to church, and they do many other things together. This could be due to the fact that the first wife is older and the two are young and so they have something in common. Again, it could be that as a first wife she has accepted her husband's decision but is still not comfortable with the idea of sharing a husband with others. Nevertheless, the younger wives still respect the senior wife and they do support one another. For instance, the firstborn son of the senior wife (secondary school teacher at Bandawe) had a wedding in 2012 and all the family supported him with the preparations, cooking and financial support.[162]

Also, children seem to get on well with each other. The first wife's other son has some white friends outside the country, and he pays school fees

---

[160] Int. Mama NyaChilalango, Mr Banda's first wife, Bandawe, 7.5.2012.

[161] Int. Mama NyaMulenje, Mr Banda's second wife, Bandawe, 7.5.2012.

[162] Int. Wales Banda, Mr Banda's son, Bandawe, 10.5.2012.

for his brother (second wife's son) who is at Chintheche Community Day Secondary School. When I asked this son to escort me to Kazando headquarters during my field research, he said he was busy, and instead he asked his step brother to escort me and he did. This shows that there is good relationship among the children.

Banda's Family and Church Life

I participated in the Sunday worship services at Munkhokwe for several weeks, but I did not see the husband. When I asked the younger wives about his absence they just laughed. I observed that the younger wives are very committed to the church's activities. They joined the *Amayi Achikondi* and they sing in the choir. However, the children, especially the older ones, have joined churches of their choice. The one who wedded is in the Assemblies of God, three go to CCAP. The remaining four sometimes worship at the Last Church but as they grow up they will probably make their own choices.[163]

The husband is not a committed member of the church and it seems he drinks beer a lot. Although the younger wives mentioned that they live together well they also pointed out that generally polygamous marriages are not good. Both of them knew in advance that Mr Banda was already a married man. When I asked them why then they decided to get involved in a polygamous marriage, the second wife said that apparently her first marriage had failed so she accepted Mr Banda.[164] The third wife confessed that it was a mistake which she was not supposed to make.[165] The first wife did not want to comment or say anything on the matter, which in a way showed that she was bitter about the polygamy.

Mr Banda's polygamous family seems to be a success story, but from the women's point of view it is not really a happy story, especially for the first wife. Some of their children are oftentimes involved in conflicts with others. Some of their neighbours complain about the children's bad behaviour. One time one of the boys severely beat another boy in the

---

[163] Int. Mama NyaMunyirenda, Mrs Banda, second wife, Bandawe, 7.5.2012.
[164] Ibid. 7.5.2012.
[165] Int. Mama NyaZgambo, Mrs Banda, third wife, Bandawe, 7.5.2012.

neighbourhood for no reason and the case ended at the police.[166] I actually saw the beaten boy on that day on his way to the hospital with a swollen face. It is not clear whether the children's behaviour is connected to their polygamous setting. But it may be difficult to inculcate the desired standard of discipline in a child who looks up to two or three "mothers" from different backgrounds.

The Significance of Polygamy in the Last Church

Polygamy played a great role in the church in the past. Its main significance was that many polygamous people found acceptance in the church. Besides that, the children born from these polygamous members were the ones that later became members in the church. The acceptance of polygamy in the Last Church really was in line with the fact that people are saved by grace through faith in Jesus Christ and not by works according to Ephesians 2:8 [For by grace you have been saved through faith, and that not of yourselves; it is the gift of God]. However, its later prohibition shows that it was not enough to accept polygamy just because great figures in the Bible were polygamous men. A Christian church is supposed to be identified with Jesus Christ and the cross. Where a church is identified as *tchalitchi la mitala* then probably that church is focusing on something minor.

Polygamy was at first mentioned as a major "tool" responsible for the fast growth of the church in its early years. The leaders of the church mentioned that the Last Church is not expanding much today compared to the past. What does this mean to the church? If the Last Church is to continue to expand then the church should find other "tools" of evangelization. I think this is the challenging part, to continue to expand as Last Church in a society where there is much choice of churches. As much as the prohibition of polygamy may seem a "positive action" it is also a challenge to the future of the church.

---

[166] Int. Mrs Chimaliro, mother of the beaten boy, Bandawe, 12.5.2012.

The Future of Polygamy in the African Last Church of God

Generally, there are very few members in the Last Church today who have more than one wife. For instance, in Chitipa the number of polygamous members has significantly decreased. In Ulambia at Kasama congregation there are only two members with two wives namely, Mr Msimbowe and Bishop Msongwe and at Kameme congregation there are also two members who have two wives.[167] Many congregations do not have any polygamous families. This decrease is not attributed to the fact that polygamy is now forbidden in the church, but mainly due to the fact that polygamy is generally not appealing to many young people today due to cultural change and the ever-rising cost of living.[168] Even though this is the case, we cannot expect polygamy to completely phase out all at once, especially in congregations that are in very remote areas and in those congregations which have defied the banning of polygamy openly.

Chibaka's story also shows that the issue of polygamy in the church continues and will continue to face challenges for some time even in those congregations which have accepted its ban.

It is unfortunate that I did not have the chance to hear Chibaka's wife's side of the story, how she took the husband's decision to send her away just like that. Maybe there is indeed a need to rethink polygamy not only in CCAP, but even in churches like Last Church. But it is clear that polygamy, for whatever reasons, negatively affects women and children.

Looking at polygamy in the Last Church over the years one observes that its decrease was not due to the fact that polygamy is "forbidden" in the Bible. Over the years, members' attitude toward polygamy started to change. I believe that this change is due to the fact that, like many other cultural practices, polygamy has been losing its appeal and essence to many people over the years. However, this has been aggravated by socio-economic factors such as the fact that it is now very costly to care for a large family due to the high cost of living. Thus, the forbidding of polygamy in 2008 was the result of a process that started slowly a long time ago in the church. The challenges in the church resulting from the

---

[167] Int. Bishop Alex Sibale, Chitipa Boma, 6.4.2013.
[168] Ibid. 6.4.2013.

prohibition of polygamy should not be interpreted as a reflection that the leaders imposed this on the members but rather as expected of any other change.

Having removed the basis of the church, other significant changes continue within the Last Church of God. The church is now manifesting some Charismatic and Pentecostal tendencies. How does one explain this phenomenon in the church that has for many years been known as "traditional"? In the next chapter, I will look at this topic.

Chapter 7: Charismatic and Pentecostal Tendencies

Every organization or religious institution, over time, experiences changes. And when the changes happen there are usually people who welcome it and others who resist it. The Last Church of God is no exception. From the beginning the church was more traditional in the sense that it took on board many traditional cultural aspects. And for a long time, the Last Church did not entertain Pentecostal or Charismatic tendencies within its domains. Even now some congregations reject these tendencies.

The Last Church is now caught in between members who would like to end some cultural aspects that were allowed in the past and those that want to continue with the old traditions. The first group, in the process of bringing change, is incorporating some Charismatic as well as Pentecostal tendencies. This is more than the "traditionalists" can tolerate. The question here is: what is behind this change in the Last Church?

The Pentecostal/Charismatic changes taking place in the church are the result of some members searching for a deeper spiritual fulfilment rather than just following traditions that have been passed on from one generation to the other. Such members want a church that will be more meaningful to both their physical and, more importantly, their spiritual lives. Yet those that are resisting change are mainly resisting the authority of the young leaders who are introducing the change rather than the change itself. These tensions become a threat to the unity of the church.

Pentecostalism as Understood by the Members in the Church

It is important to first explain the word Pentecostalism in line with the members' understanding of the word. To the members, the word Pentecostalism is a broad term covering many things. But at the center of this word is the born-again philosophy. Here there are three groups of members.

The majority of the members equate Pentecostalism to the born-again philosophy, which has speaking in tongues at its center. The other members (at Karonga) go beyond the first group by adding some other things to the word which are not necessarily Pentecostal in nature. Any change that this group does not want is referred to as a "Pentecostal tendency."

The third group (the ones for change) understands the born-again philosophy as spiritual rebirth. This group recognizes things like speaking in tongues as acts of the Holy Spirit. Their argument is that they do not want to be just like Pentecostals. They are following the word of God, and if the Pentecostals are also following the word of God then there are likely going to be similarities.[1]

In reality, the changes lean more to Charismatic tendencies rather than to what the members call Pentecostal tendencies. However, at present in the Last Church there seems to be no clear-cut demarcation between these two tendencies. For instance, while the group in favour of the born-again philosophy emphasizes the need for members to be filled with the Holy Spirit, they do not emphasize the baptism with the Holy Spirit. While they recognize the gift of speaking in tongues and the need to exercise spiritual gifts in the church, they do not seem to claim the ability to exercise spiritual gifts by all members of a local church.[2] On their prayer themes, while they do touch on faith healing, they do not emphasize material prosperity or employment opportunities, which are typical Charismatic themes.[3]

So, in my reference to the Pentecostal and Charismatic tendencies in the church I will mean the born-again philosophy as it is generally understood (spiritual rebirth together with speaking in tongues etc.) by the members themselves.

---

[1] Int. Bishop Alex Sibale, Bishop Chitipa, Chitipa Boma, 6.4.2013.

[2] Rhodian Munyenyembe, *Christianity and Socio-Cultural Issues: The Charismatic Movement and Contextualization in Malawi*, Zomba: Kachere; Mzuzu: Mzuni Press, 2011, p. 39.

[3] Ibid. pp. 40-41.

The Beginning of the Pentecostal /Charismatic Change in the Last Church

The Pentecostal tendencies began to infiltrate the Last Church of God gradually through individual pastors and members in various places. For instance, one time there was a Synod meeting at Chitete in Ntchisi before 2006 and there some pastors complained to the Synod that people were laughing at them in terms of their practices of worship. These pastors suggested the need to change certain things like beer drinking etc. But the issue was not taken any further. In Mzuzu there were pastors like Rev Mwakalenga and Rev Mwambughi of Chibavi Last Church who believed in the born-again philosophy and the power and role of the Holy Spirit in the Christian's life.

The Pentecostal tendencies in Chitipa started in 2005 when Bishop Sibale, who is the District Principal for Chitipa, went to Tanzania for a church conference.[4] There he saw that their colleagues were free in their worship and that they had incorporated many aspects of "Pentecostalism." When he came back he shared his experience with other members who agreed that it was a good thing, not good because it came from Tanzania, but because they saw the importance of things like emphasizing the need for members to be born again; the need for nights of prayer and praying for the sick.[5]

They therefore introduced the born-again philosophy first in the church at Chitipa *boma*. Sibale as the District Bishop had the opportunity of being in touch with many congregations in the district and eventually the idea spread. Essentially the stress was that people in the church should be born again. They also conduct healing and deliverance services. Apart from that they have intercessors in the church and they do have nights of prayer at times, probably once in a month, but this differs from congregation to congregation.[6]

In June 2012 those members who were not for these changes came into the open. This group of people was mainly from Karonga and Kyela in

---

[4] Int. Bishop Alex Sibale, Bishop Chitipa, Chitipa Boma, 6.4.2013.
[5] Ibid. 6.4.2013.
[6] Ibid. 6.4.2013.

Tanzania. The problem, however, was that many of the changes that this group was against had been already agreed upon in the new constitution of the church.[7]

Actually, on 18th August, 2006, a big Synod was held at Kyela in Tanzania, where it was discussed that there was need for the church to get registered with the government and to have a common seal. The leaders from the three countries (Malawi, Zambia and Tanzania) agreed that the church should be registered.[8]

During that Synod meeting the church's constitution was revisited and some changes were made with regard to it. This constitution was supposed to govern the church in all the countries where the church is found. Among other things, they agreed to stop allowing polygamy and beer drinking for members of the church. It was also agreed during the review of the constitution and by-laws that there shall be a retirement age for the clergy at seventy years. Before this decision was made clergy were supposed to serve for life.[9]

The registration exercise for the new constitution started in 2008. In 2009, the Last Church of God and His Christ International called for a big Synod which took place on 10th August 2009 at Fonkha in Zambia. The Synod was attended by three countries, namely Malawi, Zambia and Tanzania. The constitution was read and was adopted by all countries. After that the constitution was sent to the Registrar for registration in Malawi.[10]

However, on 10th October, 2009 there came a letter from Karonga refusing most of the reviewed aspects in the constitution and by-laws. The signatories happened to come from Karonga and from Kyela in Tanzania.[11] When the executive of the church met, it resolved that what was agreed and passed at the Synod cannot be reversed by just a handful

---

[7] Int. Bishop Alex Sibale, Bishop Chitipa, Chitipa Boma, 6.4.2013.
[8] Church minutes, The Last Church of God and His Christ International, nd.
[9] Ibid.
[10] Ibid.
[11] Ibid.

of members from two districts, those who are for drinking alcohol and polygamy. Thus, the registration proceeded as agreed during the Synod.

When finally, the registration was completed on 8th August 2011, it became clear that some people did agree to the review of the constitution to get the church registered while in fact they really did not want the change. This included not only those from Karonga and Kyela, but also some of the leaders at the headquarters. This group, which is led by Senior Bishop Getson Nyondo from Karonga, clearly raised the issues which they found unacceptable within the reviewed constitution and gave their reasons. Their main concern is the born-again philosophy and also other things which, according to them, are Pentecostal tendencies (though they are not generally Pentecostal).[12] These issues are highlighted below.

Preaching

The concerned group does not agree to church members conducting hospital visits or praying for the sick, and prison visitation. They argue that the church from its beginning has never gone to cheer the sick in hospital or to pray with the convicts in prison nor did they ever pray for the sick.[13]

Membership in or Affiliation with other Religious Organizations

The group does not approve that the church should join any association with other churches or organizations such as becoming a member of the Evangelical Association of Malawi (EAM) or being a member of the Malawi Council of Churches (MCC). They claim that to be part of these organizations means becoming Pentecostal.[14]

---

[12] Church minutes, The Last Church of God and His Christ International, nd.
[13] Ibid. nd.
[14] Ibid. nd.

Teaching

The group in question argues against having Sunday schools in the church. They also do not agree to the fact that pastors should be going for pastoral training (Bible School). They argue that it is said in the Bible that no man can teach the Bible but only the Holy Spirit. And that ever since the church started, no one has ever been taught at a Bible School, neither young nor old.[15]

This became an issue apparently because Bishop Sibale organizes a one-week seminar for pastors every year in Chitipa, where they are taught by people from different churches, including some from Pentecostal churches.[16] And also Pastors Mwambughi and Mwakalenga have been attending some pastoral training. Thus, for instance since 2010 Pastor Wale, a Nigerian missionary, has always been invited to come and teach. Again, Rev Mwenitete of the CCAP, Pastor Moyo from Living Waters and even some from the Assemblies of God have been called on several occasions to come and teach during the seminars at Chitipa. Some of the topics were pastoral care, effective preaching, leadership and many others. The group in question argues that some of the Pentecostal tendencies come into the church from seminars like these.[17]

Uniform

At the Synod meeting in 2006 it was discussed that there was need to change the women's uniform. The issue was raised when some people brought up the concern that when the *Amayi Achikondi* put on their uniform (white blouse and black skirt) they receive criticism from some members of some churches which were the first to use such colours as their uniform (for example CCAP). Apart from that, it was sometimes difficult to differentiate a female member of the Last Church from one of another church like CCAP.[18]

---

[15] Church minutes, The Last Church of God and His Christ International, nd.
[16] Int. Bishop Alex Sibale, Bishop Chitipa, Chitipa Boma, 6.4.2013.
[17] Ibid. 6.4.2013.
[18] Ibid. 6.4.2013.

The Synod therefore agreed to change the uniform to avoid such confusion. The new uniform was to comprise of a white blouse, maroon skirt and collar and white shoes. The maroon stands for the blood of Christ and white for the holiness which comes with the blood of Jesus. The opposing group does not want this change. Instead, they prefer the old uniform and would like to maintain it.[19]

Retirement Age

It was agreed when reviewing the constitution and by-laws of the church that the retirement age for pastors should be seventy years. This meant that leaders were no longer to serve in their positions for life. The group claims that putting a retirement age is like removing the old people or discriminating them in the church, hence they cannot agree with this.[20]

Polygamy, Smoking and Beer Drinking

In the face of the HIV/AIDS pandemic and the economic challenges being faced by the members in the Last Church of God the Synod decided to forbid the practice of polygamy by its members which at first was allowed. The Synod also agreed to prohibit beer drinking altogether. However, the faction wants to maintain the former position of the constitution on these two matters.[21] Interesting enough the former constitution did not allow smoking for its members, but this faction wants smoking to be legalized in the constitution as well.

Registration

The concerned group also argues that the church should not conduct any census for its members as the act is a seduction from the devil. They base their argument on 1 Chronicles 21:1-2 ["Now Satan stood up against Israel and moved David to number Israel"].

Apart from the above issues the group clearly stated in their letter that they had also refused the payment of K20 as membership fee by each

---

[19] Area Bishops Karonga and Kyela - the Archbishop Last Church, 10.8.2012.
[20] Ibid. 10.8.2010.
[21] Ibid. 10.8.2010.

member of the church. They also refused to pay K20,000 which was agreed upon to come from each district as a contribution towards obtaining the common seal.[22] In short, the group refuted almost everything that the Synod had agreed upon.

Looking at the issues raised above one wonders whether this group was not represented at the Synod during the review of the constitution. However, according to their letter addressed to the Archbishop, the leaders were part of the decision making with regard to the changes in the constitution. The group wrote in their letter to the Archbishop:

> The Senior Bishop with regard to the Synod we had at Fonkha, Zambia on 10/08/09 we have communicated to the whole church here, the church has rejected the rules made during that Synod. The rules are as follows.[23]

The letter then continued stating the rules which the church in Karonga had rejected. Below are the rules as stated in their letter.

(1) *Kukanizga mitala* (forbidding polygamy).[24]

(2) *Kufumyamo bachekulu* (the removing of elderly people with regard to the retirement age).

(3) *Ndalama K20 ya membership fee* (an amount of K20 for membership fee).

(4) *Ndalama K20,000 ya common seal* (an amount of K20 000 for the common seal).

(5) *Kukanizga phere* (forbidding beer drinking).

(6) *Kuluta ku sukulu ma pastor* (training of pastors).

---

[22] Area Bishops Karonga and Kyela -the Archbishop Last Church, 10.10.2010.

[23] Bwana Senior Bishop kwakuyana na umo tikakhalila ku Fonkha, Zambia pa 10 August 2009 taphalira mupingo ghose kuno, bamupingo bakana kwakuyana na malango agho ghakakakika ku Synod yila. Malango ghakhe ni agha. Area Bishops Karonga and Kyela – the Archbishop Last Church, 10.10.2010.

[24] Ibid. 10.10.2010.

(7) *Kusintha uniform ya wa mama* (the changing of *Amayi Achikondi* uniform).

(8) *Kusintha zina la Last Church kuti lichemekenge Last International Church* (The changing of the name from Last Church to Last International Church).

(9) *Kusaya bana* (the blessing of children by the pastor).

The letter was signed by the Area Bishops from both Karonga and Kyela. The group then took a further step. They wanted to get the certificate (common seal) from the Board of the Trustees of the church, insisting that the board members were introducing born again philosophy into the church.[25]

However, they met resistance there because the constitution does not permit them to be the custodians of the common seal. According to the church's constitution the church's documents like the common seal are to be kept by the board of trustees, specifically the Secretary of the Board.[26] It should be noted that some of the opposing members of the board are the ones who supported the revised constitution and also the Pentecostal tendencies in the church. The members include the Board Chairperson Bishop L.K. Mwambughi, the board Secretary Pastor H.R. Mwakalenga and Bishop Joseph Sibale, a board member.[27]

On the other hand, the Karonga/Kyela group had support also from some top leaders in the church like the Chairman and the Secretary of the Synod, Bishops Chande and L.K Longwe respectively. So, after the board denied them their request the next step was to ex-communicate the opposing board members. The first to be ex-communicated was the Chairman of the board, Bishop L.K. Mwambughi on 11th August, 2011, signed by Synod Secretary L.K. Longwe and counter signed by the Chairman of the Synod, Bishop Chande.[28] This was what was contained in the ex-communication letter:

---

[25] Church minutes, The Last Church of God and His Christ International, nd.
[26] Ibid.
[27] Int. Bishop Alex Sibale, Chitipa Boma, 6.4.2013.
[28] Letter from the Synod held in Mzimba to Bishop Mwambughi, 11.8.2011.

The Synod has sat down on the issue of born again as well as disrespecting the issue that was discussed during the Synod at Mzimba. You are one of those that cry in the Last Church so the Synod has ex-communicated you. [29]

SECTION 4. BY LAWS: OF THE LAST CHURCH
a. Disobedience (Kwambula kupulikila) [30]
b. Disrespectful to the elders (leaders) (Kwambula ntchindi ku ulala) [31]
c. Going against the ruling of the leaders without any reasonable ground (Kususka ulamuliro wa balala kwambula chandulo) [32]

Next to be ex-communicated were Senior Bishops of Chitipa District A.J. Sibale and Pastor H.R. Mwakalenga, who were ex-communicated verbally. Out of the seven members of the board three were left who were in support of the group. The group thought that when those who were defending the constitution were out of the way, then the common seal would be taken by them regardless of what the constitution says on the use and custodianship of the common seal. [33]

Nevertheless, those that were ex-communicated did not surrender the common seal, arguing that those who excommunicated them did not have any authority to do so, as what they did was unconstitutional. Hence the group took the issue to court to demand the return of the common seal from the excommunicated board members. [34]

While the conflict over the common seal continues, many congregations outside Karonga, Chitipa and Mzuzu are not aware of such conflicts. However, in the places concerned there is unrest.

---

[29] Sinodi yaja pasi pa nkhani ya boni ageni ndi kunyozera nkhani ya Sinodi yaku Mzimba sonu imwe mwewamoza muliya mu Last Church sonu Sinodi yakumikani. Letter from Synod held in Mzimba to Bishop Mwambughi, 11.8.2011.
[30] Ibid. 11.8.2011.
[31] Ibid. 11.8.2011.
[32] Ibid. 11.8.2011.
[33] Int. Joseph Sibale, Bishop Chitipa, Chitipa Boma, 6.4.2013.
[34] Ibid. 6.4.2013.

Mzuzu

When the members heard about the excommunication of their Area Bishop Mwambughi they decided to write a letter to the Archbishop. The letter was written by members from several congregations, mainly Msongwe, Chibavi, Mchengautuwa and Ekwendeni. It was signed by the pastors of these congregations, probably representing their members. They wrote to this effect;

> The reason for writing this letter is that, with regard to the news that has reached us concerning the ex-communication of our Area Bishop Mwambughi, we your children in Mzuzu have looked into the matter and do not agree with the ex-communication of the Area Bishop. We have seen that you, our leaders, do not agree with our way of worship, therefore we have decided that it is good for us your children in Mzuzu to separate from you and be independent, we are still in the Last Church but have accepted to worship independently. We don't have any grudges with you but only God should guide us all.[35]

The letter was signed by Pastors from Msongwe (Rev Njoka Phiri), Chibavi (Pastor H. Mwakalenga), Mchengautuwa (Pastor M.C Kaonga) and Ekwendeni (Rev Mwabwalwa). Sibale said that these members thought that the Archbishop was going to call them as the leader so that they bring their grievances before him. But the Archbishop took no action when he received the letter.[36]

---

[35] Chakulembera kalata iyi ntchakuti kuyana na nkhani iyo yatisanga Ise yakusezgeka kwa Area Bishop withu Mwambughi sono ise wana wino Wa Mzuzu takhala pansi nakuyowoya kuti ise tazomerezezgha kuti yaye kusezgeka Kwa Area withu sono tawona kuti imwe walongozgi withu kupemphera uko Tikupemphera mukukolelana nako yaye sono lekani takana nakuganiza kuti ntchiweme kuti ise wa Mzuzu tifumeko kwa imwe na kuyima patekha tiri wa Last kweni yakuzomera kupemphera payekha. Kweni chifukwa na imwe tilije kweni chiuta ndiyo wamanye kutilongozga tose pamoza. Pastors Last Church of God Mzuzu Congregations - Archbishop S.C.K. Chikosera Phiri, the Senior Bishop Chairman of Synod Chande and the General Secretary Y.P. Longwe, 23.8.2011.

[36] Int. Bishop Joseph Sibale, Bishop Chitipa, Chitipa Boma, 6.4.2013.

The situation was more serious in Chitipa district where it crystallized in open conflicts between these two groups and the case even reached the District Commissioner's Office.

Chitipa

When the members in Chitipa heard that their District Bishop Sibale was ex-communicated from the church on the grounds of "born again philosophy," they too decided to write the Archbishop to notify him concerning their stand. Like their colleagues in Mzuzu they titled their letter *"malayilo"* (farewell). It is interesting that these members used the address of the Last Church of God Mwanza headquarters in Tanzania. The contents of the letter were as follows;

> Sir, the reason for writing this letter is to inform you that we your children of the Last Church at Chitipa *boma,* we are very much concerned with the ex-communication of our Senior Bishop A.J. Sibale. For this reason, we have discussed and have rejected the ex-communication of Mr Sibale. Therefore, Sir, we have concluded that you and us will never agree on the way of worship because we are used with the way we pray of which you do not agree. As such, we are saying farewell that we have separated ourselves from Msondozi and will now belong to Mwanza headquarters, where we have been welcomed with two hands. There are no grudges between you and us. But God should guide us all. All of us in Chitipa have agreed on this issue and if there is one of us who holds a position there appoint someone in his/her place because we will be serving in Tanzania with regard to Synod, session and anything which might be there.[37]

---

[37] Badada chakulembela kalata iyi ntchakuti timumanyisheni kuti ise tawana Winu ba Last Church ba Chitipa boma kuti ntchito yose iyo yikachitika ku Synod Yakubimika balongozi withu ba senior, Bishop A.J Sibale takhuzika nayo chomene. Kwaichi takhala pasi nakuzomelezgana kuti ise taba Chitipa takana kuti ba Sibale bayimikike. Sono bwana tafikapo kuti ise na imwe tazamukoleranako chara chara pa Nkhani ya kapemphelero chifukwa tazgowera nakapemphelero kithu aka imwe mu Kukana. Sono ise tikumulayilani kuti uko ku Msondozi tafumako taluta ku Mwanza headquarters uko ise tapokeleleka na maoko yabiri. Palije kaheni pakati paise naimwe. Kwene Chiuta ndiyo watidangilire ise tose. Ise tose taba Chitipa tazomerezgana pa nkhani iyi nakuti pala alipo yumoza uyo anaudindo kwa imwe uko mubikepo munyakhe pamalo yakhe. Chifukwa tose titebetelenge ku Tanzania. Kwamba Synod Executive, session na ivo vingabako. Last Church of God Mwanza Headquarters - The

The letter ended with signatures from Area Bishops and Head Pastors from Chitipa Central, South (Nthalire), West (Wenya), North (Kameme) and Chitipa East (Misuku). But again, it seems that there was no response from the headquarters, even after this letter. A look at the two letters above raises the question of whether these people (Mzuzu and Chitipa) discussed and shared what to include in their letters. The contents of the two letters are quite similar.

The other question that one can ask is why the Archbishop as the overseer of the church chose to remain silent over such a crucial issue, which is clearly threatening the unity and peace of the church. Probably an explanation could be found from events that later emerged from Karonga.

The situation in Chitipa came to its climax in 2012 when the leadership of the church in Karonga decided to organize a meeting at Siyombwe in Chitipa. They wrote the invitation letters to some churches within Chitipa as follows;

> Dear Christians – Chitipa
> THE MEETING AT SIYOMBWE
> With regard to the meeting scheduled on 29th June, 2012 at Siyombwe-Chitipa, the Christians and leaders that are coming include; The Archbishop Chikosera Phiri, the General Secretary Longwe and the following senior Bishops, From me the Secretary to the Senior Bishop Katonje Makwakwa on behalf of Karonga D.C.C.[38]

Sibale commented that the surprising thing was that the leaders of the church in Chitipa were not communicated to; they just heard rumours from some members that there was a letter that was circulating with regard to the above meeting. However, according to the church's norm,

---

Archbishop S.C.K. Chikosela Phiri, The Synod Chairman Senior Bishop Chande and the General Secretary Y.T. Longwe, 21.8.2011.

[38] Kwakuyana na ungano uwu wuli pa 29 June, 2012 ku Siyombwe- Chitipa, ba Khristu na Ulongozgi uwu bukwiza ndi uwu: Ba Archbishop Chikosera Phiri, Ba General Secretary Longwe na ma senior Bishop agha. Ndine Secretary wa Senior Bishop Katonje Makwakwa, M'malo gha Kalonga D.C.C. Ba Archbishop Chikosera Phiri, Ba General Secretary Longwe na ma Secretary - Senior Bishop, Katonje Makwakwa to the Christians in Chitipa, 12.5.2012.

if the Archbishop was coming to an area for a meeting, it was a big event and all the members and congregations were to be informed.[39]

Again, the fact that the meeting was called by members outside the district was unheard of since every district is expected to organize its meetings and activities within its area of jurisdiction.[40] This was the time that the Archbishop showed that he was on the side of the Karonga group. At the same time, the action showed that not all members in Chitipa district were in support of the revised constitution. These were the ones that welcomed the visitors from Karonga and the Synod leaders that came for the meeting.

The meeting took place as planned. One significant thing that happened was the appointment of the new office bearers for Chitipa District by the Archbishop and the dismissal of the old office bearers. The following new leaders were elected on 29th June, 2012:[41]

> Senior Bishop for Chitipa was Rev Getson Nyondo.[42]
> Senior Secretary for Chitipa District was Rev Lazarus Mbughi.[43]
> Bishop for Kameme was Rev Kingstone Msukwa.
> Bishop for Bulambia was Rev Charles Nyondo.
> Bishop for Nthalire was Rev Mubeka Kaira.
> Rev Kapesa Kayira was appointed pastor for Wenya congregation.[44]

The Archbishop wrote a letter submitting these new names to the District Commissioner and a copy of the same was sent to the Police Officer in charge of Chitipa Police. The letter also advised the two offices above that:

> Mr Sibale has no authority on the ownership of the Last Church of God and His Christ International, since he was suspended (Removed from the office) by the Synod last year 2011 at Euthini in Mzimba and he himself

---

[39] Int. Bishop Joseph, Sibale, Bishop Chitipa, Chitipa Boma, 6.4.2013.
[40] Ibid. 6.4.2013.
[41] The Archbishop, The Last Church of God and His Christ International - The District Commissioner, Chitipa, copied to The Police Officer In-charge, Chitipa Police, 17.8.2012.
[42] Ibid. 17.8.2012.
[43] Ibid. 17.8.2012.
[44] Ibid. 17.8.2012.

confirmed this suspension by joining another body of Church which its Headquarters is in Mwanza Tanzania. He wrote a letter to the Archbishop telling him that they had joined Last Church of God based in Tanzania and its Headquarters in Mwanza.[45]

When the news reached the Board of Trustees of the church they too wrote a letter to the District Commissioner for Chitipa informing his office "that the names of Chitipa Office bearers remain unchanged, contrary to the circular dated 17th August 2012, signed by Katonje Makwakwa as Board Chairman and T. Longwe as Board Secretary who are in fact not members of the Board."[46] The Board gave more names of the office bearers in Chitipa district as follows:

>Senior Bishop Alex Joseph Sibale
>District Secretary Christopher Sichinga
>Bishop Glyn Mwakalenga (Kameme area)
>Bishop Justine Kamuela (Misuku area).
>Bishop Den Songaa (Bulambya area)
>Bishop Grate Siyame (Nthalire area)
>Bishop Kapesa Kayira (Wenya)[47]

When the D.C. received these two contradictory letters, he called both parties to a meeting on 17th July 2012.[48] However, he discovered during the deliberations that the issue between the two parties was already in court, therefore he just asked both parties to exercise discipline and wait for the outcome from the court.[49]

The problem on the ground, however, was on the use of the church buildings in some areas. For instance, in January 2013 Mr Simbeyi and some other followers of the group came to the church at Chitipa *boma*

---

[45] The Archbishop, The Last Church of God and His Christ International - The District Commissioner, Chitipa, copied to The Police Officer In-charge, Chitipa Police, 17.8.2012.

[46] Board of Trustees, Last Church of God and His Christ International - The District Commissioner, Chitipa, 4.10.2012.

[47] Ibid. 4.10.2012.

[48] Minutes. Meeting concerning wrangles over the ownership of the Last Church and His Christ International held in the Office of the District Commissioner, 17.7.2012.

[49] Ibid. 17.7.2012.

disrupting church activities and threatened bloodshed if Sibale continued to use the church building. They argued that they too contributed to the building of the church, so they questioned why Sibale's group should be the only one using it. [50]

When the issue reached the police, Sibale was advised to temporary stop using the church building for fear of his life. However, later in the same month he was told to continue using the church and the other group led by Simbeyi were strongly warned that if they will cause any more trouble they will be arrested. For the period when the church was closed they used to gather at Sibale's house.[51] Sometimes the other group would come and make noise outside. At another time, they disrupted prayers during a night of prayer that was organized by the youth at the church.

On the same, at Kameme, Rev Msukwa, who is in support of the group, has taken over the church building there. Bishop Sibale went there to try to resolve the matter, but it seems he was not successful. Two of the pastors that were chosen in the new office were those that had been temporarily removed from the church on drinking grounds before the group came in the open.[52]

Karonga

The above account may lead one to conclude that all the members in Karonga are against the changes that have taken place in the church, including the absorption of some of the Pentecostal tendencies. But this is not the case. Bishop Sibale mentioned that in fact some members from Karonga have complained to him that they are not happy with what their leaders are doing. When I asked him about what action those members have taken so far, he said that the members are afraid of being bewitched if they do this. In fact, Sibale too has been openly threatened but he said that he had told them that he trusts in God who protects him.[53]

---

[50] Int. Bishop Joseph, Sibale, Bishop, Chitipa Boma, 6.4.2013.
[51] Ibid. 6.4.2013.
[52] Ibid. 6.4.2013.
[53] Ibid. 6.4.2013.

Nevertheless, there are some pastors in Karonga who have come into the open that they are for change in the church and these have also allowed Pentecostal tendencies in their congregations. For instance, Pastor Mwakalewera of Ngerenge congregation is born again and in his congregation, they speak in tongues, pray for the sick and have nights of prayer. He was temporarily removed from the church but he told the leaders in Karonga that there was no problem he was going to build a separate church that will be under the church in Chitipa and will continue in the way they were worshipping. The leaders thought about the consequences such an action was going to bring, therefore they immediately reinstated him but advised him to just concentrate on his congregation and not to poison other congregations with such kind of worship in the district.[54]

Other pastors and congregations which have welcomed the change in Karonga include: Rev Kasisi at Mpata congregation, Rev Petros Mwambinga at Wovwe congregation, Rev Mwakikunga and Rev Ngosi at Songwe congregation and Rev Kayange at Ngana congregation. From this it is clear that it is not the whole church in Karonga that is against change but that it is mainly some of the leaders in Karonga and even at the Synod level that are not for change. The church leaders in Karonga were also successful in persuading even the Archbishop to come to Chitipa and appoint those new office bearers, though it was against the church's constitution.[55]

The Archbishop's Side of the Story

The Archbishop Chikosera Phiri had his own side of the story to tell concerning the matter in question. He said that the Board Secretary Rev Mwakalenga took the church's register and that he (Mwakalenga) wants to change the church's headquarters to Tanzania.[56] When I asked Chikosera how Mwakalenga accessed the church's register, he said that Mwakalenga was given the register to process the issue of the Common Seal. Once the process was done he kept the register until the issue of

---

[54] Int. Bishop Joseph, Sibale, Bishop, Chitipa Boma, 6.4.2013.
[55] Ibid. 6.4.2013.
[56] Int. Bishop Chikosera Phiri, Archbishop, Masasa, 10.10.2011.

speaking in tongues arose in his church at Chibavi. When he was told by the leaders of the church to bring the register, he brought photocopies instead. They (Mwakalenga and his group) even went to the DC to change the headquarters, but they were turned back.[57]

However, the argument given by Archbishop Chikosera Phiri is not satisfying when one considers the fact that the Last Church in Tanzania is already well established, unless if Mwakalenga is going to start a new church there. From the above accounts, one can conclude that the Archbishop is partly responsible for what is happening in the church between Karonga, Chitipa and Mzuzu congregations. As a leader of the church the Archbishop is expected to assist in solving the problems and bring unity between the two groups, but he actually seems to be widening the gap by deliberately acting contrary to the constitution which he is supposed to uphold.

The Archbishop seems to be siding with one group. It is also suspected that he is acting out of fear of the group in Karonga.[58] Either fear of being bewitched or of being removed from the position makes him to go along with their wishes, even if it is against the constitution. He is not the only one trapped in fear. Some members in Karonga feel unable to voice their views on the issue to the church leaders there because they are afraid of being bewitched and of being removed from the church.[59] Again this raises the question, should a Christian compromise the truth due to fear? And should one strive to protect oneself or one's position at the expense of the future of the church? What about Jesus' teaching on not fearing those who can only kill the body but cannot touch the soul (Lk 12:4)?

The Sibale group had written the letter themselves declaring that they were separated from Msondozi headquarters and were now joined to Mwanza Headquarters. So, they too should not put the whole blame on the Archbishop. They should have thought of requesting an audience with the leadership of the church first before rushing to make declarations. Whatever the case, good leadership is about ensuring good

---

[57] Int. Bishop Chikosera Phiri, Archbishop, Masasa, 10.10.2011.
[58] Int. Bishop Sibale, Bishop Chitipa, Chitipa, 6.4.2013.
[59] Ibid. 6.4.2013.

relationships and also the ability to manage conflicts amicably with the purpose of moving forward. There is still time for the Archbishop and his administration to do something and save the church from another split. Taking into account that Karonga and Chitipa are the districts where the African Last church of God has many of its members, I think the unity of the church in these two districts is of much significance to the church.

Controversy about Pentecostal and Charismatic Tendencies

The current conflicts happening in the Last Church of God and His Christ International can be examined at three levels: geographical location, modernity, and Pentecostal winds of the time.

Geography

Looking at the conflict in question one observes that the issue crosses the border to Tanzania. It is not clearly understood how the church at Kyela got itself involved with the issue in Malawi. Again, the churches in Chitipa wrote the Archbishop that they were welcomed with two hands at Mwanza headquarters in Tanzania. This may look simple on the surface. But in reality, it means Mwanza headquarters will have to be involved with the life of the church in Chitipa. If that happens, Mwanza headquarters will be partly responsible for magnifying the conflicts in the church in Malawi. Similarly, we do not see the leadership in Malawi redirecting the members at Kyela to the right authorities.

One, however, ought to be careful here to avoid concluding that the Mwanza headquarters are siding with the churches in Chitipa. It could be that they were acting in good faith to say if these members were no longer accepted by Msondozi headquarters then they are free to worship under Mwanza headquarters. This means that the members in Chitipa were not necessarily encouraged by Mwanza headquarters to separate from Msondozi headquarters. We do not know exactly what these members said to Mwanza headquarters. Nevertheless, Tanzania should have at least tried to find out from Malawi about the conflict before accepting these members. This is one church whether in Malawi or Tanzania, so they should work together where necessary to maintain the unity of the church.

The issue of Kyela still remains a puzzle. The church there should have raised their concerns to the leadership at Mwanza headquarters where they rightly belong. Whatever the case, one thing is clear, that even in Tanzania there is division as far as Pentecostal tendencies are concerned. These two instances are a serious call for the headquarters in Tanzania and Malawi to examine the issue of Pentecostal tendencies and to try to iron out the differences in the church and map the way forward.

Modernity

In the past, the leadership positions in the church, be it at congregational or national level were given to elderly people, probably because culturally we expect elders to lead. Another reason may have been that in the past the Last Church comprised of more elderly people as compared to the younger ones; and because these positions were for life, younger members did not stand a chance to lead. In the end, it became like a tradition that only old people could lead. Thus, it was unimaginable then to find for example a thirty-year-old member becoming a pastor or bishop in the church. In such a setting decisions from the Synod were easily welcomed.

We are no longer living in the past. Things have changed. Where they used to have more elderly people the opposite now applies. The younger members are the ones now taking up many leadership positions. For instance, the National Board of Trustees of the church is not headed by elderly people. This means that decisions of the church at the top are now being influenced mainly by the young generation. This does not go well with some older members in the churches. The change in the church is being initiated to a large extent by young pastors who think that some of the old practices do not fit the modern times. In this way, the conflict is between modernity vs. continuity of old traditions by older members. This is evidenced by the reaction of the members at Karonga.

It is true that people will not just accept anything for the sake of change. At the same time, it is questionable if people reject everything that comes with change even those things that will be of benefit to them. This is what the group at Karonga did. One wonders how the issue of membership fee, retirement age and change of the women's uniform among others are related to the born-again philosophy.

The argument given by the group that they cannot change because such things have never happened in their church before seems to cover up their real reason. Should the church not involve itself in praying for the sick, having Sunday school and even visiting those in prisons, just because it is not part of the church's tradition? What should come first between Christ and tradition or culture in a Christian's life? On the other hand, the young pastors should be careful with the changes they are trying to make in the church. It is not a question of just moving with the times, but whatever change they desire should be in line with God's word. Both sides should not let their wisdom and culture dominate their faith, instead they should let their culture be dominated by faith.[60] When both sides can put faith first, then it will "colour" everything in their lives.[61] Then the conflict at this level will vanish.

Pentecostal Winds of the Time

Apart from the issue of modernity the Last Church, like other churches such as the mainline churches, has been caught up in the Pentecostal winds of the times. But the question here is, to what extent is this a cause of conflict in the church? Is it true that the born-again philosophy is indeed the cause of conflict in the church? Whenever people revise the constitution, they do it in order to meet the needs of the people at a specific time. I believe the things that are regarded as "Pentecostal" by the Karonga group were introduced in an attempt to assist members to live an effective Christian life. It was not just a matter of doing away with old traditions. But rather it was a question of assessing whether the old traditions are meaningful to the members today.

One wonders why the other districts are silent on the matter as if this issue does not concern them. However, the born-again philosophy has also penetrated some congregations in Nkhatabay. The Head Pastor between Tukombo and Dwambazi, Rev Milanzi, and Pastors Chibangamakani Nyirenda and Bwanali are all in support of the born-again philosophy. Again, some churches in Nkhotakota and Ntchisi

---

[60] Steven Paas, *The Faith Moves South: A History of the Church in Africa*, Zomba: Kachere, 2006, p. 240.

[61] Ibid. p. 240.

display the born-again philosophy. The reality on the ground is, many Last Church congregations in the country in general do not look at the changes in the constitution nor understand them as Pentecostal tendencies in the way the group at Karonga perceives them. So, for instance, the forbidding of polygamy and beer drinking, the retirement age and even the need for pastors' training have been welcomed by many churches as positive changes that will transform the Last Church of God for the better. These are not seen as Pentecostal tendencies.

However, what many of these churches reject is the born-again philosophy only which has to do with the way of worship, specifically speaking in tongues, and deliverance as it happens in Pentecostal/Charismatic circles. Praying for the sick, on the other hand, has been and is happening in many of these churches, though differently. As the situation stands many churches do not incorporate this born-again aspect in their worship, and they have put a blind eye to those churches that are practicing it. Thus, these congregations clearly state that they do not practice Pentecostal tendencies, especially in the sense of born again philosophy. But they have not openly denounced those congregations which practice born again philosophy, except for the Karonga group.

Another question is how to explain this born-again philosophy in the Last Church. Should it be seen as a youth phenomenon as Rijk van Dijk in his study of the "Born Again Network" would interpret it?[62] Even though this might appear to be true when considering the fact that some of the pastors in the church who support this are youths, it is still an inadequate explanation. For how does one account for entire congregations in Chitipa and the ones in Mzuzu that are in support of this phenomenon? These congregations are composed of both adults and youths. These people are united in their quest to live a prayerful life and the need to rely on the power of the Holy Spirit both as individuals as well corporately as a church. Besides, the issue of Pentecostal or Charismatic tendencies is not a new thing in the Last Church of God. From early times, there have been some individuals who longed for something deeper in their spiritual life than mere traditions. And I think many

---

[62] Klaus Fiedler, "The Charismatic and Pentecostal Movements in Malawi in Cultural Perspective," in *Religion in Malawi*, 1999, pp. 28-38.

people misunderstood them because when they prayed in the power of the Holy Spirit and things happened, people would say they relied on or used traditional medicine. We are told this of Ben Ngemela. He is described by some as being "like" a prophet.[63] Why not just call him a prophet? Probably people would not imagine a prophet in the Last Church of God, more especially in the 1930s. Ngemela can be said to have been a Pentecostal son of his time. The other case is that of White Longwe in the 1960s. Those who knew him say that he was charismatic.[64]

It can therefore be concluded that from the early times of the church there has been a desire in members for a deeper spiritual fulfilment which they could not find in mere observance of the traditions.[65] The changes that are happening in the church are a result of members genuinely searching for that fulfilment. It is not just a desire to be like or to worship like the Pentecostals. I agree with Klaus Fiedler that what is happening in the Last Church today is a revival situation.[66] Sooner or later it will reach out to many other congregations, even in the very rural areas. Those that are resisting change are, as a matter of fact, resisting the "young" authority and not necessarily being against Pentecostal tendencies.

While the Pentecostal/Charismatic tendencies have reached some congregations of the African Last Church I have not heard of this scenario within the Reformed Last Church of God. However, they may be present in some of the congregations. Since there is a gap between the headquarters and the grassroots congregations some of these things may be taking place in the congregations without the headquarters' knowledge.

In order to appreciate how far these tendencies have affected the church, it is necessary to look at the Sunday worship in one of the congregations within Mzuzu city.

---

[63] Int. Bishop Sibale, Chitipa Boma, 6.4.2013.
[64] Int. Rev Chiuli Manda, retired Area Bishop, Munkhokwe, 10.10.2012.
[65] Klaus Fiedler, "The Charismatic and Pentecostal Movements in Malawi in Cultural Perspective," in *Religion in Malawi*, 1999, pp. 28-38.
[66] Ibid.

Chapter 8: Sunday Worship and Preaching Service in the Last Church of God and His Christ International

In this chapter, I will discuss the Sunday service of the African Last Church of God by describing the services of two congregations, one from the congregations that have not been affected by Charismatic tendencies and the other one from a congregation that has welcomed Charismatic tendencies. The aim is first to find out how these Charismatic tendencies are manifested within the Last Church service of worship. Second, to find out if the Charismatic tendencies have also affected the teaching, especially the themes of concentration in the Last Church. While others are of the view that much of the teaching of Charismatics reflects the "prosperity gospel,"[1] one will notice that while the Charismatic tendencies have indeed transformed the nature of worship in the concerned congregations, the teaching so far remains unchanged.

Sunday Worship in the African Last Church of God

The Sunday service in many Last Church of God congregations starts around 10:00 a.m. and is usually directed by the church secretary. Sometimes the pastor may choose preachers in advance so that they prepare, but sometimes he appoints preachers on the same day. There are supposed to be at least three preachers and each one has to use three texts from the Bible in his or her preaching. But this tradition is dying in some congregations as they only choose one preacher. After the preachers have been chosen there is an opening prayer. Thereafter choirs available on the day are given a chance to sing, followed by a hymn from the hymn book.

Soon after the first hymn the first preacher comes forward to preach. There are always two people involved here, the preacher and the one reading the scripture chosen by the preacher. As one reads the scripture,

---

[1] Klaus Fiedler, "The Charismatic and Pentecostal Movements in Malawi in Cultural Perspective," in *Religion in Malawi,* 1999, pp. 28-38.

the preacher explains each verse. The first preaching is followed by a choir, then the second preaching.

The second hymn is sung and finally the third preacher wraps up the preaching of the two preachers. When he is through, offerings are collected while a choir is singing. The third hymn is sung and if there are any announcements, they are made by the secretary. Finally, a closing prayer is offered.

Just like a Sunday service in one CCAP Congregation may be similar to the service in all CCAP churches, so it is with the service in the Last Church of God congregations. Below is a description of a service in a congregation that has not been affected by Charismatic tendencies. I visited Munkhokwe congregation on 12th September, 2010 and this was how their service was done.

Sunday Service at Munkhokwe African Last Church of God in Nkhatabay

People started coming to the church around quarter past nine in the morning but the pastor and his wife were among those that came earlier. The pastor sat in front while the wife sat with the rest of the members in the pews. Members who arrived earlier were greeting each other and chatting, waiting for the service to begin. The service began around 10:00.

The church secretary made a few announcements, after which an opening prayer was offered. The Pastor announced the main scripture for that day as Galatians 6:4 ["But let each one examine his own work, and then he will have rejoicing in himself alone, and not in another."] The theme was *"we yose wajiyese ntchito zake"* (everyone should evaluate his or her own works). Then the pastor appointed two women to prepare for preaching. *Amayi Achikondi* were asked to sing. They sang two songs. One of them (in Tonga) said:

> What is to build the church?
> To build the church is to love one another,
> On my own I cannot build the church.

This song is not from their hymn book. Afterwards the pastor commented on the words of the song. That indeed love was important in the church. And all members were asked to stand and sing a song from their Tonga hymn book.

After the song was over, the church secretary, who was leading the service, called for the first preacher to come forward. She prayed and told the congregation that her message was *"Limbikani mtima ndikuchita zinthu mwamphanvu"* (Be strong at heart and do things diligently). This theme was different from the one introduced by the pastor. Her first text was Habakkuk 2:20. One of the leaders in front opened a Chichewa Bible and as he was reading the preacher was also preaching. He read, ["I am in my holy temple. Let the whole earth be silent in front of me."] She spoke to the audience that the word of God was clear. They were in God's house; therefore, they should be quiet before the Lord. Then she instructed the reader to open 2 Kings 6:5 which reads ["One of them was cutting down a tree. The iron blade of his axe fell in the water. "Master!" he cried out. "The axe was borrowed!"]

She explained that people's lives are like the axe in the story in the sense that life is borrowed. Happy are those who walk with Jesus, for even if they die they will be raised back to life. She continued that the prophet in the story was lucky, because they had Elisha in their midst. Finally, she asked the one reading the Bible to find Deuteronomy 31:6 ["Be strong and brave. Don't be afraid of them. Don't be terrified because of them. The Lord your God will go with you. He will never abandon you."] She ended by appealing to the audience to go out and serve God with courage and not to be afraid of people because He has promised to be with them always.

After the first preacher, the *Amayi Achikondi* were also asked to give two songs before the second preacher was invited. It was the Pastor's wife. Her first text was taken from Psalm 32:2, ["Blessed is the man whose sin the LORD never counts against him."] She explained that happy are those people whose sins have been forgiven by God. Her second text was John 1:4-5 ["Life was in him, and that life was the light for all people. The light shines in the darkness. But the darkness has not understood it."] She expounded that Jesus is the light that shines in darkness, but unfortunately many people have rejected him. Then they sang another song from the Tonga hymn book.

Lastly, the Pastor summarized both preachings and emphasized the theme he gave earlier (Galatians 6:4). He told the audience that each one of them should evaluate his or her own works in accordance with God's word. He then opened Psalm 31:24 ["Be strong, all of you who put your hope in the LORD. Never give up."] He urged the members to go out and do God's work without fear. He asked the reader to use the Tonga Bible. When the preaching was over, it was time for offerings. For those who did not make it to the church but managed to send offerings, their names and the amounts were announced to the congregation. Finally, a closing hymn was sung.

But before the final prayer was offered, the secretary called the names of two women to come forward. They stood before the pastor and five women deacons stood behind them. The pastor asked each one of them to confess before the congregation the sin they had committed that led them to be temporarily removed from the church. Their sin was that they got married outside the church, that is, by eloping. Now they stated that they were ready to be fully re-incorporated into the church. Apparently, they had been disciplined by the church for six months.

The Pastor asked the secretary to read Psalm 51:1-2 in which David asks God to wash away the sins he had committed and make him pure. After commenting on the scripture, he asked the congregation to welcome them. As the two women went to sit down, the secretary also called names of two people, a man and woman, who came forward. They too stood before the Pastor and he asked the woman why she came to the front. She answered that at first, she belonged to CCAP, but she had decided to follow her husband to Last Church. The Pastor read Philippians 2:29, where Paul was asking the believers to welcome Epaphroditus with joy. Finally, a closing prayer was offered and the people dispersed. There had been 47 members present, 21 women, 16 men and 10 children.

I observed several things from their Sunday services: firstly, many members do not have hymn books, so the songs are tuned in such a way that almost everyone can join and sing easily even without a hymn book. Preachers are free to read and use Bibles of any language of their choice within the service. Choruses are not allowed in the church.

The other thing is that the services of the Last Church are more relaxed in the sense that there is no "solemnity" as is characteristic in some churches. As members are waiting for the service to begin, they freely greet and chat with one another, even with the Pastor already in the front. One, of course, may argue that this is possible because members are usually from the same vicinity and hence they know each other.

Nevertheless, the "discipline" that is found in some churches is disturbing, as sometimes people do not even care to greet the person sitting next to them. It has become a common practice to hear the preacher saying "before I start preaching please greet your neighbours." The church is supposed to be a place of fellowship and togetherness where various kinds of people who usually cannot associate outside the church should find an opportunity to interact and know each other as a family of God. The church should be about relationships.

The choosing of preachers during the service makes the preachers to speak on different themes altogether. Even if the pastor gives the theme at the beginning of the service, the preacher without preparation will use the scriptures that she or he is familiar with. It happened during this particular service that the theme given by the pastor was that everyone should evaluate his or her works, but both preachers came up with their own themes like be strong at heart and work diligently. Apart from that, the way the preacher will preach without preparation is different to the way she or he would preach if they had prepared in advance for the task.

Nevertheless, the three preachers add variety and keep the concentration level of the audience from slipping too low.[2] Some congregations, however, do appoint preachers before the day of the service in order to give them ample time for preparation. In Chitipa they have moved away from the tradition of having three preachers during the service. Instead they only have one preacher and s/he is not restricted to three Bible readings. Bishop Sibale stated that they saw that when three people were preaching, they each came with a different

---

[2] Ulf Strohbehn, *The Zionist Churches in Malawi. History – Theology - Anthropology*, Mzuzu: Mzuni Press, 2016, p. 159.

theme and so there was no correlation of the messages.[3] It is interesting to note that there seems to be no reason for demanding three preachers during the service. The idea seems to have come from contact with African Independent Churches, together with the pastor's robe, head dress and staff (now in the process of being discarded).

The Sunday Service as Observed at Mchengautuwa Last Church of God in Mzuzu

I observed four services of worship at Mchengautuwa for four consecutive Sundays. This church is one of the churches that agrees with the issue of being born again.

I arrived at the church at 9 a.m. and by that time the church was already cleaned up. Chairs for the leaders were arranged in front. A mat and some chairs for the rest of the members were also ready by that time. But there was no one in the church. The service began at 10 o'clock with thirteen adults and seven children. The pastor started with a prayer. He began to lead the service since the secretary had not yet arrived. The pastor called for two choruses which he started himself. We were all asked to stand and sing. The first chorus went like this:

| Aliyemweyo Yesu aliyemweyo x3 | Jesus is the same x3 |
| Aliyemweyo Yesu samasintha | Jesus does not change.[4] |

After the above chorus, the second one went like this:

Ndineneletu, ndineneletu ine x2	Let me declare x2
Ndineneletu Yesu ndi mfumu ya mafumu	Let me declare that Jesus is King of Kings
Ndi fumu Yesu, Yesu ndi fumu eeh x2	Jesus is King, Jesus is King x2
Yesu ndi fumu ya mafumu	Jesus is King of Kings[5]

It was then time for what they call time for praise songs and only one song was sung. After this song, everybody was supposed to confess his/her sins. The praise song was:

---

[3] Int. Bishop Sibale, Chitipa Boma, 6.4.2013.
[4] Amayi Achikondi choir, Mchengautuwa Last Church of God, 24.11.2013.
[5] Amayi Achikondi choir, Mchengautuwa Last Church of God, 24.11.2013.

Palibe amene angafanane naye x2	There is no one who can compare with him
Fumu ya mafumu, karonga wamtendere	King of Kings, King of Peace
Palibe amene angafanane naye	There is no one who can compare with him

When the praise song came to an end, members started praying individually. Finally, the pastor said "up, up Jesus" to which the members replied "up, up Jesus" and then the members were told to sit down. Then the pastor told the congregation that from that Sunday they will start something new; apart from the preaching they will be having a teaching. He had a small booklet that contained several topics and it was written in Tumbuka. The first topic was "*Chisinkhu Chachipulikano*" (The root of our faith). There were 12 points under this topic. Since it was a teaching the pastor invited members to answer questions and participate. The points were as follows:

- All peoples on earth believe in God (Jews, Christians and Muslims).
- All these believe that God is one but differ on three points: The Jews do not accept the revelations of Jesus in the New Testament. The Christians accept the Old Testament and believe that the New Testament (Christ) is the fulfilment of the Old Testament. Muslims accept Jesus as a great teacher but believe that Mohammed is the greatest prophet.
- God is Spirit and He is good. At the same time, He is not limited by time or space.
- God is all knowing concerning the past, the present and the future.
- God is holy in all His ways
- We cannot properly relate with God without parting with evil.
- God is powerful and nothing can fail Him or even prevent His will from being done.
- God does not change. He does not have any beginning and will always remain the same.[6]

---

[6] Amayi Achikondi choir, Mchengautuwa Last Church of God, 24.11.2013.

These were some of the points that were discussed and at the end the pastor asked questions and the members gave their responses. Mama NyaLola asked a question *"waYuda na Yesu Khristu ubale ulipo?"*[7] (Is there a relationship between the Jews and Jesus?) To this question, the pastor answered *"ubale ulipo kweni ngwakulepwelera"*[8] (The relationship is there but it is loose). According to my opinion the response given was not very satisfactory.

Then the preacher prayed for the teaching and the programme continued. The first hymn that was sung was no. 50 from their Tumbuka hymn book.

Kukunozga ku chanya nkhwakung'azima	Heaven is joyful and dazzling and those
Awo walikuyako wakung'azima	Who have gone there are dazzling
Chorus	
Wampingo tiyeni titemwanenge	Church members, let us love one another,
Wonani nyaliyo	See the lamp
Nyali yithu ndi Yesu mpingo wose	Our lamp is Jesus for the whole church

After the hymn, a choir was called to sing one song:

Sindizasiya kuimbira Yesu	I will not stop singing for Jesus
Nangawanji wangayowoya viwi	Even if others talk much to discourage me
Sindizasiya kuimbira Yesu	I will not stop singing for Jesus
Chorus	
Yerere mama sindizasiya kuimbira Yesu	I will not stop singing for Jesus.[9]

The preacher that day was Mr Mtambalila. He asked the pastor to open and read John 3:16 ["For God so loved the world that He gave his only begotten son, that whosoever believes in Him should not perish but have everlasting life"]. **Upon the reading of the scripture the choir was called again to sing another song:**

Nanga wanji wangayowoya viwi	Even though some can talk much
Pakutondeska kuti	In order for me to fail
Ndimusopani kweni ine	To worship you
Nditondekenge cha pakuti	But I will not fail
Mukunditemwa	Because you love me

---

[7] Mama Lola, church member, Mchengautuwa, 24.11.2013.
[8] Mr Chibaka, Acting Reverend, Mchengautuwa, 24.11.2013.
[9] Amayi Achikondi choir, Mchengautuwa, 24.11.2013.

Chorus
Mulikundipa moyo	You have given me life
Mulikundipa chuma kusazgira pa ichi	you have given me wealth above that
Mulikundipa charu ndicho nkhukhalamo.	you have given me the earth, that's where I live.[10]

The preacher then took over and started preaching in Tonga. He first referred to the passage that had already been read (John 3:16). The message was that God sent Jesus to die for us who are sinners and not for the righteous. Then he asked the pastor to read 1 Cor 13:13 ["And now abide faith, hope, love, these three; but the greatest of these is love"]. He continued that the Bible says that Jesus came on earth so that we should be one, whether Last Church of God in Nkhatabay, Karonga etc. We should be one. But above everything, what is important is love.[11] Then he started a song in Tonga:

Kale Achiuta mungutemwa charu	Lord you loved the world long time ago
Mungutama Yesu	and you sent Jesus.[12]

But he failed to continue with the song and the members could not assist him, as it was clear that they were not familiar with the song. He continued with the preaching. "God sent Jesus so that we should be saved, it is not me saying this, and if we understand less we will go to hell and if you do evil, God will judge you." He asked the pastor to open 2 Chr 29:29, but he could not find the passage and instead was asked to open Matthew 23:27 ["Woe to you, scribes and Pharisees, hypocrites! For you are like whitewashed tombs which indeed appear beautiful outwardly, but inside are full of dead men's bones and all uncleanness."]. After the reading the preacher continued: "Is there anyone who has not understood the Bible? Those of us who are alive should pray to God. We should not be like tombstones, beautiful but useless inside. Amen!"[13]

The preaching was over and the offerings were called for. Two deacons were invited to the front, one male to collect offerings from male

---

[10] Amayi Achikondi choir, Mchengautuwa, 24.11.2013.
[11] Mr. Kambalila, preacher, Mchengautuwa, 24.11.2013.
[12] Ibid. 24.11.2013.
[13] Mr. Kambalila, preacher, Mchengautuwa, 24.11.2013.

members and a female deacon to collect offerings from female members. In the meantime, the church's youth choir was singing:

Mumangoti Yesu mumkonda	You just say that you love Jesus
Koma zopereka mukana ndiboza zedi	But you refuse to give that is a lie indeed.[14]

The second offering song went like this,

Ten kwachanso timaponya	Even Ten Kwacha we give
Tipeleke nsembe kwa Mulunguyo	Let us give sacrifice to God.[15]

Preacher Msuku prayed for the offerings. The pastor told the members that it was testimony time and anyone who wanted to testify about anything the Lord had done for them was welcome. The pastor was the first.

Rev Chibaka's Testimony

Running to and fro amidst *alleluias* Rev Chibaka told the congregation that he had two testimonies. He told the members that he had some problems when he started the process to get his first wife back.[16] The wife's parents wanted him to pay *lobola* first, but he did not have any money. The first time he went he was chased by the wife's relatives and he was not even allowed to see his wife. Then he prayed and fasted. He asked God to enter the hearts of the wife's relatives. After this, he took the money that he had amounting to MK 4,000 and went and apologized to the parents. This time, he was welcomed and was told not to leave his wife again, but was told to pay the *lobola*. The wife would come to his house soon.[17]

The Second Testimony

Rev Chibaka said that his second testimony concerns a woman who had a very visible tumour on her neck for seven years. When she came to him

---

[14] Youth Choir, Mchengautuwa, 24.11.2013.

[15] Ibid. 24.11.2013.

[16] The story of Mr Chibaka has already been explained under marriage and polygamy.

[17] Mr Chibaka, Acting Reverend, Mchengautuwa, 24.11.2013.

he assured her that the operation, which had not been accepted for all this time, will now be done. He prayed for her and gave her some water to drink. He told her to add some of the water to her bathing water. The woman underwent the operation and came back to him on 18th November without the visible tumour but only small stitches. The woman was very happy and has invited him to go to her home in Karonga one of these days.[18]

Mama Lola's Testimony

Mama Lola thanked God for keeping her alive. She testified about her daughter who two weeks before had her heel pricked. She went to the hospital, but she did not get well and she was even failing to walk. They resorted to prayer and the pastor, Mr Chibaka, prayed for her. The girl is now fine.[19]

Mr Banda's Testimony

He said that one day his one-year old son had fever. He woke up around 3 a.m. and found that his son was not breathing well. He started singing praises to the Lord and praying. In the morning, his child was fine. He said that when this was happening, his wife was sleeping.[20]

After the testimonies were over, visitors were called to the front. The pastor welcomed them as the rest of the congregation were singing *alendo talandirawa tiyamike Yesu, hosanna alemekezeke hosanna tiyamike Yesu* (the visitors we have received, we should thank Jesus, hosanna, Jesus should be praised).[21]

The pastor then called for those who had problems and needed prayer to say so. *Mama Lola* raised her hand and said that she had a dream. She was asked to tell the dream and the pastor was to interpret it.

---

[18] Ibid. 24.11.2014.
[19] Mama Lola, church member, Mchengautuwa, 24.11.2013.
[20] Mr Banda, church member, Mchengautuwa, 24.11.2013.
[21] Amayi Achikondi choir, Mchengautuwa, 24.11.2013.

Mama Lola's Dream

She dreamt that she, together with other members, were in a vehicle going to a church meeting, but the road was winding up and down and was slippery. Showers were falling. Only Mama Lola knew that the vehicle was in danger and was going to have an accident. She started praying and suddenly they found themselves at a certain house, but they did not know how the vehicle had left them.[22]

Chibaka's Interpretation of the Dream

Chibaka said that a woman stands for the church. The Last Church is moving up and down. There is truth and lies; there is also good and bad in the church. The dream is a revelation to the church. There is need to pray for the church so that it should move smoothly. If not, the church at Mchengautuwa will have an accident (will end). Sometimes the leaders might not know that something is going wrong.[23]

Mama NyaLwanda's Dream

A NyaLwanda dreamt that she was together with her brother in the house, when her brother realized that a dog had eaten his relish. The brother started chasing the dog. The owner of the dog started chasing her brother. NyaLwanda left the house and found herself at a big river, which she had to cross, but there were only two small sticks across the river. She and two of her children started to cross to the other side. One of her children (Brian) fell into the water and started to drown. She jumped into the water and rescued him and they continued. Brian again fell into the water and she rescued him again. They eventually reached the other side of the river where she found many shoes as if everyone crossing the river had left their shoes there. A woman told her that she too had to take off her shoes.[24]

---

[22] Mama Lola, church member, Mchengautuwa, 24.11.2013.
[23] Mr Chibaka, Acting Reverend, Mchengautuwa, 24.11.2013.
[24] Mama NyaLwanda, church member, Mchengautuwa, 24.11.2013.

Chibaka's Interpretation

He said that the dream was a revelation for her house. Brian's drowning in the river means Satanism is involved. The child is being used by Satanists. He explained to the congregation that there are demons of the air which are eight, demons of the land (eleven) and these include death, and demons of the sea which are the leaders of demons. Therefore, the Satanists want to anoint the child as a leader. This is a revelation that the parents should pray for the child. The prayers will save the child.[25]

Mama NyaManda's (Mrs Siyatu) Dream

In her dream, she saw the *Apostoli* (members of the Apostolic Church who dress in white) praying to marry her daughter. The daughter was refusing and they wanted to kill her.[26]

Chibaka's Interpretation

He said that this dream was direct. This is happening already. Either the girl is already in a relationship with someone from the Apostolic Church or someone from that church is praying to marry her. Chibaka said, if the mother does not want her daughter to be married to someone from that church, then she should pray against it.[27]

This particular Sunday service was long and we got out of the church around 2 o'clock after the pastor had offered the benediction prayer.

I was interested in Chibaka's dream interpretation, so I decided to ask him about it. He explained that as the person explains the dream he knows its meaning, but he prays first to God to interpret the dream. He further said that sometimes he does not interpret the dreams immediately, and he has to pray first.[28]

Sometimes God reveals things directly to the pastor. For instance, on one Sunday Chibaka told the congregation that he had a revelation in which

---

[25] Mr Chibaka, Acting Reverend, Mchengautuwa, 24.11.2013.
[26] Mama NyaBanda, church member, Mchengautuwa, 24.11.2013.
[27] Mr Chibaka, Acting Reverend, Mchengautuwa, 24.11.2013.
[28] Mr Chibaka, Acting Reverend, Mchengautuwa, 24.11.2013.

he was told that there are 200 women who have been sent to Mzuzu to destroy pastors and their ministries and the true worshippers. He said he asked his fellow pastor about it (whose name he did not mention), who confirmed that it was true. Chibaka said that sometimes revelations come to him through dreams, visions or through discernment and even just as a thought. But usually God speaks to him through dreams and discernment (thoughts).[29]

"Traditional" vs Pentecostal/Charismatic Tendencies in Worship

The two services of worship described show remarkable differences. One may not be wrong to conclude that the service at Mchengautuwa congregation is far removed from the traditional service of the Last Church (like the service at Munkhokwe congregation).

There were some similarities, though. The first concerns the time for beginning the service. Both services began around ten o'clock in the morning. This probably can be explained that usually there is only one service in all Last Church congregations as compared to other denominations that often have two or more services.

The second is the practice of having one person read the verse as the preacher preaches on which still continues even at Mchengautuwa congregation. This practice has been in the Last Church for a long time.

The seating arrangement for leaders also remains intact in both congregations. Usually male leaders sit in the front facing the rest of the members. On one Sunday, church elder Banda at Mchengautuwa urged the *alalakazi* to be sitting in the front lines while the children and the others sit behind them. Female deacons were also reminded to be putting on their *duku* (head covering) when they come to the church. It was observed that during offering time female deacons failed to stand in front to collect the offerings because their heads were not covered.

Another area of similarity is that of preaching. In both congregations, there seems to be no programme written in advance concerning who is

---

[29] Mr Chibaka, Acting Reverend, Mchengautuwa, 24.11.2013.

to preach and what the themes are. They also both have the same way of singing their hymns.

Despite the above similarities, it is the differences between the two services that seem to be more magnified and make one wonder whether congregations that have adopted Charismatic characteristics are not leaving behind their identity as far as worship is concerned in the traditional Last Church of God.

The first one is the issue of choruses. Rev Kaundama mentioned that they do not allow the singing of choruses because it is like becoming Pentecostal.[30] Thus one observes that there are no choruses or the shouting of *aleluya* at Munkhokwe church, a feature that is prominent at Mchengautuwa. In addition, Mchengautuwa church has changed from the traditional three preachers and three texts each to only one preacher within the service. The old practice still continues at Munkhokwe church.

Another interesting aspect at Mchengautuwa is the confession time which involves the singing of choruses and then praise songs (which are also choruses but concentrate on exalting God and on people's surrender to God). As individuals publicly pray and confess their sins to God they open their hearts to God. All these are a "taboo" at Munkhokwe church.

Mchengautuwa church also emphasizes the importance and the significance of the Holy Spirit. Thus, they recognize the speaking in tongues of its members, especially during nights of prayer, whereas Munkhokwe church, while they believe in the Holy Spirit, does not emphasize the subject.

The testimony time and the time to pray for those with problems including dream interpretation is a practice found at Mchengautuwa congregation and not at Munkhokwe church.

Lastly, the benediction at Mchengautuwa church caught my attention. The pastor at Munkhokwe church would just say a "simple" payer after everything, but at Mchengautuwa he offered a benediction similar to the way the CCAP does it "the love of God our Father, the grace of our Lord

---

[30] Int. Rev Kaundama, Kamsita, 10.9.2011.

Jesus and the fellowship of the Holy Spirit be with you both now and forever."[31]

Understanding the Differences

Having looked at the differences in the services of worship between the two churches above it is necessary to examine the possible causes of the differences. The differences lie mainly in the nature of worship. Mchengautuwa, together with other congregations, has incorporated some Pentecostal, Charismatic and even mainline tendencies. Some can explain this by the fact that, since Mchengautuwa is in town and surrounded by different churches, it is easier to be influenced by them. This seems to make sense for instance, the church is near to God's Will Pentecostal Church, where people say miracles are performed and people receive prophecies. Sometimes members of the Last Church go there with their problems to get assistance. Mr Chibaka mentioned that one day he went there just to see for himself.[32] While I cannot deny the possible influences from other churches, this alone is an insufficient explanation. For how do we explain the same tendency in Kameme congregation in Chitipa?

Another explanation may have to do with the issue of modernity. Some can argue, for instance, that Mr Chibaka is a young man in his thirties and other pastors in favour of this change are also relatively young compared to the past when all the pastors in the church used to be old men. As much as there seems to be some truth in this, again this does not adequately explain this phenomenon. For should we assume that other congregations have not been affected by this issue of modernity?

In order to understand these differences in worship, I go back to the issue of some members seeking deeper religious fulfillment in a church that for many years was "dead". In their quest for that, they have adopted some Charismatic and Pentecostal practices. This does not make their quest a "mere" copying of what others are doing, as Chibaka and others emphasized, it is not just a matter of wanting to worship like

---

[31] Cf. 2 Corinthians 13:14.
[32] Mr Chibaka, Acting Reverend, Mchengautuwa, 24.11.2013.

Pentecostals, but rather of seeking God in earnest.[33] As a revival this phenomenon will reach out to many other congregations.

The Significance of the Differences to the Last Church of God and His Christ

Mchengautuwa congregation represents those churches that have aligned themselves to the born-again philosophy. These include some congregations within Mzuzu, Chitipa and some parts of Karonga. The Charismatic phenomenon that is characterizing some parts of the Last Church has much significance to a church that for a long time served largely as a "social institution." This might seem to be an exaggeration, but even the members themselves testify that in the past what used to happen in the church was sometimes not befitting a church. Sometimes members, including the preacher, were very drunk to the extent that the preacher would fail to preach on the pulpit.[34] What is happening is a revival, to make the church what it is supposed to be, "a house where people can truly worship" (Luke 19:46). This should not be interpreted as human doing but rather as the Holy Spirit moving the church toward that direction through people that have opened their hearts to Him.

Apart from that, this born-again phenomenon is in a way a wakeup call for the Last Church of God as a whole. Like the Protestant Reformation, instead of rushing to avoid this challenge, the church should re-examine itself in terms of its purpose and calling as far as preaching the gospel is concerned.[35] Instead of it being looked upon as a negative thing as some seem to view it, it might actually prove to be of benefit to the church.

While these Charismatic tendencies might be a good development in the Last Church, it matters a great deal how the phenomenon is handled. Otherwise, what was initially a good thing, may prove to be disastrous.

---

[33] Mr Chibaka, Acting Reverend, Mchengautuwa, 24.11.2013.

[34] Int. Rev Joseph Sibale, Bishop Chitipa, Chitipa, 4.5.2013.

[35] Klaus Fiedler, "The Charismatic and Pentecostal Movements in Malawi in Cultural Perspectives," in *Religion in Malawi*, 1999, pp. 28-38; Klaus Fiedler, *Conflicted Power in Malawian Christianity: Essays Missionary and Evangelical from Malawi*, Mzuni Press, 2015, pp. 322-349.

As the situation stands there is already a threat of a "split" hanging in the air, especially with the Mzuzu/Chitipa born-again factions. However, looking at it critically, this faction does not intend to leave the church as it is the case with Charismatic movements in some churches.[36] This means the leaders can properly channel and direct the existence of this movement in the church, thereby maintaining the unity of the church. At the same time, this also calls for the born-again faction to wisely and responsibly handle the issue. What is happening now in the Last Church is not a peculiar case. It is a well-known fact that the "Charismatic movement has remained within the Catholic Church, within the Anglican Church, and within the CCAP."[37]

Teaching/Preaching in the Last Church of God and His Christ International

I observed the preaching at Mchengautuwa congregation for four consecutive weeks trying to find out whether at all the Charismatic tendencies have infiltrated even the teaching or the gospel message during the services. Apart from Mchengautuwa I also attended a few worship services at Chibavi congregation and at Chitipa *boma*. However, I will just present the message as observed at Mchengautuwa and try to incorporate the ones at Chibavi and Chitipa in my interpretation. My interest was ignited when I realized that usually the message(s) in the "traditional" Last Church services revolve around rebuking people's sins and calling them to repentance. Many times, they do not go beyond these two themes. The question is, have the Charismatic tendencies influenced the message in the Last Church? And if so, to what extent?

First Preaching

On this particular Sunday, the one preaching was the acting Rev Chibaka and he preached from John 3:1-7 about Nicodemus and his theme was Jesus and Nicodemus. The reading was in Tumbuka and the preacher read the passage himself. The following was his message.

---

[36] Ibid. 1999.
[37] Ibid.

Nicodemus wanted friendship with Jesus and was told to be born again. Ask your neighbour, are you born of water and the spirit? (Members asked each other). Congregation, people disappoint, but Jesus does not. Nicodemus was a worshipper, but he lacked Jesus. Mary, the mother of Jesus, was like an envelope, but what was needed was the letter. Her pregnancy was like a stamp showing that inside was a letter (Jesus). Therefore, today there is no need for *tikuoneni Maria* (behold the holy mother Mary). Likewise, if you go to welcome visitors at the bus depot you wait for the bus, but it is visitors that you welcome. In the same way, Mary is the good mother, but it is Jesus that we need. If you have Jesus, you have a very precious thing, even if others fight against you, they will not overcome you. So, stand with Jesus, and you will not stop praying. But if you trust in men they will disappoint you and you will even stop coming to church. Nicodemus wanted to make friendship with Jesus, but people today have filled born again churches in order to be rich, but we want to preach Jesus.

You can heal the sick, cast out demons, but it does not always mean that it is God at work, even the devil can do that. Shadrach, Meshach and Abednego refused to worship idols and were thrown in the fire. But when they were checked later they found four people instead of three. The fourth one looked like the son of God. If you have Jesus, even if you are thrown into the fire, beaten or insulted, you have a big thing (here he gave his own testimony). When I started a church in my village, I was tested. People would say I was young and will not go far with it. One night a bright light appeared in my house, so I started reading my Bible and praying as I recited Psalm 23. Suddenly an old woman said "are you praying" and she pleaded to be let out. I didn't know how she had got inside in the first place. Therefore, we need to be filled with the Holy Ghost and be born again. Lastly, we don't have to pray in body but rather in spirit. Amen.[38]

At the end of the service the pastor asked those who wanted to be born again and to be led by the Holy Spirit to raise up their hands. No one did. He explained to the members that to be born again does not mean to speak in tongues or crying, but rather to receive Jesus in their hearts. Still, nobody raised their hand. The programme continued.

Second Preaching

The preacher on this Sunday was again Mr Chibaka, and his message was from Matthew 26:41 ["Watch and pray. Then you won't fall into sin when you are tempted. The spirit is willing. But the body is weak"]. He started with a question to the audience. What does it mean to keep watch? Some answered to be clever while some said it is to be prepared. He then continued with the message:

> Tell your neighbour we should begin together, don't slumber. When Jesus was walking with the disciples he told them to keep watch and pray. But he found them asleep. The bodies of the disciples of Jesus were weak. The physical body wants good cabbage, bread, prostitution, lies, insults etc. Brethren, what I want to say is that you and me want to go to Jesus, but the devil comes. You walk with Jesus, but if he is not rooted in you the devil also stays close to you. The devil comes with his demons. The demons cannot do evil by themselves, so they use people. But God wants us to have the shield of Jesus, to protect us so that the devil should not use us. If you have Jesus you have a very precious thing. If you have a child and you put charms on his neck, when the devil comes he goes straight to the child, because it is like an aerial. But if the evil one comes to Mavuto's house and find the fire of the Holy Ghost, he/she will pass with great speed because of fear of being burned.

---

[38] Mr Chibaka, Acting Reverend, Mchengautuwa, 27.10.2013.

> So, Jesus told his disciples to keep watch. If the devil wants to destroy the pastor he does not come directly, he goes to one woman and she comes and says "pastor you impress me very much, only that I married early." If the pastor does not have Jesus, he will reply "but some men ill-treat beautiful wives, come tomorrow afternoon I am free." The devil blinds a person. We had friends we used to worship together in Last Church but they are tired. But Jesus is coming. You pray and at the same time you insult others. Even up to now you still mix God? You are still doing prostitution, witchcraft, telling lies etc. We are quick to point out the sins in others, but we are blind to our own sins. We should walk with Jesus at all times. Amen.[39]

Third Preaching

The preacher on this day was church elder Master Banda. He preached from Job 13:4 ["But you spread lies about me and take away my good name. If you are trying to heal me, you aren't very good doctors."] Mr Banda did not give a theme for the day, but his message was as follows:

> Firstly, God has decided that his word should be preached through me. It's not me preaching, but God. When Job was suffering, his spirit was not sick. If we can be like him then we are rich. If you are suffering for example, you don't have food, but you have Jesus then you are rich. In the past, the children of Israel were told to fast for forty days, they were eating the word of God only.[40] You can have everything on earth but have nothing in heaven. The passage we have read, it is you who tell lies, but God sees the truth. We don't know the hearts of people. People should come to church for Jesus and not following someone because you will be disappointed. You can only be good doctors if you

---

[39] Mr Chibaka, Acting Reverend, Mchengautuwa, 3.11.2013.

[40] I can find no reference to this in the Bible.

believe in Jesus. The word continues that you should have kept quiet and you would have been wise. For instance, I met a man one day who wanted to make me join his church. I asked him, do you pray to Mary, Mohammed or Jesus? The man was defeated. We should walk in the way of Jesus. Do not follow your pastor, secretary or preacher. We should pray to God who created all of us. If God says do not do this, don't do it. In this earth there are two, God and the devil. When God says, do not curse, the devil says the opposite. When we come to church we should have one mind. When the pastor says every Sunday that we should stop our sins we really repent, but the moment we go home we do contrary to the word of God. Amen.[41]

Observations on the Preaching

No one would deny the changed nature of worship in those congregations that manifest the Charismatic tendencies. The services of those who manifest the Charismatic tendencies are characterized by the singing of choruses, exclamations of Hallelujah's, testimony time etc, one may be led to assume that their message should also lean more to popular Charismatic themes like the "prosperity gospel." Yet, a look at the messages above and even messages at Chitipa and Chibavi shows that the central message was the need for repentance and salvation in Jesus Christ. The audience was encouraged to give up their sins and live for Christ. Sins like witchcraft, lies, prostitution, gossip etc. were pointed out and denounced. In fact, in one of the services at Chitipa the preacher's message emphasized against "storing of wealth on earth." He called the members to be heavenly minded since worldly wealth will pass away.[42] Another point of emphasis in the message was the role of the power of the Holy Spirit in assisting the believer to overcome sin, the devil and evil. These are recurrent themes in the "traditional" Last Church services. I did not hear any message to do with prosperity of the

---

[41] Mr Banda, church elder, Mchengautuwa, 10.10.2013.
[42] Mr Nyondo, preacher, Chitipa, 6.5.2013.

members at least in the services I observed. This does not mean that the members do not believe in the power of God to make them rich, but the approach to this teaching is quite different from the Charismatics. Again, at the end of the various services, when people were called to be prayed for, material wealth and employment opportunities were not the prayer themes requested, but rather family issues and health problems. In this case, the tendencies leaned more to the Pentecostal side.

The question remains, how do we explain this situation whereby the worship is characterized by Charismatic manifestations, while the message during the worship remains unchanged? It should be mentioned that while the Last Church is now found in towns like Mzuzu, the majority of its members remain the "poor" and are not very educated. Thus "if preachers were to emphasize the "prosperity gospel," the message would be ill suited and would not even make sense to many. The preachers try to deliver a message which people can easily understand. As it is observed by others, the prosperity message fits well in an urban, well-to-do middle-class context.[43]

Other Observations with regard to the Sunday Message in the Last Church of God

A look at the messages in the Last Church shows that there was an attempt oftentimes by preachers to expound the biblical texts read. However, in agreement with Mijoga's observations, the texts were often not explained in a systematic manner with regard to their historical, political or socio-cultural setting.[44] There was, however, an exception to this at Chibavi congregation, where the pastor gave a socio-cultural

---

[43] Klaus Fiedler, "The Charismatic and Pentecostal Movements in Malawi in Cultural Perspectives," in *Religion in Malawi*, 1999, pp. 28-38; Klaus Fiedler, *Conflicted Power in Malawian Christianity: Essays Missionary and Evangelical from Malawi*, Mzuni Press, 2015, pp. 322-349.

[44] Hilary Mijoga, *Separate but Same Gospel: Preaching in African Instituted Churches in Southern Malawi*, Blantyre: CLAIM-Kachere, 2000, p. 17.

setting to the story of the healing of the ten lepers.[45] But this was a rare occurrence. The preachers also tried to apply the message of the passage read to people's life experiences. Thus, for instance, we saw Chibaka telling the members at Mchengautuwa that like Nicodemus they needed to be born again.

However, I found a difference when it came to the preacher's preference as far as choosing of biblical texts is concerned. Mijoga had observed that there is a preference for narrative texts by AIC preachers. On the contrary, I discovered that often preachers in the Last Church selected a few "separate" individual biblical texts, not even from narrative stories or texts. I do not have an explanation for their choice, but that is what I observed.

In my opinion members at Mchengautuwa church and also at other congregations of Last Church I had observed are likely to have problems as far as spiritual growth is concerned. Their preaching seems not to go beyond getting saved. But the thing is after getting saved, what next? That is where the church has to come in and teach its members how to grow spiritually and not remain babes in spirit. I believe that this is also a cause for the conflicts going on in the church today. Spiritual maturity determines the way a person responds to issues, challenges and problems that arise in their life or in the church.

The other point concerns Bible interpretation. In some cases, the preacher did not give a "correct" account and a fair interpretation. For instance, to say that "the children of Israel were told to fast for forty days," there is no such story in the Bible. And to tell the people that even if you do not have food, but if you have Jesus, then you are rich. As much as there could be truth in this, I wonder whether this would make sense to someone in that situation.[46]

---

[45] The Pastor explained to the members how the lepers were treated at the time of Jesus by isolation and he also explained why Jesus instructed them to go and present themselves to the priest.

[46] The preacher could also have checked his statement against James 2:15-16 "If a brother or sister is naked and destitute of daily food, and one of you says to

Sometimes the preacher would wander away from the passage before he came to it again. For instance, when preaching on Nicodemus, the preacher brought in some issues that were not related to the topic, like the issue of Mary, the mother of Jesus. And I think by the time he came to the conclusion, he (and probably the audience as well) had forgotten his own theme which was Jesus and Nicodemus.

I think their preaching would be enriched if the leaders would make an effort to draw a preaching programme in advance and come up with themes or topics that they think would be of great help to their members. They could also leave room sometimes for preachers to come up with their own themes. They can also consider special times or seasons like Christmas, Easter etc as they come up with a preaching programme as other churches do. This will serve as a guide to the preacher and the person can prepare well for the day.

It seems that some find problems in finding the appropriate passage and theme for the preaching. For instance, Mr Banda did not give the theme and it was not very clear what he wanted to teach from the passage he had chosen (Job 13:4). Mr Chibaka did not put his message in its context on keeping watch (Matt. 26:41). Jesus said those words while he was in Gethsemane on the night of his arrest, but throughout the preaching nothing concerning that was mentioned. There is need to be organizing inside training where members themselves, especially those who take preaching roles, can share how best one can preach. They can even invite others to come and speak to them on the matter.

The members should also be encouraged to own Bibles and read them frequently. If they are to grow spiritually, they have to make individual effort. This will not only do them good, but even the whole church will benefit. To have a quality church requires quality members.

These observations show that even though Mchengautuwa church differs in many ways from churches in Nkhatabay like Munkhokwe, the messages in their preaching are similar (the message still remains typical of the message in traditional Last Church). For those churches also emphasize

---

them, 'Depart in peace, be warmed and filled,' but you do not give them the things which are needed for the body, what does it profit?"

salvation, but also the challenges they encounter in preaching are the same in both congregations. While the Pentecostal/Charismatic tendencies have infiltrated some congregations of the Last Church, they are yet to touch and transform the message preached in those congregations.

Chapter 9: Becoming Mainline Again

In addition, the changes that have taken place in the Last Church of God, especially to do with polygamy and the Pentecostal/Charismatic tendencies, there seem to be other changes in quite a different direction. The Last Church seems to be in a position where on one side it is moving forward in terms of "adopting" other practices; at the same time, it is moving backward not in its' spirituality, but to the practices which it denied in the beginning. The Last Church began as a "sect" denying some of the things within the mainline tradition. Thus, by saying "becoming mainline again" I simply intend to emphasize that the Last Church actually sprouted from the mainline tradition.[1] The founder, Jordan Msumba, while he had tried a "break up" with the main line in terms of preaching, dressing, polygamy etc, the church seems to be going back to the very same ways it came from. This move seems to have started way back with Msumba himself and has been gradually working itself out over the years and continues up to now. The move toward becoming mainline is mainly the result of the church's desire to be like other churches.

There seem to be several factors responsible for this process of change in the church. Among them is modernity. The young generation wants to move with time and some old traditions seem to be less appealing to them. Younger people want a church that is lively. More importantly, these people interact with others from other denominations in the community and naturally they do not want to be associated with a church that looks so "backward" in society. As a result, the Last Church began to change to accommodate itself to the changing culture to make it more compatible with the surrounding culture.[2]

Apart from that, there are also some members in the church who feel that some of the practices in the church are not biblical truths and these would like to reform the church from within. By doing that in some ways

---

[1] Ronald L. Johnstone, *Religion in Society: A Sociology of Religion*, Upper Saddle River: Roberts, 2004, p. 89.
[2] Ibid. p. 97.

they are going back to mainline characteristics. For instance, these members argue that beer drinking and polygamy are not biblical.[3] But, of course, this is debatable. Nevertheless, this is their argument.

It also appears that there is a need in some members to be just like the other churches. The traditional practices in the Last Church made them in a way to be separated from the other churches. The need to belong is also contributing towards becoming mainline again.

There is also a realization in the church that for a long time many people outside the church did not take the church seriously because of certain practices. For instance, in the past when there was a conference, members would actually bring pots of beer to the church. During break time members (who drink beer) would sit round the pots and drink. Sometimes even the preachers would drink to the extent that they failed to preach on the pulpit. This led to the outsiders in Chitipa and Karonga calling the church "church la *mulyafyosa*" (the church which eats/takes anything).[4] Therefore, some members would like to change the face of the church so that it should be regarded like other churches. Here one may agree with the sociologists' theory of social deprivation. Since its beginnings, the Last Church has oftentimes been deprived of prestige, social status and opportunity for participation in various activities by other churches.[5] For a long time they would not even be invited to participate in choir festivals organized by mainline churches. This in a way seems to have forced the members to do something about the situation. There are a number of fields where the African Last Church is becoming mainline again.

Doctrine

When Msumba established the Last Church he only added certain practices, but the doctrine remained the same as that of mainline churches. The Last Church of God, just like mainline churches, is less

---

[3] Int. Rev Chiuli Manda, retired Area Bishop, Munkhokwe, 10.10.2012.
[4] Int. Rev Joseph Sibale, Bishop Chitipa, Chitipa, 5.4.2013.
[5] Ronald L. Johnstone, *Religion in Society: A Sociology of Religion*, Upper Saddle River, New Jersey: Roberts, 2004, p. 92.

focused on doctrine and does not emphasize much soliciting new members. Again, like mainline Protestants, the church is less concerned with personal conversion.[6] The Last Church does organize conferences, but their main target are the members and not necessarily to convert unsaved people outside the church. So, it can be argued that from the beginning the church started manifesting characteristics of the mainline tradition.

Clerical Dressing

From the beginning of the church until the early 1960s the Last Church had adopted the Zionist way of dressing during worship. The pastors' clerical dressing used to comprise of a headgear (*vilundu*) and long robes (*mikhanjo*) and they used to carry a staff or rod. However, when Longwe became the General Principal in 1962, he initiated change to this type of dressing. The headgear and the rod were removed. However, Longwe did not manage to bring uniformity as far as the clerical dressing is concerned. Longwe observed that the former dressing was one of the contributing factors for many youths' reluctance to join the church.[7] At present there are six different clerical dressings. For instance, in Mzuzu the pastors' clerical dressing comprises of a black gown with a black ephod and white collar. In Karonga alone there are three uniforms. One is a white gown with a black ephod and a white collar. The other set comprises of a pink gown with a black ephod and white collar and the third one is a black gown with a sky-blue ephod and white collar. In Ntchisi it is a black gown sewn together with a white collar and no separate ephod. This change in regalia, especially the black gown and white collar, is a move towards mainline, specifically CCAP. Different from the Last Church, the Zionist Churches have maintained the traditional garb and have largely lost the appeal for the youth.[8]

---

[6] www.theopedia.com/mainline_church. 2.5.2013.

[7] Int. Rev Chiuli Manda, retired Bishop, Munkhokwe, 12.10.2012.

[8] Ulf Strohbehn, *The Zionist Churches in Malawi. History - Theology - Anthropology*, Mzuzu: Mzuni Press, 2016.

Number of Preachers during the Service

The Sunday services in the Last Church, typical of many AICs like Zionists, were characterized among other things by three preachers. The significance of the three preachers is not known. Many congregations are still continuing with this tradition. However, some congregations in Chitipa and Mzuzu have only one preacher during the service. These argue that having three preachers within a single service causes confusion as each one of them preaches a different message. This is indeed true. In many cases the preachers are not told in advance to prepare for the service. The argument being that Christians are soldiers, hence they are supposed to be ready at all times,[9] and sermon preparation is seen as a human meddling in divine affairs.[10] They believe that the Spirit's inspiration is a sudden and unforeseeable event, hence there is no need for sermon preparation.[11] However, during the service, even if the chairperson may give the theme, the ones who have been taken unawares to preach would each preach the message or from the passage that they are well familiar with. The lack of any justification for having three preachers during the service seems to indicate that Msumba copied a Zionist practice. This is probably the reason why some are going back to a single preacher in a service.

Women's Guild (Umanyano)

Many churches have got well established organizations within the churches, and the most common one is the women's guild. This is called by different names depending on the church one belongs to, such as *Umanyano, Mvano, Chigwirizano* etc. In the Last Church, the women's guild was adopted in the 1970s. During one of the synod meetings at Msondozi pastors were asked to facilitate the starting of this guild in their respective congregations. In certain congregations, the guild was started much earlier than in others, depending on the pastor.

---

[9] Int. Rev Kaundama, Kamsita, 10.9.2010.

[10] Ulf Strohbehn, *The Zionist Churches in Malawi. History - Theology – Anthropology*, Mzuzu: Mzuni Press, 2016, p. 159.

[11] Ibid.

In the Last Church, this guild is referred to as *Amayi Achikondi*. However, in some places they also call themselves *Umanyano*. Their uniform is even similar to that of *Umanyano* of CCAP, only with a different belt. The *Amayi Achikondi* is not as organized as, for instance, the *Umanyano* in Livingstonia Synod in terms of objectives etc. The *Amayi Achikondi* do not have written objectives. However, they are involved in similar activities like the *Umanyano* such as sick visitation, teaching each other on home management, Bible sharing, choir, etc. With the direction the church is moving now, the *Amayi Achikondi* may be reshaped with clear written objectives and improved organization. However, this may take some time.

Pastoral Training

From the beginning the Last Church has been known as one of those churches which do not believe in the necessity and usefulness of theological training for its pastors. They argued that as long as a person is able to read and understand the Bible, then he can preach the word to others. Apart from that, the Holy Spirit is there as a faithful teacher, hence no Bible school can teach better than the Holy Spirit. There is a man in Mpherembe nicknamed *Mtchayabwekwa* (one who beats anyhow); he just demands anyone to read any passage or verse and he interprets it. He argues that the Bible was meant for people, therefore anyone can interpret it.[12]

It should be mentioned that the church did not, however, forbid anyone who had the desire and means to go for such training to do so. The issue in question was one of the several topics that were discussed and included in the revised church constitution (2008). The constitution, however, does not clearly state how these pastors are to acquire such education and who will be responsible for the costs of such training.

With time, there has risen a group of people in the church who believe in the importance of theological education for the leadership of the church. Some of these have taken individual initiatives to go for leadership training. Such people include Rev Mwambughi and Rev Mwakalenga

---

[12] Int. Rev Mwakalenga, Chibavi, 12.10.2013.

(Chibavi). These two have undergone leadership training offered by the Christian Missionary Foundation. This is a Nigeria based organization and they did the training for one year. The courses they covered included: discipleship, wealth creation, the person and ministry of the Holy Spirit, evangelism and spiritual warfare and victorious Christian living.[13]

The two pastors also did a six months' course under the International Leadership Institute. This is an American based institution and it targets leaders from various churches. Once these have been taught, they are expected to go and teach fellow leaders in their churches. Rev Mwambughi and Rev Mwakalenga are currently involved in the teaching of fellow pastors within Mzuzu at Chibavi congregation. However, Rev Mwambughi is also currently doing another leadership course, together with Rev Sibale of Chitipa.[14]

The beginning of these leadership trainings may look small at the moment, but in the long run they may bring a significant transformation to the church. However, this may take years, since at the moment it is only those who can afford to pay for the courses that are engaging in such education. Another challenge is that many congregations are in the rural areas and we do not know whether pastors there see the need for such training and again whether they have the financial resources needed.

Despite these individual attempts, I think that the church is very far from achieving the pastoral training that is stipulated in their new constitution. I believe they wanted their pastoral training to be like the ones done by the mainline churches. There people are trained before actually becoming pastors, and the church is usually responsible for their training costs. To achieve such pastoral training the Last Church needs to really work hard from the grass root congregations. Nevertheless, the beginning is vital.

---

[13] Int. Rev Mwakalenga, Chibavi, 12.10.2013.
[14] Ibid. 12.10.2013.

Polygamy

For a church that was known as *tchalitchi la mitala* (church for polygamous people) to come to a point of forbidding the very basis of the church is no small thing. This has met opposition in some areas but to a large extent many members have accepted the church's stand on the issue. Jordan Msumba resisted the mainline churches' stand on polygamy as he thought that it was discriminating and left many people outside the kingdom of God. While Msumba tried to inculturate the gospel into the traditional culture, todays' generation wants to inculturate it into modern society. The current position of the church on polygamy is thus going mainline again. This prohibition will be in a way liberating to the majority of women who do not like the practice, but it will leave polygamous women and men again without a church.

Dedication of a Church

Another area where the church seems to be going mainline is in the area of dedicating a newly built church. It has been a tradition for the mainline churches to set apart in a special way a new church building before its official usage. These churches do also dedicate other things such as new uniforms, chairs etc. The Last Church has adopted this tradition and shaped it to their taste.

It should be mentioned that the process of "becoming mainline again" is also taking place in the Reformed Last Church, only that it is happening more slowly. The Reformed Last Church has not so far tackled the issues of pastoral training and retirement age of pastors. They are still continuing the practice of having three preachers during the service and acceptance of beer drinking. I think the Reformed Last has not yet sat down to revise their constitution in a manner the African Last has. Even the prohibition of polygamy seems to have been just orally communicated without any written reference point. This I attribute to their leadership management. Nevertheless, I believe with time they are slowly moving in the same direction as the African Last.

From the above observations, it is clear that in various ways the Last Church is a case of an "independent church" becoming "mainline" again.

The Last Church has undergone changes in the direction of mainline churches thus rejecting its origin. The church may not realize that the changes taking place are moving towards becoming mainline again, but that is actually what is happening. The changes are not mainly dealing with any biblical interpretation but rather have to do with sociological considerations. This is seen in the way the church stands in relation to other churches in the society. When the church repudiated some of the mainline traditions and incorporated some of its own practices, it separated itself in a way from the other churches. Not only that, some of the practices it adopted made the mainline churches look down upon the Last Church. This made the Last Church socially deprived of its prestige, social status and participation with other churches as it made them distinct. This has forced the new generation to keep on changing some of the practices hence moving toward mainline characteristics in an attempt to be seen on the same level as the other churches and in the process losing their identity. Thus, in this area the Last Church seems to be driven more by a desire to belong as opposed to seeking for a deeper spiritual fulfillment. There is, however, a danger in trying to be like the others as people may be taken up by the outward practices while neglecting the true worship which God desires.

The process of becoming mainline again like the Pentecostal/Charismatic tendencies in the church has a bearing on the church. The church has lost its original salt and has become one among the others. What remains for them now is history and structure, not necessarily their theology or teaching. With these changes taking place years from now the Last Church might become completely different from what the founder started. More importantly, if they do not clearly define how they are to uniquely worship as Last Church, then the church will be easily tossed around by any wind of change or teaching. The Charismatic/Pentecostal tendencies in the church are a case in point as they have already produced a threat to splits.

Bibliography

Oral Sources

Amayi Achikondi choir, Mchengautuwa Last Church of God, 24.11.2013.
Amayi Achikondi choir, Munkhokwe Last Church of God, 24.9.2011.
Banda, Mama, church member, Munkhokwe, 19.9.2012.
Banda, Master, church elder, Mchengautuwa, 10.10.2013; 24.11.2013.
Banda, Mr, church member, Mchengautuwa, 24.11.2013.
Banda, Rev Mboya, Munkhokwe, 12.7.2010.
Banda, Wales, Bandawe, 10.5.2012.
Buwani, Mama NyaManda, Chairperson *Amayi Achikondi*, Munkhokwe, 12.7.2010.
Bvula, Katsache, General Chairman, Kasamba, 26.28.2012.
Chibaka, Acting Reverend, Mchengautuwa Last Church, 24.10.2013; 24.11.2013; 27.11.2013.
Chimaliro, Mrs, Bandawe, 12.5.2012.
Chimbaza, Gogo, retired Reverend, Munkhokwe, 8.7.2012; 16.7.2012.
Chimuliu, Rev, Area Bishop, Msondozi, 10.10.2010; 20.10.2010.
Chirwa, Chimuliwu, Area Bishop, Msondozi, 20.10.2011.
Chirwa, Fanny, Chairperson *Amayi Achikondi*, Munkhokwe, 16.9.2010; 25.10.2010.
Youth Choir, Last Church, Mchengautuwa, 24.11.2013.
Dube, Mrs, former Last Church member, Chitipa, 5.4.2013.
Kambalila, Mr, preacher, Mchengautuwa, 24.11.2013.
Kaundama, Mrs Rev, Kamsita, 12.10.2012.
Kaundama, Rev, Kamsita, 10.9.2010; 8.10.2010; 9.10.2012; 10.10.2010; 16.2.2011; 12.7.2011, 10.9.2011; 10.8.2012; 24.9.2012; 9.10.12; 12.10.2012.
Lola, Mama, member Last Church, Mchengautuwa, 24.11.2013.
Mahemani, Wales, youth, Munkhokwe, 13.7.2010.
Manda, Chiuli, retired Bishop, Kamsita, 17.9.2011; 25.10.2012.
Manda, Chiuli, retired Area Bishop, Munkhokwe, 25.10.2010; 19.2.2012; 30.7.2012; 31.8.2012; 17.9.2012; 10.10.2012; 12.10.2012.
Manda, Chiuli, retired Area Bishop, Kamsita, 31.8.2012; 19.2.2012.
Masinda, Mrs, Kazando, 6.11.2011.
Masinda, O, General Principal, Kazando, 21.9.2011; 15.4.2012; 28.8.2012; 6.11.2012;
Matola, Rev, Katoto Last Church, Chintheche, 27.10.2010.

Mughogho, Mrs, Wife to CCAP Rev K.T.R. Mughogho, Bandawe, 19.2.2012; 3.5.2012.
Mvula, G.D., church member, Maulawo, 28.8.2012.
Mwakalenga, pastor, Chibavi Last Church of God, Chibavi, 4.4.2013, 12.10.2013; 5.11.2013.
Mwambughi, Bishop, Chibavi, 15.10.2013.
NyaBanda, Mama, church member, Mchengautuwa, 24.11.2013.
NyaChilausipa, Mama, Bandawe, 7.5.2012.
NyaLwanda, Mama, church member, Mchengautuwa, 24.11.2013.
NyaMunyirenda, Mama, Bandawe, 7.5.2012.
NyaZgambo, Mama, Bandawe, 7.5.2012.
Nyondo, Mama, church member, Msondozi, 6.4.2013.
Nyondo, Mama, church member, Chitipa *bom*a, 6.4.2013.
Nyondo, Mr, preacher, Chitipa, 6.5.2013.
Phiri, Chikosera, Archbishop, Msondozi, 10.10.2011; 4.4.2012.
Phiri, Mugubu, General Secretary, Kazando, 11.3.2011.
Phiri, Chikosera, Archbishop, Msondozi, 24.6.2011; 1.1.2012; 4.4.2012; 12.10.2012.
Phiri, Mugubu, Church's General Secretary, Kazando, 11.3.2011.
Sibale, Joseph, Bishop, Chitipa boma, 5.4.2013; 6.4.2013; 4.5.2013.
Youth Choir, Last Church, Kazando, Munkhokwe, 19.9.2012.
Youth Choir, Mchengautuwa, 24.11.2013.

Unpublished Sources

Chikometsa, Nelson, Death Rites in African Instituted Churches: The Watchman Healing Mission and the Restoration Church, BA, University of Malawi, 2005.
Kamwela, Bonnet, Mbulu as a Pastoral Problem in Mzimba in the Northern Malawi, BA, University of Livingstonia, 2013.
Kapito, Lucy, Women in African Instituted Churches in Ndirande and Mbayani Townships, Blantyre City, BA, University of Malawi, 1995.
Lwinga, Godwins, Gospel and Culture in Malawi: A Missiological Examination of the Relationship between Ndali Traditions and Christianity (1900-2012), MA, Mzuzu University, 2013.
Malanga, Oliver, Women's Participation and Contributions to Pentecostal Movements: A Case Study of Four Congregations, BA, Mzuzu University, 2012.
Manda, J.D., Independency in Nkhatabay District Area from about 1930 to Current Times, BA, University of Malawi, 1970.

Mlenga, Moses, A Critical Examination of the Issue of Polygamy in the Synod of Livingstonia: Biblical, Moral and Missiological Implications, PhD. Mzuzu University, 2013.

Mlenga, Moses, History of Livingstonia Mission: 50 Years of Post-Missionary Leadership 1958-2008, PhD Module, Mzuzu University, 2009.

Mphande, Chanju, The History of Independent Churches in Malawi: An Investigation of the Last Church of God and His Christ among the Tonga of the Lakeshore (Nkhatabay), BA, Mzuzu University, 2009.

Mwale, Jemiter, The Establishment and Development of African Abraham Church in Malawi (1929-2000): A Case Study on the Major Changes in Doctrines and their Impact (Chamchere Mission Station), BA, University of Malawi, 2000.

Mwangupili, Ndongolera, Grassroots Perception of the Trinity: The Case of the Catholic Church and the Last Church of God in Champhira, MA module, Mzuzu University, 2009.

Mwase, Towera, The Marriage Instructions for Girls and Women in Mzuzu Churches, MA, Theology and Religious Studies, Mzuzu University, 2012.

Sikanda, B.J.K, The Last Church of God and His Christ in Karonga: An Historical Analysis of its Development, History Seminar Paper, Chancellor College, 1975-1976.

Sitima, L.M., The Last Church of God and His Christ in Dowa District: Its Impact on the People, BA, University of Malawi, 2007.

Letters, Minutes

Acting Chief Secretary to the Government to The Chief Secretary to the State (Nyasaland), 22.9.1939.

Church minutes by the Last Church of God and His Christ International (Msondozi), nd.

Letter from the Synod held in Mzimba to Bishop Mwambughi, 11.8.2011.

Minutes concerning wrangles over the ownership of the Last Church of God and His Christ International held in the office of the District Commissioner (Chitipa), 17.7.12.

Minutes of Msondozi Headquarters, nd.

Minutes Reformed Last Church of God Kazando Synod, 19.10, nd.

Pastors Last Church of God Mzuzu Congregations to The Archbishop S.C.K. Chikosera Phiri, The Senior Bishop, The Chairman of Synod Chande, The General Secretary Y.P. Longwe, 23.8.2011.

Rev Masinda, P.G.O. to Wilson and Morgan (Legal Practitioners), 4.11.1992.

The Provincial Commissioner (Northern Province) to The Chief Secretary of the State, 18.10.1927.

The Provincial Commissioner (Northern Province) to The Chief Secretary to the State (Nyasaland), 22.9.1939.

The Secretary to the Senior Bishop (Katonje Makwakwa) to The Christians in Chitipa, 12.5.2012.

Published Sources

Anderson, Allan, *An Introduction to Pentecostalism: Global Charismatic Christianity*, Cambridge University Press, 2004.

Anderson, Allan, *Bazalwane: African Pentecostals in South Africa*, Pretoria: UNISA, 1992.

Banda, Godfrey A. and Peter G. Forster, "The Last Church of God and His Christ" in *Journal of Religion in Africa*, vol. 29, 1999.

Banda, Rachel NyaGondwe [Fiedler], *Women of Bible and Culture: Baptist Convention Women in Southern Malawi,* Zomba: Kachere, 2005.

Barret, David (ed), *World Christian Encyclopaedia: A Comparative Survey of Churches and Religions in the Modern World A.D. 1900-2000*, Nairobi, New York, Oxford; Oxford University Press, 1982.

Breugel, J.W.M. van, *Chewa Traditional Religion*, Blantyre: CLAIM-Kachere, 2001.

Chakanza, J.C., *African Ancestors' Religion – Chipembedzo cha Makolo Achikuda*, Zomba: Kachere, 2004.

Chakanza, J.C., *Voices of Preachers in Protest. The Ministry of Two Malawian Prophets: Elliot Kamwana and Wilfred Gudu*, Blantyre: CLAIM-Kachere, 1998.

Englund, Harri, "Christian Independency and Global Membership: Pentecostal Extraversions in Malawi," *Journal of Religion in Africa*, vol. 33, 2003, pp. 83-111.

Fiedler, Klaus, "For the Sake of Christian Marriage, Abolish Church Weddings" in: James L. Cox (ed), *Rites of Passage in Contemporary Africa. Interaction Between Christian and African Traditional Religions*, Cardiff University Press, 1998, pp. 46-60.

Fiedler, Klaus, "For the Sake of Christian Marriage, Abolish Church Weddings," in: *Religion in Malawi*, 1995, pp. 22-27; revised in: Klaus Fiedler, *Conflicted Power in Malawian Christianity: Essays Missionary and Evangelical from Malawi*, Mzuni Press, 2015, pp. 6-21.

Fiedler, Klaus, ''The Charismatic and Pentecostal Movements in Malawi in Cultural Perspective'' in *Religion in Malawi,* 1999, pp. 28-38; revised in: Klaus Fiedler, *Conflicted Power in Malawian Christianity: Essays Missionary and Evangelical from Malawi*, Mzuni Press, 2015, pp. 322-349.

Fiedler, Klaus, *Conflicted Power in Malawian Christianity: Essays Missionary and Evangelical from Malawi*, Mzuzu: Mzuni Press, 2015.

Hara, Handwell Yotamu, *Reformed Soteriology and the Malawian Context*, Zomba: Kachere, 2008.

Ifemeje, Charles Okechekwu, *African Independent Churches: A Pastoral Challenge to the Church in Igboland-Nigeria*, Aachen: Shaker, 2002.

Johnstone, Ronald L., *Religion in Society: A Sociology of Religion*, Upper Saddle River, New Jersey: Roberts, 2004.

Kalu, Ogbu U. (ed), *African Christianity: An African Story*, Trenton: African World Press, 2007.

Kitschoff, M.C. (ed), *African Independent Churches Today. Kaleidoscope of Afro-Christianity*, Lewiston: Edwin Mellen, 1996.

Langworthy, Harry, *"Africa for the African." The Life of Joseph Booth*, Blantyre: CLAIM-Kachere, 1996.

Makondesa, Patrick, *The Church History of Providence Industrial Mission*, Zomba: Kachere, 2006.

Meyer, Birgit, "Christianity in Africa: From African Independent to Pentecostal Charismatic Churches, in *Annual Review of Anthropology*," vol. 33, 2004.

Mijoga, Hilary, *Separate but Same Gospel: Preaching in African Instituted Churches in Southern Malawi*, Blantyre: CLAIM-Kachere, 2000.

Mlenga, Moses, *Polygamy in Northern Malawi. A Christian Reassessment*, Mzuzu: Mzuni Press, 2016.

Munyenyembe, Rhodian, *Christianity and Socio-Cultural Issues: The Charismatic Movement and Contextualization in Malawi*, Zomba: Kachere; Mzuzu: Mzuni Press, 2011.

Mwale, P.V.J., "The Last Church of God at Nkhunga" in J.C. Chakanza, *An Annotated List of Independent Churches in Malawi 1900-1981*, Zomba: TRS, 1981.

Mwasi, Yesaya Zerenji, *Essential and Paramount Reasons for Working Independently*, Blantyre: CLAIM-Kachere, 1999.

Paas, Steven, *The Faith Moves South: A History of the Church in Africa*, Zomba: Kachere, 2006.

Pauw, Martin, "African Independent Churches in Malawi: Background and Historical Development" in M.C Kitschoff (ed), *African Independent Churches. Today. Kaleidoscope of Afro-Christianity,* Lewiston: Edwin Mellen, 1996.

Phiri, Isabel Apawo, "African Traditional Women and Ecofeminism: The Role of Women at Chisumphi Cult in Preserving the Environment," *Religion in Malawi*, 1996, pp. 14-19.

Pretorius, H.L, *Historiography and Historical Sources regarding African Indigenous Churches in South Africa: Writing Indigenous Church History,* Lewiston: Edwin Mellen, 1995.

Ranger, Terence O., *The African Churches of Tanzania*, Historical Association of Tanzania, Paper No. 5, Dar es Salaam: East Africa Publishing House, 1972.

Strohbehn, Ulf, *The Zionist Churches in Malawi: History - Theology – Anthropology*, Mzuzu: Mzuni Press, 2016.

Sundkler, Bengt, *Bantu Prophets in South Africa*, Cambridge: James Clarke, 1948.

Uprichard, R.E.H., *What Presbyterians Believe*, Ahoghill: The Oaks, 2011.

Web Sources

Wikipedia: http://en.wikipedia.org/wiki/African_Initiated_Churches, 13.7.2013.
www.theopedia.com/mainline_church.02/05/2013.

Index

African Abraham Church 78f, 89, 103, 119, 137f
African Independent Churches 7, 9-12, 15-18, 20-22, 24-26, 137, 176
African Indigenous Churches 9, 11-14, 16f, 19, 22
African National Church 29, 40, 45, 58, 66
Alalakazi 79, 81, 86, 101, 108, 110, 126f, 184
Amayi Achikondi 43, 80-82, 92, 97, 102, 108f, 112-117, 128-130, 144, 153, 156, 172f, 176-179, 181, 201
American Mission Church 11
Ana a Mulungu Church 22, 25
Banda, Rachel NyaGondwe [Fiedler] 87, 113f
Banda, Alexander 58
Banda, Frida 84
Banda, Isaac Mkhuta 7, 31
Banda, Joseph Mboya 84
Banda, Kananga 108
Banda, Kaphinya 57, 61-67, 69-73, 76, 94
Banda, Khumbo 31
Banda, Kubema 108
Banda, Master 191
Banda, Mboya 77, 79, 83f, 86f, 89-91, 93, 126
BaNgemela 30, 53
Barret, David 9, 13f
Beer drinking 38, 42, 89, 117, 122, 150f, 154f, 169, 198, 203
Beza, Bishop 71
Blantyre 16, 19, 22, 25, 28f, 50, 56, 58, 60, 76, 88, 94, 140, 193
Booth, Joseph 28f

Brotherhood of the Cross and Star 16
Buleya, Mrs 115f
Chande, Bishop 98, 107, 156, 158, 160
Charismatic 15f, 26f, 36, 86, 93, 127, 134, 137, 147-150, 166, 169-172, 184-188, 192f, 196f, 204
Chibaka, Mr 140-142, 146, 178, 180-183, 186-188, 190f, 194f
Chibanzi, Mr 51
Chibavi 52-54, 99, 105, 138-141, 150, 158, 165, 188, 192f, 201f
Chifira village 50
Chigawinga, Rev 50
Chigwiti 50
Chikhasu, Rev 55
Chilembwe, John 11, 19, 25, 40
Chilibwanji, Mr 51, 97, 115
Chilibwanji, Mrs 115
Chilowamatambe, village 55
Chimbizi, Gogo 70
Chimchele, Principal 55
Chimcheli, Rev 71
Chimuliu, Bishop 98, 105-107, 111, 121, 125
Chimwalira, Bishop 107
Chintheche 32f, 41, 74, 77, 98, 102-104, 118, 121f, 144
Chipangano 33f, 45f, 66, 108
Chipolopolo 66, 76
Chipuliko, Rev 11
Chirwa, Chimgogu 77, 89
Chirwa, Nkholozo 57
Chirwa, Timon 28
Chisonga, Mr 74
Chisumphi Cult 23
Chitete 150

Chitipa 49f, 53f, 60, 72, 75, 91, 99, 104-106, 110f, 117, 119, 129f, 135, 146, 149-151, 153, 156-166, 169f, 175f, 186-188, 192, 198, 200, 202

Chiwirira, principal 55

Chiwole 50

Chizi 50

Christian Catholic Apostolic Church 19

Church of the Ancestors 23

Daneel, Inus 24

Mlenga, Daniel 54

Dar es Salaam 59

Democratic Republic of Congo 21

Den Songaa 162

Dowa 50, 55f, 60, 65, 71-73, 76, 85, 141

Dowie, John Alexander 20, 49

Dube, Mrs 105

Durban 28

Dwambazi 50, 66, 107, 168

Ekwendeni 99, 138, 158

Elangeni 54, 65, 71, 99

Emanuel Church 45, 58

Enukweni 140f

Ethinzini 54

Ethiopian 10, 18-21, 25

Ethiopianism 10, 18, 25

Euthini 54, 65, 99, 161

Fiedler, Klaus 11, 15-17, 26, 49, 100, 130f, 169-171, 187, 193

Forster, Peter G. 27f, 30, 40-42, 44f, 52, 61, 95

Galileya 55

Gudu, Wilfred 16, 19, 22, 25

Gutamu, *Mama* 84

Herero Church 23

Holy Christian Church 140

Holy Spirit 24, 39, 85, 99, 149f, 153, 169, 185-187, 190, 192, 201f

Independent Bantu Churches 18

Jere, L.L. 42

Johannesburg 58f

Kachali, Agness 43

Kachere 10f, 13, 16, 19, 22f, 25, 27-29, 36, 45, 87f, 94, 113f, 134, 137, 149, 168, 193

Kaira, Mubeka 161

Kajiriwi 50

Kalowa 50, 57, 98

Kamanga, Sala 120

Kambalila, Mr 139

Kameme 53f, 99, 104, 146, 160-163, 186

Kameme, Phillip 53f

Kamende, Rev 56

Kampetewu, Michael 84

Kamsita 31f, 39, 42f, 45f, 48f, 51, 96-101, 108-110, 113, 116-118, 120-124, 132f, 135, 185, 200

Kamuela, Justine 162

Kamukungu 108

Kamwana, Elliot 11, 16, 19, 22, 25

Kamwana, Kenani 25

Kang'oma, village headman 65

Kanyalumwala, Rev 71

Kaonga, M.C. 158

Kaonga, Rombani 139f

Kapako Native Mission 58

Karonga 29-35, 41, 47f, 50-53, 56, 58-60, 72, 91, 99, 107, 133, 138f, 149-152, 154-157, 160f, 163-169, 179, 181, 187, 198f

Kasambala, church secretary 74

Kasantha 53

Kasewe, Debadeba 65

Kasisi, Rev 75, 164
Kasungu 48, 50, 56, 60, 76, 78, 85, 99
Kaswamphande, Rev 107
Katenga, Mr 62, 67
Kaulambwi 50
Kaunda, Isaac Chazuka 31-35, 84
Kaunda, Katenga 67
Kaundama, Rev 39, 45, 49, 51, 96-101, 108-110, 113, 116-118, 120-124, 126, 132-135, 185, 200
Kaunga, Mr 55
Kawalazi 67, 107
Kayange, Rev 164
Kayira, Kapesa 161f
Kazando 36, 45, 47, 56, 58f, 61-63, 66f, 70-74, 76-78, 81, 85, 87, 90, 92f, 126, 144
Kenya 59, 106
Kimbangu 21, 24
Kimbanguist Church 21
Kinna, Mr and Mrs 84
Kitwe 57
Kulinji, Rev 74
Kuwirwi 50
KwaZulu-Natal 21
Kyela 150-152, 154-156, 166f
Lenshina 24
Livingstonia Mission 27
Livingstonia Synod 37, 42, 44, 113f, 201
Lola, *Mama* 178, 181f
Lola, Rhoda 139
Longwe, Bandawe 54
Longwe, James 66
Longwe, L.K. 156
Longwe, L.M. 107
Longwe, Mskalu 120
Longwe, Mwasoni 57

Longwe, Nkhulambwi 115f
Longwe, T. 162
Longwe, White 45, 61-68, 70f, 73, 76, 94-97, 107, 116, 160, 170, 199
Longwe, Y.P. 158
Longwe, Y.T. 160
Nyirenda, Luka 31, 47, 50, 54, 66f, 76, 95, 140, 168
Lusaka 40, 70
Lwazi 50
Lweya 50, 107
Mabungo, Mrs 120
Mackenzie, D.R. 44
Madondolo, Rev 71, 98
Mahemani, Mrs 120
Makondesa, Patrick 11
Makwakwa, J.F. 107
Makwakwa, Katonje 160, 162
Makwenda, George 106
Makwenda, village 50
Manda, Azikonda 115
Manda, Chiuli 7, 27, 30f, 33, 35, 42f, 46-48, 50f, 54-58, 71-74, 94-96, 98, 106-108, 132-134, 170, 198f
Manda, Mselu 107, 111
Masinda, O. 36, 45, 56, 58f, 63, 76, 78, 81, 85, 89f
Masoakakula 55
Matola, Rev 98, 102-104, 118, 121f
Matridi, missionary 46, 108
Mazawamba, Mr 120
Mazawamba, Mrs 120
Mbamba 50, 64
Mbeya 58f
Mbizi, Y. 42
Mbozi 59
Mbughi, Lazarus 161
Mbuna, Bishop 55

Mchengautuwa 99, 139-142, 158, 176-188, 190-192, 194f
Messianic 12, 21f, 25
Mgodi, village 50, 74, 77
Mhone, Harrison Truegodi 31
Mhone, Stanwell 96, 107
Misuku 54, 99, 104, 160, 162
Mkandawire, A.G. 107
Mkangali, principal 55
Mkhuta, Isaac 7, 31, 35, 47, 62, 106
Mkulu, Mai 79
Mkweu, Yakobe 42
Mlenga, Moses 117, 132-134, 136f, 142
Mokone, Mangena M. 18f
Mozambique 56, 58, 85, 106
Mphande, Changombo 57
Mphande, Chanju 22-24
Mphande, Katongo 31, 45, 47, 50, 62, 65
Mphande, Mtegama 57
Mponela 55, 71f
Msadala, Mr 120
Msadala, Mrs 120
Msimbowe, Mr 146
Msiska, Mr 138, 139
Msondozi 7, 28, 30f, 33-35, 46f, 50, 60, 64-67, 70f, 75, 78, 82, 90, 94, 97, 105f, 111f, 121, 125f, 159, 165f, 200
Msongwe, Bishop 99, 146, 158
Msuku, Preacher 180
Msukwa, Elias 139
Msukwa, Kingstone 161, 163
Msumba, Jordan 7, 25, 27-37, 40f, 46f, 49-51, 54, 59f, 70, 75, 94f, 106, 131-133, 197f, 200, 203
Mtambalila, Mr 178

Mtengowanthenga 55
Mufulira 57
Mughogho, K.T.R. 43, 54, 99
Mugomo, Agrippa 57, 65
Mukuwazi 34
Mulowoka, Mr 65f
Muluzi, Bruno 107
Munkhokwe 7, 27, 30, 33, 35, 47f, 50f, 54-58, 62, 70-74, 76f, 79-87, 89f, 92-98, 106-109, 112-116, 118, 120f, 126-130, 132-134, 144, 170, 172, 184f, 195, 198f
Muzguri 57
Mvula, A.J. 67
Mvula, C.C. 42
Mvula, G.D. 54
Mvula, Keliment 62
Mvula, M.J. 42
Mvula, Maxson 57
Mvula, Maxwell 42
Mvula, Rev 77
Mwabwalwa, Rev 158
Mwakalenga, Glyn 162
Mwakalenga, H.R. 52-54, 110, 138f, 150, 156-158, 164, 201f
Mwakikunga, Rev 164
Mwale, Barness Lowokani 57
Mwale, Behappy Macley 78
Mwale, Jemiter 79, 89, 119, 137
Mwale, Walter 59
Mwalilino, Mr 52
Mwambinga, Petros 164
Mwambughi, L.K. 110, 138, 141, 150, 156-158, 201f
Mwangasi, village 31, 52
Mwanjisi, Timothy K. 58
Mwanza 7, 35, 59f, 159, 162, 165-167
Mwanza, G. 42

Mwasi, Henry K. 107
Mwasi, Yesaya Zerenji 19, 94
Mwenitete, Rev 153
Mzimba 32, 48, 50f, 54-57, 60, 71, 76f, 97, 99, 133, 156f, 161
Mzuzu 20-24, 26f, 36, 39, 49, 83f, 90f, 95, 98f, 107, 117, 129f, 132-134, 136-138, 140, 142, 149f, 157-160, 165, 169f, 175f, 184, 187f, 193, 199f, 202
NaKalagho, Ivy 117
NaKalumbi, Rose 117
NaKamba, Ellen 117
NaKayange (Mrs Kanthonga) 117
Namibia 23
NaMkoko, Alesi 117
NaMsongole, Eunice 117
NaMtowe, Sofia 117
Nazareth Baptist Church 21
New Guinea 23
New Religious Movements 11, 15f
Ng'oma, Mutepelera 31, 47
Ngemela, Ben 30f, 35, 41, 52f, 59f, 170
Ngosi, Rev 164
Ngulube, Z. 99
Nigeria 10, 15f, 20-22
Njikho, Mrs 113
Nkhana, Zifa 84
Nkhata, Chipolopolo Isaac 76
Nkhatabay 7, 11, 22-24, 29, 31-33, 43, 45, 50, 54, 56, 58-60, 62, 72, 75f, 78, 83, 85, 97f, 103, 105, 107f, 111, 115f, 120, 133, 143, 168, 172, 179, 195
Nkhotakota 50, 60, 65, 71f, 74, 76, 98, 138, 168
Ntchisi 50, 55, 71f, 85, 98, 150, 168, 199
Nthalire 54, 99, 160-162

NyaChilausipa 143
NyaChirwa, Fanny 115, 120, 129
NyaDalapalapa 52
Nyakyusa 30
NyaLola, Mama 178
NyaLwanda 182
NyaManda, Buwani 80-82, 115, 183
NyaMchimba 53
NyaMunyirenda 143f
NyaSaka, Donifasi 115f
NyaUhango 52
NyaZgambo 143f
Nyerere, Japhet Wanzagi 60
Nyirenda, J.B. Phonji 76
Nyirenda, Malisao 67
Nyondo, Charles 161
Nyondo, Getson 152, 161
Nyondo, Ridwell 105
Pengapenga, Rev 56, 58
Pentecostal 12-16, 20, 23f, 93, 121, 127, 147-153, 156, 163f, 166-171, 184-187, 193, 196f, 204
Peter, Kyungu 41, 52
Phiri 31, 33, 50, 62, 64, 66, 83, 160
Phiri, Chikosera 28, 97-99, 107, 111, 136, 158, 160, 164f
Phiri, Guvu 78
Phiri, Idress 78
Phiri, Isabel Apawo 23
Phiri, Jali 98
Phiri, Muguvu 58
Phiri, Njoka 158
Phiri, O. Masinda 78
Phiri, S.C.K. Chikosela 160
Polygamous arriages 89, 128, 134-136, 144
Polygamy 27, 30-33, 36-38, 42, 44, 46-48, 89, 101, 117, 122, 128, 131-139,

142, 144-146, 151f, 154f, 169, 180, 197f, 203
Pretoria 18f, 21, 28
Providence Industrial Mission 11, 19, 86
Rijk van Dijk 169
Roman Catholic Missions 44
Rumphi 50, 60, 99
Rungwe 30, 35, 52, 58f
Salima 21, 50, 55f, 76, 140
Sanga, Malenga 67
Scottish Mission 44
Seventh-day Adventist 105
Shaba, Agillipa 54f
Shembe, Isaiah 21, 24
Shepperson, George 28
Sibale, Alex Joseph 49, 60, 99, 104-106, 110f, 117, 119, 130, 135f, 146, 149-151, 153, 156-165, 170, 175f, 187, 198, 202
Sichinga, Christopher 162
Sichinga, Sam 41
Sichoni 75
Sichula 54
Simbeyi, Mr 162
Siyame, Grate 162
Siyatu, Mrs 183
South Africa 7, 12, 18-22, 28-31, 33, 56, 58f, 85, 106, 140
Sundkler, Bengt 12, 17-22, 24f
Susa 54
Tambalaweku, Mr 62, 67
Tanzania 7, 30, 33, 35-37, 47, 52f, 56, 58-60, 74f, 85, 106, 111, 131, 150f, 159, 162, 164-167
Thembu National Church 18
Thembuland 18
Thotho 55, 107f

Tile, Nehemiah 18
Turner, Harold 12, 17, 22, 24f
Ukinga 59
Ulambia 54, 99, 104, 146
Usisya 7, 31, 36
Vula, Rotani Makeseni 65
Wale, Pastor 153
Watch Tower Society 27-30, 37, 40, 49
Watchman Healing Mission 19, 25, 103
Wenya 54, 99, 160-162
Wesleyan Methodist Church 18
Witwatersrand 18
Yokamu, Rev 78
Zambia 56f, 60, 70, 85, 106, 111, 151, 155
Zimbabwe 56-59, 85
Zion 19, 21, 49, 83
Zionist 18-22, 24f, 49, 83f, 86, 90f, 95, 99, 175, 199f
Zoe Harvest Ministry 140
Zululand 18

www.ingramcontent.com/pod-product-compliance
Lightning Source LLC
Chambersburg PA
CBHW071204240426
43668CB00032B/2079